Love & Limits: Achieving a Balance in Parenting

Love & Limits: Achieving a Balance in Parenting

BY

Ronald Huxley, MS
Sullivan Center For Children

Singular Publishing Group, Inc.
401 West A Street, Suite 325
San Diego, California 92101-7904

19 Compton Terrace
London N1 2UN, UK

e-mail: singpub@mail.cerfnet.com
Website: http://www.singpub.com

Typeset in 11/13 Jason Text by Shepherd, Inc.

Printed in the United States of America by Bang Printing

Library of Congress Cataloging-in-Publication Data

Huxley, Ronald.
    Love and limits : achieving a balance in parenting / by Ronald
    Huxley.
        p.   cm.
    Includes bibliographical references (p.).
    ISBN 1-56593-936-0 (soft : alk. paper)
    1. Parenting.   2. Parent and child.   I. Title.
    HQ755.8.H895   1998   98-5413
    649´.1—dc21   CIP

For information on holding a *Love & Limits* seminar in your area contact Ron Huxley at (209)–299–4759 or e-mail at REHuxley@aol.com.

I would like to thank my family for putting up with my early and late hours of typing of this book. Also, thank you for giving me the "courage to be imperfect."

A special thank you to Dr. Giri Hegde for your support and making this book possible.

And most importantly, thank you to all parents I have worked with who asked for this type of book to be written.

Table of Contents

Parents' Quick Reference Problem Guide

Attention Seeking/Annoying
Diagnostic Questions
DR's
Dirty Words
Dramatic Play
Expressive Arts
Family Meeting
High Fives
Negative Reinforcement
Public Recognition
Quality Time
Reflections
Removing Yourself from the
    Situation
Rewards
Selective Ignoring
Signs In The Window
Storytelling
Structured activities
Touching

Angry or Aggressive
All or Nothing
Call the Police
Diagnostic Questions
DR's
Expressive Arts
Family Therapy
Freeze Play
Time-in/Time-Out
Medical Checkup

Monitoring
Monkey See, Monkey Do
Parental Disappointment
Redirection
Reflections
Saying "No"
Structured activities

Anxiety
Bedtime Rituals
Choices
Consistency
Expressive Arts
Family Therapy
Habits
Mealtime
Medical Checkup
Reflections
Rituals
Separation Serenity
Structured activities

Argumentiveness
Broken Record
Choices
Choose Your Battles
Rubber and Glue
Saying "No"
Swinging to the Mood Music
Verbal Warning

Charity
Awards

Diagnostic Questions
Dramatic Play
Humor
Moving the Furniture
Reflections
Removing Yourself from the
    Situation
Rituals
Storytelling
Structured Activities
Time Cushions

Stubbornness
Broken Record
Choices
Choose Your Battles
Rubber and Glue

Substance Abuse Prevention
Discussion
Family Meeting
Growing Pains
Monkey See, Monkey Do
Peer Grading
Puberty Preparedness Training
Quality Time
Reasoning
Storytelling
Swinging to the Mood Music

Swearing
Behavior Penalties
DR's
Freeze Play
Parental Disappointment
Time-In/Time-Out
Saying "No"

Teamwork
Awards

Encouragement
Family Meeting
Helping Others
Huddling
Job Description
Mutual Problem Solving
Negotiation
Privileges
Rewards
Storytelling
Supply and Demand

Trust
Attachment
Quality Time
Reflections
Reasoning

Whining
Diagnostic Questions
DR's
Freeze Play
Removing Yourself from the
    Situation
Saying "No"

Withdrawn
Conversation Extenders
Diagnostic Questions
Distraction
Dramatic Play
Expressive Arts
Faith Building
Family Therapy
Reflections
Separation Serenity
Swinging to the Mood Music

Part
1

Balancing Acts: The Personal and Social Forces that Create Family Imbalances

Balancing love and limits is one of the biggest challenges for contemporary parents. Change has come to almost every area of a parent's life. The roles, relationships, and responsibilities of yesterday are no longer applicable for the parents of today. Discipline, or the way in which we teach our children about right and wrong, has come under great debate. On the one hand, society states that hitting or spanking is no longer an acceptable way to discipline our children. On the other hand, simply loving our children has failed to teach them how to behave appropriately. As a result, parents are more confused than ever about how to deal with their children. Many contemporary parents have come to realize that it is difficult to do something they have never been taught to do—namely, balance love and limits. This book will provide parents with practical, solution-oriented methods and ideas they will need to regain that balance with their children.

All of the problems and ideas in this book were chosen specifically to answer the problems and struggles experienced by contemporary parents. They come from a wide variety of settings, including: multicultural parenting hot lines, volunteer and court-ordered parenting classes, prison facilities, statewide conference workshops, keynote addresses, corporate and community seminars, and marriage, family, and child therapy sessions. Only by asking parents what troubles them most can a parenting book hope to be of any significant value. All of the "textbook" knowledge included here has been tested, to one degree or another, in the parenting "trenches."

In addition, this book takes into consideration that contemporary parents include both traditional, two-parent families and nontraditional, multistructured families. As we will discover, the nontraditional family of yesterday is fast becoming the traditional family of today. This includes single, divorced, step, adoptive, and foster parents and grandparents raising their grandchildren. In 1987, the National Survey of Families and Households reported that 33% of the U.S. population was some type of step family or remarried family (Glick, 1991). It has been predicted that by the year 2000 step-families will outnumber traditional two-parent families (Glick & Lin, 1986). Currently, the divorce rate is estimated between 50 to 85%, and although researchers have difficulty deciding the exact percentage, the fact remains: it is the majority, not the minority, in American society. Therefore, it would be a serious error to not include nontraditional along with traditional parents in seeking a balance of love and limits.

The primary question raised by both traditional and nontraditional parents is, "If a parent cannot spank or yell at their children to get them to behave (which is the manner in which most parents today were raised) and loving a child is not enough to teach children right from wrong, what should a parent do?" A recent survey by *Child* Magazine (Lombardi, 1995) on the most common discipline practices of parents reported that 90% used time-out on a regular basis. Of those 90%, only 30% felt that this method was an effective strategy with their children. That leaves over two thirds of the parents using something on a daily basis even though they believe it doesn't work at all! Why? And if time-out doesn't work, what does? These are some of the questions that will be addressed in *Love & Limits*.

The first section of the book is called "Balancing Acts." Parents must contend with various social and personal forces that create feelings of imbalance in the parent and family. Imbalance is the feelings of confusion, conflict, and helplessness parents experience when disciplining their children. Balance, in contrast, is the state of serenity parents feel when making a connection with their children. This connection translates into acts of cooperation when children are self-responsible and work together with their parents. Unfortunately, many parents experience this balance only in small, rare doses. Some parents might even go so far as to claim they have never felt it.

Another way of describing the experience of balance is when parents' inner values and beliefs agree with their outer behaviors and actions. When these are not in alignment, parents feel as if they are incompetent and ineffective at the job of parenting. Stated another way, they feel like "bad" parents because they are not living up to their values and beliefs about how to be a "good" parent. Usually, the truth is that they do not have the right tools to do the job. Although their intentions are good, their methods and strategies are not as effective as they would like. At one time those methods and tools might have worked just fine. Perhaps, when the parents were children some 20 or more years ago, those tools were the right tools for the job. Today, they may be outdated and no longer acceptable to society. And when parents lack right tools to do the job, children often take over control of the home through their out-of-control behaviors.

Furthermore, balancing love and limits will depend on the parents' ability to cope with the personal and social forces that make up their lives. Specifically, these personal and social forces include **Defining Love & Limits, Confusing Social Messages, Family Systems: The Imbalance that Keeps a Balance, Power Plays: The Games Families Play, The Rise of the Nontraditional Family, and The Perfect Parenting Standard.**

Throughout the book, parents will have the opportunity to complete several value clarification exercises. These exercises are designed to assist parents in identifying the values they use to balance love and limits. *Values* are defined as the individual beliefs systems parents have about what it means to be a "good" or "bad" parent. These belief systems are often subconscious or not discussed with other parents and partners. The premise of this book is that if parents' values are in sync with their behaviors, then they will feel satisfied and in control. In other words, they will have achieved a balance of love and limits. Although these exercises are optional, parents will find them an excellent aid in clarifying why they do what they do. From there, parents can learn what to do differently. In addition, using these exercises will allow parents to discriminate between conflicting beliefs they hold about parenting and come up with alternative beliefs and behaviors to practice. Parents will gain the power to stop acting on a problematic belief once they are aware of its force in their behaviors. It is not the point of these exercises to instill values in parents. Parents must decide which values they treasure and want to pass on to their children and which values they would like to eliminate.

The next section is entitled "The Four Styles of Parenting." The intent of this section is to help parents uncover HOW they balance love and limits. It will also demonstrate how their childrens' self concept is affected by these styles. Parents will discover their strengths and weaknesses and gain an in-depth look at how to have both high love and high limits. In addition, various parenting tools and exercises are provided along with each style to better equip parents in balancing love and limits.

The last section may be one of the greatest assets for contemporary parents in achieving a balance of love and limits. It gives parents what they have always wanted: tools to do the job. It answers a common question: "What else can I do?" Parents will have over 100 parenting tools to answer that question. The parenting tools are listed in alphabetical order with a quick reference at the end of each on the recommended age of the child and its strength as a tool for increasing love or limits or both. These tools are used throughout the book to help parents learn to balance love and limits. Terms in boldface throughout this text refer to toolbox entries.

An additional aid is the *Parents' Quick Reference Problem Guide. It lists* common problems parents experience with their children and various parenting tools to use for them.

Professionals who work with parents will note that no single theoretical orientation has been used in the design of the ideas or tools cited throughout the book. Effort was made to concentrate on various practical concepts and ideas and to avoid the suggestion that there is only one right way to parent. The advantage to this approach is that parents can choose what works best for them, based on their own experiences, backgrounds, cultures, and personalities. It's doubtful that parents care much for the theory behind a parenting technique or discipline method. They are much more likely to want to know how well it works than its particular theoretical orientation.

Professionals who can appreciate this attitude will find their work with parents much more effective and less resistive; they may even find it helpful in their own roles as parents. Some might consider this just another way to try to please all of the people all of the time. Just the opposite is the goal here. Not every parenting theory is cited in this book, or at least not every aspect of every theory. Only that part that has been most effective in my experience has been utilized to help parents balance love and limits.

This text allows for personal discrection discretion in selecting orientations for assisting parents in achieving a balance of love and limits. As such, a cognitive approach is offered to help parents overcome "perfect parenting standards" or beliefs about what they must, should, or ought to be doing. An existential approach is designed to help parents deal with the feelings of grief and loss. A Bowenian perspective primarily is used for the chapter on family systems, and so on. This is not to say that other approaches would not be equally as effective in answering these problems. The suggestions here are simply ones parents have found helpful.

In addition, the tone of this book is purposely authoritative and direct. It comes from the cry of many parents for an "expert" to give them direction and answers to their problems in balancing love and limits. The primary goal of this book is to empower parents to choose the best "tool for the job" while challenging their personal values and beliefs about parenting and discipline. The hope is that parents will decide, on their own, if what they are doing is effective or ineffective and then make the necessary changes to their beliefs and/or behaviors. As any professional, who deals with helping others change, knows, individual resolve and personal commitment is the most effective means to making a change.

Overall, *Love & Limits: Achieving a Balance in Parenting* is designed for contemporary parents, both traditional and nontraditional, who want to regain control over their lives and their children. To accomplish this, parents will be both equipped and empowered to balancing love and limits with their children.

Chapter
1
Defining Love & Limits

Love and limits are difficult to define. Although parents often assume they have the same definitions of love and limits, they may discover that the meanings the parents give the definitions are very different, even complete opposites. Parenting partners rarely have the same definitions of discipline. One parent may define love as the "providing of food and shelter" while another defines it as "spending time playing with a child." One parent may equate limits with "spanking" and the other with "reasoning or talking."

Parents do not come up with these definitions on their own. They are usually inherited from the examples of parental figures in their own lives. Adults either follow the practices of their own parents or guardians or they reject their examples as too abusive or relaxed. Unfortunately, knowing what one does not want to do is much different than knowing what one needs to do instead. And so, the struggle to define love and limits demonstrates why so many people seek more balance in their parenting. To illustrate, try this value clarification exercise.

Value Clarification Exercise: My parenting values
Write three words that represent how you (not someone else) define love and limits. Don't be concerned with having the "right answer." Simply write the first thing that comes to mind. First, write three words that represent love and then three words that represent limits, as indicated below.

Love   Limits
1.   1.

2.   2.

3.   3.

Next, take each word listed under love and each word listed under limits and compare them to one another. Circle the words in each list that are most important to you. Compare the top-ranking word from each list to one another. If possible, place a star by the word that has a higher priority or importance to you.

Parenting partners can compare their answers. Notice how similar or how different your definitions are. The more different, the more likely that parents will have power struggles over discipline. Even if the words are identical, the meaning each parent gives to them may be very different. Discuss the meaning you have for the word you wrote.

Relationship Discipline and Action Discipline

Parents who consider love more important than limits often attempt to balance their parenting through what might be called *relationship discipline.* They use their attachment and bond with their children to teach right from wrong. They do this by spending a lot of time with their children, communicating and negotiating with them. Their definitions for love might include "spending time with" or "being available for" their children. Their definitions for limits might include such things as "listening" or "reasoning" with children. Balance between love and limits centers on "increasing a child's self-esteem," "making a child feel special," and "letting the child know they are loved."

On the other hand, parents who consider limits to be the most important component often use external control and action to discipline their children. For these parents, "respect" is a common definition for love, just as "obedience" is for limits. Negotiating a rule or chore goes against their idea of respect. The parent's decision is final and not usually subject for discussion. These parents are quick to act rather than negotiate or reason with their children; thus, their form of parenting is called *action discipline.* Balance between love and limits focuses on "teaching children respect," "modeling consistency," and "providing structure."

Of course, love and limits are both important in parenting. For simplicity, we will refer to these contrasting approaches to discipline as love and limits throughout the book. Emphasis will be on balancing both love and limits. Too much emphasis on one form of discipline over the other leads to feelings of imbalance in parents and children and can result in *power plays* between parenting partners. To begin, let's look at where these values for love or limits originate.

Values and Parenting

Values are a system of beliefs that parents have about themselves and the world around them. Values have a strong influence on our parenting and come from a variety of sources. The strongest influences are childhood experiences with one's parents or a parental figure. Mothers and fathers play a big role in our values. They express their beliefs about how to be and act by telling their children what they want them to do or what not to do. This expression might come from parents directly, through what parents say, or indirectly, through what parents do. They might be conscious beliefs used in the home or unconscious beliefs that all family members follow but never openly express. Either way, parents are the first teachers on what it means to be a parent parenting.

For example, parents might tell a child that talking with your mouth full is not polite, or they might send them to their room or even spank them for their behavior. Either way, the child has learned the rule: "Don't talk with your mouth full!" Values are evident in household rules and the consequences (or lack of them) for certain behaviors.

Most young children do not question the values of their parents until they are much older. One reason for this is because disobeying one's parents may result in punishment or rejection. Children come into the world highly dependent on their parental figures, both emotionally and physically. The idea of questioning a parent's values is unthinkable. Because these values are passed down at such a young age, during the formative stages of life, these beliefs are deeply ingrained and largely unconscious.

As children become school-aged, peer groups become an important source of beliefs. As a result, older children are less dependent on their parents and more independent or interdependent on children their same age. Old beliefs are reinforced and new ones are learned through playing and interacting with peer groups. If a child's peers hold beliefs that are similar to their parents, the parents' beliefs are reinforced. But when the values of peers are different, discomfort sets in and a parent's beliefs may become less important or more frequently questioned. Not accepting another child's values may result in being isolated and/or negatively labeled by other children. To illustrate the power of peers in children's beliefs and behaviors, observe children interacting on the playground. Notice the harsh ways in which they treat each other and the lengths some children go to be in sync with other children. It is not uncommon to hear a child say, "I won't be your friend" when a playmate is not doing what he wants. Observe the distress this causes in the playmate. Even words of comfort from a parent may fail to reassure the child, who now feels excommunicated by his friends.

The formation of an identity is an important developmental goal of the older child, especially after the age of 10 years. Preteens and teenagers want to be separate from adults and make their own mark on the world. Although younger children can reject the pressures of other children, the adolescent finds this much more difficult. The idea of becoming ostracized or considered different by one's peers is difficult for most older children to bear. Children (and adults) can be merciless when it comes to labeling one another as "geeks," "nerds," or "squares." Some children will do anything to avoid these labels. Look at how many parents advocate against drugs by their words and their deeds, and yet children still cave into peer pressure.

Heroes are another source of values. These are people, real or fictional, who are admired for certain attributes they possess. Modeling is an important aspect of how children learn. Some theorists feel that it is the most important variable for learning values (Bandura, 1977). Children model their heroes or the people they most want to be like. These heroes could be celebrities, comic book heroes, teachers, relatives, friends, or parents. Television is often a reflection of what society as a whole considers to be parenting heroes. Over the years, models of family life have changed drastically. The parenting heroes of yesterday, the Ozzies and Harriets and the "fathers who know best" have been replaced by Marge and Homer Simpson, not to mention numerous examples of single parent and stepparent family programs seen today. What society considers to be acceptable heroes and models of parents have drastically changed.

Personal goals and self-image are another source of values. What parents believe to be a nice house, car, education, or job has a lot to do with their values. One parent's shack is another parent's mansion. How a parent spends time and money reflects these personal goals and self-images. Parents who spend time instead of money on their children are communicating a value that goes deeper than any money or gift. Parents who want their children to have more out of life than they have work harder and push their children harder than other parents who do not share that value. Parents who value fair play become much more upset by two children fighting over a toy than parents who value solving one's own problems. Parents who value nonviolence have stricter rules about toy weapons and playing fighting games than parents who are not as concerned about this type of play.

Values are not a topic parents usually sit around and discuss. The reason for this is that values are largely unconscious. Parents are seldom aware of the values they learned as a child. Consequently, parenting partners rarely share these values with one another or find them discussed in parenting books. Many parents don't know why they do what they do. They gravitate toward other parents who share their values and move away from those who do not. They choose partners who appear to share their values, or at least complement them, and avoid partners who do not.

Relationships seem to have an unspoken contract built into them (Watlawick, Weakland, & Fisch, 1974) Parents expect certain behaviors or responses from their partners or their children. They judge others by their own values about what they feel to be a "good" parent or "good" child. And they avoid what they believe to be a "bad" parent or "bad" child. Making their values conscious is the first, most important step parents must take in changing their relationships with their partners and their children. This requires open communication, something many parents never witnessed, or valued, in their homes when they were growing up.

The most important aspect about values and parenting is that values can change over time. Many of the values parents held when they were children are different from the values they hold as adults. As their goals, self-image, heroes, education, and experiences change, so do their values. Older children make conscious choices to hold different values than their parents. In fact, just by reading this book, parents are on the way to changing their values and their relationships with their partners and their children. If values did not change, parents would be stuck doing more of the same (Weiner-Davis, 1995).

As an experiment, ask yourself if you are the same person now, in beliefs and behaviors, as you were as a young child. How about as an adolescent or young adult? The answer is usually yes and no. Yes, in that you still bear some of the old beliefs and behaviors, and no, in that you have adopted new, different beliefs and behaviors. Even if parents have never challenged the values of parental figures in their life and their society, they can still ask themselves the simple question of whether or not their values are producing satisfying, effective relationships with their children.

Parents might be forced to question their values when they go against a social norm. For example, a parent might believe that children should respect their elders. The same parent might use physical discipline to teach a child this value, resulting in a bruise on the child and the intervention of a law enforcement agency in the parent's life. Is the value "bad" because society opposes the hitting of children? Not necessarily. The value appears sound, but the method used to convey it goes against a social norm. American society seeks to protect children from undue physical punishment, and so it becomes necessary for the parent to change the method of discipline, not the value or belief. This need to adapt is a daily reality experienced by parents who come from different cultures. Multicultural parents may have learned different methods for teaching values and beliefs than those valued in American society. The approach of this book is to help parents, regardless of their culture or family background, develop more flexible values and beliefs if those values are the cause of the problem and/or to change their methods of parenting if they wish to maintain their existing parenting values.

Whether or not parents change their values, their beliefs, or their methods, they can still balance love and limits by gaining insight into the values and beliefs they already carry around with them. Without this insight parents will continue to experience the same difficulties over and over again.

Defining love and limits is the first personal and social force that creates a feeling of imbalance in families. These definitions reflect values or a system of beliefs that parents inherited from various sources but primarily come from their own parental figures. Values are powerful because values guide a parent in what it means to be a "good" or "bad" parent. Values also reflect society's expectations about what it means to be a "good" or "bad" parent. We will continue the discussion on the power of values and beliefs in balancing love and limits in the next chapter, which explores how these values make up the confusing social messages about what is appropriate parenting behavior.

Chapter
2
Confusing Social Messages

How many parents do you know who would like to have Dr. Spock for an uncle, T. Berry Brazelton, M.D., for a grandfather, or some other parenting guru in the family? If they did, they could pick up the phone or stop by for a visit to ask for suggestions about raising their children. If they could, parents wouldn't feel so confused by all of the social advice available on any given subject. They could just listen to that "expert relative"—at least until the expert's suggestions didn't work. One social force that creates feelings of imbalance in a parents' balance of love and limits is the confusion of social messages.

Our balance of love and limits is determined, to a large degree, by society's view of what is acceptable or unacceptable when disciplining children. At one point in history, parents were urged to spank their children. It wasn't uncommon to hear parents say, "What that child needs is a good spanking." The underlining value was that children needed more limits. But the method for imposing limits confuses parents who now follow society's belief that children should not be harmed. Yesterday, society admonished parents not to "spare the rod and spoil the child." Now, society admonishes parents not to hit or spank a child. Or as one parent humorously put it, "it's time to spare the bod, not the rod."

This confusion would be easier to untangle if parents had a resident parenting expert to help them. Unfortunately, parents do not have a parenting guru to consult whenever problems with children pop up or they are frozen with inaction about how to set firm limits. Professionals who are available for advice usually tell parents what not to do (Never strike your child. Do not raise your voice.) and forget to tell them what to do instead. If a pediatrician, social worker, teacher, counselor, relative, or friend does tell parents what to do, that advice usually boils down to a universal, magical technique like time-out. *Time-out* is a favorite tool of contemporary society. Parents have come to believe they can send their child to their room for any problem that arises. Unfortunately, research indicates that time-out works only 30% of the time (Lombardi, 1995). Parents either use the technique incorrectly or they use it for every problem with every one of their children. In some cases parents may have too small a home to send a child to their room or they might have aggressive or extremely hyperactive children who cannot handle the control and isolation that time-out requires. These children might go into a rage and destroy their room from the stress of being confined. And what about older children? Time-out often transforms into grounding when children become teenagers. Even then, grounding is not always effective.

And so, the problem remains, that parents don't know what to do instead of *time-out*. After they are stripped of their only discipline tool (be it right or wrong), they are not equipped with anything to replace it. The same research that shows time-out to be predominately ineffective also reveals that more than 60% of the parents who used time-out continue to do so long after they come to believe it to be ineffective. Why? Because they don't know what else to do! Maybe time-out should be used only as a technique for frustrated parents rather than for disobedient children.

It is not a lack of sources of information that confuses parents. It is the abundance of information that bombards parents through parenting magazines, books, audiotapes, news media, computer programs, and the internet. The problem is trying to make sense of all this information and to choose a technique that works. As an experiment, parents can go to their local library or bookstore and ask for a list of books on a common parenting topic, like toilet training. Parents will be shocked by how many titles there are on the subject and how many different approaches there are to its solution.

Another experiment would be to survey professionals and friends on what is the best form of discipline for handling a difficult developmental transition, such as the terrible twos or the teenage years. One source might advise the parent "to get tough" while another suggests "relax" or "don't worry, it is just a stage." No wonder parents feel unbalanced in their love and limits. They don't know which bit of advice to follow.

Magical Wands or Parenting Tools?

One of the reasons parents are confused by social messages is that they mistake helpful advice to be a magical wand rather than a parenting tool. Just wave this bit of advice over yourself, your parenting partner, or your child, and all of your problems will disappear. Right? Wrong! Advice is simply a tool. Sometimes it works for you and sometimes it doesn't. Although it is possible that parents may use a tool incorrectly, it is more likely that the tool is simply not the right one for a particular parent with a particular problem. Rather than feel like a "bad" parent because the tool failed, it is easier to get rid of it and find one that is right for the job.

A *tool* is an instrument designed for a specific task. It has no inherent magical abilities. A parent wouldn't use a hammer to repair every item in the house. That would break more things than it would fix. So, why would a parent want to use the same discipline method for every problem with their child? Time-out, spanking, or any single tool can create more problems than solutions if that is the only strategy a parent uses.

In addition, children react differently to different types of tools. Individual differences alone will dispel the notion of a magical wand. Some children will faint if you look at them cross-eyed. Others could be hit with a two-by-four and tell you, with a smile, to get a bigger stick. All children are different. And all parents are different. The more tools parents have in their tool belt and the more practiced they become in their use, the more adept they will be at handling parent/child problems.

Value Clarification Exercise: Picking a tool

Pick a topic that you would like more information on for a particular parent/child problem. Go to the library, bookstore, or the internet to look up your topic of interest. Notice how many different titles and advice are available on that topic. Use the frame of mind that advice is simply a tool. Pick one or two tools to try. Do your best to use them in the home. If in 2 to 3 weeks the tool is not producing the results you want, get rid of it and go back for newer, more appropriate ones. Don't let yourself become overwhelmed or angry the tool failed. Instead, try another tool that might do the job.

Just as you would not give parents only a hammer for all home repairs, neither would you tell them to go fix everything without giving them a list of what needs repair. Parents need to be empowered and equipped to balance love and limits. They need the right tools for the job and they need an accurate concept about what needs fixing. Setting goals is one way to overcome the imbalance of confusing social messages and balancing love and limits more effectively.

Setting Goals

A parent wouldn't set out on a trip without knowing their destination. They would just be driving around. Parents need to decide what their goals are for themselves and their children. This goes back to a parent's values. Each parent must decide their own goals. Regardless of the goals, here are three suggestions to help parents achieve them:

1. Be Specific.   The first error that parents make when setting goals is not being specific enough. Vague and ambiguous goals are difficult to achieve. If parents were told to balance love and limits without defining love and limits, they would never be able to achieve that goal. In fact, they might end up worse off, feeling frustrated or inadequate because they can't balance love and limits when everyone else seems to be doing it.

Being specific means narrowing a goal down into concrete terms. Parents must explain what it is exactly that they want from their children. For example, parents who state that they want their child to get good grades without being more concrete will sabotage their efforts. Parents must ask themselves, "What does getting good grades actually mean?" What one parent decides are good grades may differ drastically from another parent's expectations.

Goals that are not specific can be overwhelming. They reside somewhere in never-never land and feel impossible to reach. One way to be more specific is to ask yourself: "How will I know when my child has gotten good grades? Will she have earned an A or a B or a C? Must she receive those grades for all of her classes? Must those grades show up on her report card or on all of her work? On what percentage of her daily work would a lower grade be acceptable?" Get the point? Define the goal in behavioral terms. This may seem more difficult, but it is a much more effective way of achieving goals.

Sometimes it's easier for parents to be specific when they use their senses and describe to another person what they would see, hear, or feel if the child was getting good grades, being respectful to adults, or playing cooperatively with siblings. Parents must describe in as much detail as possible what must transpire to achieve the goal they've set. This would help parents form an achievable goal that can be translated to observable behaviors.

2. Be Realistic.   Some goals are never reached because they are not realistic. The abilities, situations, or present attitudes of parents and children must be considered when setting goals. A child who is getting Ds and Fs on his report card is probably not going to get As or even Bs overnight. Make goals realistic by focusing on small steps toward improvement. Ask: "What would be the smallest amount of change that needs to take place for me to feel that my goals for my children have been achieved?" Perhaps it would mean the child starts getting Cs during the next semester or on his next spelling test. The next step would be to work toward Bs, then As. In fact, some children may never be able to do A work. That does not mean they are stupid or have not worked their hardest to get those grades. In making realistic goals, always compare children's successes with their own past behavior, not with other children's progress or other parents' interactions with their children.

Being realistic also means being developmentally appropriate. Some parents expect more out of their children than they can accomplish, given their age or stage of development. What constitutes chores for a 4-year-old child will be different from the chores for a 14-year-old. Even children who are the same age may have different developmental abilities. For example, when parents are making the decision whether or not to let their 12-year-old child stay home alone after school or find a baby-sitter, age is not the only factor to consider. Because maturity levels differ in children, some 12-year-olds are more mature than some 16-year-olds in taking responsibility for staying home alone. Treat each child uniquely and look realistically at the total circumstances.

3. Be Positive.   In addition to being specific and realistic, parents must be positive when setting goals. Parents need to state what they want to happen, not what they don't want to happen. After all the work parents have had to go through in being specific and concrete, they shouldn't sabotage it by setting a negative goal, such as "no more bad grades" or "stop yelling in the house." Set positive goals by stating the positive: "my child will get Cs, "talk quietly in the house," or "play ball outside."

Use Prevention to Avoid Pitfalls

When making a trip, parents not only need a map and a destination, they also need to know what pitfalls might occur along the way. For instance, parents taking a trip would check with the weather station or road conditions before heading out. Being prepared for possible dangers along the way make the journey all the more successful and satisfying.

Parents can predict at least 80% of the problems that will occur with children. Sound impossible? It's not, if you stop and observe the patterns of behaviors that occur between you and your child. Parents usually have no problem explaining what problems are occurring in their families. They know just how their child will react or just what the child will say when they try to implement a change in a behavior or give a directive. The reason is that they have experienced these problems many times before and are likely to experience them again. Once parents are aware of the problems, they can predict when and how these problems will occur in the future and thus prepare to meet them and change them.

This strategy could be called *preventive parenting*. Although it appears revolutionary in concept, it is not new at all. The eastern philosopher Buddha stated something similar to this concept in one of his Four Noble Truths (Peck, 1978). One noble truth states that life is difficult. He went on to state that anyone who will accept this truth will find that life will cease to be so difficult. Why? Because of prevention. Once parents accept the truth that problems will occur and that parenting is difficult, they will no longer be surprised when problems occur or be unprepared to meet them. It is easier to prevent something you know will happen than stop something you don't expect. If, for example, a parent knows that every night a child will get out of bed with an excuse, such as wanting a drink of water, remembering unfinished homework, or asking silly questions, the parent can stop feeling upset by this behavior because they know that it is going to happen.

Prevention also means focusing on what works and letting go of what does not. Don't do more of the same. Do something else—anything else! If parents acknowledge that problems will occur at least 80% of the time, then that means that there is at least 20% of the time that they will not. What is different about that time? When parents strive to do more of what works, parenting becomes less difficult.

Value Clarification Exercise: What works log

Keep a log or a journal for approximately 2 weeks. During this time, record both the good times and the bad times with your child. What was different about the good times? Did the child get a better night's sleep? Did you use a quieter tone of voice when upset? Did dad support mom's decision rather than contradict it? Look for the exceptions.

Chapter
3
Family Systems: The Imbalance that Keeps a Balance

Another powerful force that affects a parent's ability to balance love and limits is the family itself. The family is a highly complex relational system that affects the life of its individual members as well as being affected by those members. This mutual interaction, occurring on various levels and striving toward a common goal, is what makes the family such an important force in balancing love and limits. Unfortunately, many parents do not understand the relevance of the family when disciplining their child. Without this insight, they find balancing love and limits even more difficult.

The family, as a system, provides it members with various functions, including: economy, protection, education or socialization, status, and affection. These functions are similar to other systems (i.e., institutions) that provide family members with income (business), protection (police), or education (schools). These functions may be divided up among family members and become specific roles. Traditionally, the father has played the role of breadwinner and protector while the mother is responsible for the childrens' socialization and affection (Nye & Berardo, 1973). Who occupies each role is determined by the rewards and costs that the member experiences in that role, and by necessity. A single mother may not want the role of breadwinner, but be forced into it out of sheer necessity. The oldest sibling may not want the role of educator or protector, but feel the overwhelming pull of the family system to do so if one of the parents is absent, emotionally or physically, from the home. Consequently, family roles are rapidly changing as the nontraditional family continues to rise in American society.

The family, like other social systems, is organizationally complex, open, adaptive, and goal-directed (Kantor, 1975). Each of these areas will be discussed in more detail later. For now, the most unique feature of the family system, in terms of balancing love and limits, is its ability to regulate itself. This is the concept of homeostasis.

Homeostasis: The Family Feedback System

The primary consideration of the family as a system is its inherent ability to maintain its own unique balance, even if that balance is an imbalance. Complex systems have feedback mechanisms that provide the system with information on how far away or how close they are to approaching a state of balance, or equilibrium.

Feedback mechanisms commonly are found in machines. For instance, a home's heating or air conditioning system has a feedback mechanism to regulate or stabilize the temperature. If the feedback mechanism interprets the temperature in the house to be too high, the air conditioning system will turn on to cool it down. If the temperature is too low, the air conditioning system will turn off. This process, whereby the feedback mechanism regulates the temperature of the home, is called *homeostasis*. The purpose of the feedback mechanism is to make sure the system keeps its homeostasis. If the system deviates too far from the homeostasis, the feedback mechanisms kick in to govern or stabilize the system.

The family can also be said to have feedback mechanisms which maintain homeostasis. These concepts were first applied to behavioral and social systems by Gregory Bateson (Goldenberg & Goldenberg, 1991). He took what was originally a mathematical and engineering concept and began applying it to psychological constructs. These terms have allowed psychologists and family therapists to better explain the behavior of an individual influenced by and influencing the family system. Predominately, they look at the exchange of communication between family members and how communication is used to regulate family homeostasis. If family members deviate too far from what they determine to be an homeostatic balance, they engage in behavior to return the member and the family to its original balance. Take, for example, two children fighting over a toy. Parents might step in when the battle becomes physical to prevent anyone from being hurt. Perhaps the parents scold the children, lecture them, or send them to their rooms. Regardless of the technique, the parents attempt to return the children to the expected balance of playing cooperatively and not hurting one another.

This type of balance is said to be circular rather than linear in interaction. At one time, professionals looked at human behavior as a linear function. The linear view considers human behavior in a limited, one-event-at-a-time fashion. Circular, or systems thinking allows professionals to see the individual as both influencing his or her environment and influenced by his or her environment. This process has been called *mutual causality*. In other words, an individual's behavior can be described in terms of its relation to the whole rather than simply by cause and effect. Using the above example, parents might walk into a room where two children are fighting over a toy and ask, "Who started the fight?" One child might claim that his sister started the fight and that he had the toy first. In defense, the girl might respond that she intended to get the toy first and the her brother took it before she had a chance to play with it. In this situation, who would be right? Actually, both children would be right and both children are to blame for the fight. It is not a case of linear causality but circular or mutual causality. These chains of interaction occur continuously every day in every family. A family cannot be completely understood without recognizing the simultaneous influences that each member of the family exercises on one another.

Another way of stating this interaction is that balancing love and limits is a two-way street. Although the emphasis of this book is on the role of parents in balancing love and limits, children also play a part. It is much easier to discipline a child who has a flexible or easy-going temperament than one with a difficult, feisty temperament (Thomas, Chess, & Birch, 1968). The feisty child is more likely to test a parent's limits. In addition, parents often find it easier to discipline children with the same temperament as their own and find it harder with those with opposing temperaments. Nontraditional families find it easier to balance love and limits with biological children over their nonbiological children. This is due to many factors, including similar histories, emotional bonding, prior comfort with parenting styles, and genetic similarities. Children in a stepfamily, for instance, may work toward turning their life backwards, to the way it was before mom or dad remarried. They may prefer having only one parent telling them what to do or find they do not have their biological parent's full attention as they did before. In response, they may resist all attempts by the nonbiological parent to parent them and struggle to keep the biological parent all to themselves. This is another example of how children influence the family system to return it to its former balance.

Children also influence one another. Sibling relationships, with all of their love and hate feelings, are one of the first models of relating that children experience, especially when it comes to getting along with peers. More on how sibling birth order affects love and limits will be discussed later.

The Imbalance that Keeps a Balance

The balance that is maintained in the family system is an emotional balance (Newman, 1994). It is dynamic and constantly changing. It evolves over the course of the life span of parents and children. In fact, the right balance of change is vital to the family system. Too much change or too little creates dysfunctional cycles of interaction among members and may even result in physical or psychological disorders in individuals (Bowen, 1994). Home-ostatsis is so powerful that many families continue to maintain unhealthy balances. This is why the family system can be said to have an imbalance that keeps a balance.

Two of the drives that must be dealt with if families are to be emotionally healthy and achieve a balance of love and limits are the forces of *togetherness and separateness* (Newman, 1994). Togetherness is the force that pulls the family together, while separateness is the force that pushes individual members to be independent and unique. These forces are often contrary to one another and create feelings of imbalance in parents who are attempting to balance love and limits. But both are necessary as children grow up to be independent, responsible adults.

The force of togetherness is necessary for children to feel secure and protected. This force allows members to experience the home as a haven from worldly stress. It allows family members to return from school or work to a place of comfort and familiarity. Togetherness can be expressed in the way that the family spends time together, by the amount of affection shown to one another, and in the manner in which they cope with crisis together. In terms of love and limits, parents use the side of love to express care and nurturing for children and limits to express security and structure.

Separateness is also necessary for children as they mature and become independent from parents. This is most evident in the 2-year-old's tantrum and the teenager's rebelliousness. In terms of love and limits, parents use love to negotiate chores, rules, and privileges rather than impose them in an authoritarian manner. Limits are used to set consequences on a child's behavior when it goes outside the boundaries of acceptable rebelliousness. Although some rebellion is developmentally normal for children, it can violate family values and/or children's safety when it goes too far.

Murray Bowen (1994), one of the pioneers of family system theory, described the need for *self-differentiation*, which allows parents and children to maintain their own sense of self-separateness from the identity of the family as a whole. Balancing love and limits can be used to create self-differentiation. If love and limits are not balanced, the forces of separateness and togetherness becomes instable. If separateness outweighs the force of togetherness, family members can become self-centered, cruel to one another, overly rebellious, disrespectful, and uninterested in one another. They become emotionally cut off from the family, express false emotions and thoughts, have difficulty trusting, feel rejected, and suffer low self-esteem (Newman, 1994). If togetherness outweighs the force of separateness, members can become jealous and emotionally overinvolved. They may feel a lack of privacy, punish all negative feelings, have a low sense of self, feel rejected for being different, gossip about one another, and feel overly anxious.

Parents can use love and limits to negotiate the forces of togetherness and separateness. Some suggestions include:

♦ Encourage free expression of thoughts and ideas.
♦ Set up family meetings to discuss problems and family outings.
♦ Actively listen to one another's feelings.
♦ Allow a healthy amount of negative feelings.
♦ Permit privacy.
♦ Identify each person's uniqueness.
♦ Show appreciation for cooperative and creative behaviors.
♦ Allow children opportunities to make their own decisions and experience the natural consequences of their behaviors.

More concrete examples are given in the final section, the **Parenting Toolbox.**

The Identified "Problem Child"

Another way in which families feel an imbalance of love and limits, and thereby maintain an emotional imbalance in the family, is by labeling one member of the family as the "problem." Parents are familiar with the term, "problem child." This describes a child who resists all parental efforts at discipline, is constantly mischievous, and appears to enjoy the attention that getting into trouble provides.

Virginia Satir (1972), another leader in the field of family systems, discovered that the symptoms of the "identified problem child" are often a reaction to the family's state of imbalance. The behavior of the "identified problem child" may be an effort, albeit unconsciously, to alleviate the family's pain. The child becomes a stabilizing force to reduce stress and thereby return the family to its previous state of balance or to its imbalanced norm. A teenager's acting out, a school-age child's poor grades, a young child's temper tantrums—all may be efforts to stabilize an unstable system. For example, a child's F in math may be her way of trying to save her parents' marriage from ending up in divorce by bringing them together to deal with her problems and taking focus away from the pain of the divorce. At the very least, the F is a symptom of the pain the child feels about the divorce, especially if she was a straight A student prior to the separation. To focus only on the grades and not the pain of the divorce would be taking a linear approach to the problem. A circular or systems-oriented approach would be to help the family cope with the pain of divorce and perhaps let the grades take care of themselves.

When children misbehave they are often said to be "acting out". But what are they acting out, exactly? According to family systems theory, they are acting out the family's pain. Stated another way, when the family experiences sudden change, for better or worse, members undergo stress and the "problem child" pops up ready to stabilize the family system. Take, for example, an overly aggressive child. Sometimes, children who hurt other children are expressing their own feelings of being hurt. Due to their poor communication abilities, many children will demonstrate their own internal state: "I hurt, therefore I will hurt others." These are statements to parents or any adult who will pay attention to the cry for help. In this case, simply addressing the problems of the child would be inadequate. The whole family needs to be involved to adequately resolve this issue. Helping parents understand this dynamic will help them balance love and limits.

The Structure of the Family System

All of the forces we have described take place within a structure. A family's structure gives form to the relationships that occur within the family system. In addition, it delineates the various subsystems within the overall family system that must perform specific roles, rules, and responsibilities.

In contemporary American culture, these subsystems consist of an executive or marital subsystem, parental subsystem, and sibling subsystem (Minuchen & Fishman, 1981). Figure 1 illustrates these subsystems. This illustration is called a *genogram* and is often used by family therapists to map out the family structure.

The foundation of the family system is the executive or marital subsystem. Family therapists have placed special emphasis on this subsystem because many family problems, even individual problems, reverberate from the condition of the marital subsystem. Generally, the more secure the marital subsystem, the more secure the child. The more insecure the marital subsystem, the more insecure the child. While this book is not specifically about the marital subsystem, this is often the focus parents make to balance love and limits in children.

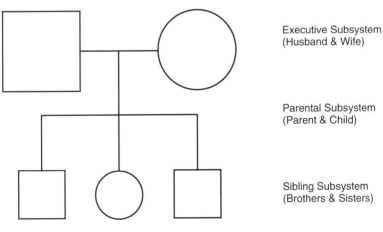

Executive Subsystem
(Husband & Wife)

Parental Subsystem
(Parent & Child)

Sibling Subsystem
(Brothers & Sisters)

Figure 1   Family Genogram.

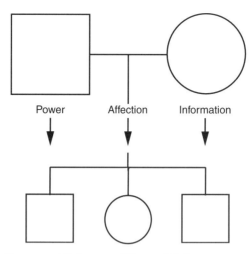

Figure 2   Downward Influence of Parental Subsystem.

Another important subsystem is the parental subsystem. This subsystem consists primarily of one or two parents and their child(ren). In some cultures this might also include grandparents and older children who take a turn at parenting responsibilities. Figure 1 demonstrates the vertical relationship of this system versus the horizontal alignment of the executive or marital subsystem. This vertical relationship outlines the differences in power and responsibilities between parent and child. The parent's role is to care for, watch out for, and guide the behavior of the child who is dependent on, looks up to, and must be guided by the parent. Power, affection, and information about the world, other people and oneself all come "down" from the parent to the child via the parental subsystem (Fig. 2).

The primary emphasis of this book is on the parental subsystem. To balance love and limits, parents must be the primary stimulus for change. How a parent provides power, affection, and information directly influences the balance of love and limits. For example, an overapplication of power might create a balance of too many limits and not enough love, while an overapplication of affection and information might create a balance of too much love and not enough limits.

This downward influence can also affect love and limits by what has been called the *parents' projection process* (Bowen, 1994). This process projects parents' unresolved issues, from their families of origin, down to one or more of their children. Unfulfilled dependency needs, fears, insecurities, and even family secrets can be passed down to children (Bradshaw, 1995). Children closely identify with their parents and often try to meet these unconscious needs left unresolved in parents. Parents may not feel they received the kind of love and affection they deserved as a child and consequently become emotionally enmeshed with their own children. A proper balance of love and limits is difficult in this situation, where a parent's relationship with a child more closely resemble siblings or buddies rather than parent and child. Here again, the child needs to self-differentiate to develop into a responsible, emotionally healthy adult. Another example is when a child closely resembles, in appearance or personality, a parent's own parental figure; if he or she has unresolved feelings for that parent, he or she may treat the child like that parental figure rather than as a unique person.

The third subsystem is the sibling subsystem, including all children in a household that are cared for by the marital or executive subsystem. This subsystem makes up children's first peer group. Their ability to form significant relationships in later life at work, home, and school begin within this subsystem (Toman, 1962). Sibling birth order affects the quality of the emotional relationships of one child to another. It also affects children's feelings of attachment to their parents and the attitudes children form about themselves through life.

Sibling Birth Order

Sibling birth order not only provides information on how a family is organized sequentially; it also speaks a lot about its emotional makeup (Bradshaw, 1995). This emotional makeup is characterized by family members' feelings of togetherness or separateness. Both are necessary in a healthy family. But the way in which they are experienced are determined to a large degree by sibling birth order. Older children will have experienced more separateness, because they did not have any siblings when they entered the family, than will later born children who already have brothers and sisters present. The following material was inspired by the work of Walter Toman (1976) and later expanded upon by Kevin Leman (1985). While this information is not empirically verified, parents will find it very close to their own realities.

Birth order affects a child's perception of how he or she fits in the family system (Leman, 1985). Every child has an innate need for belonging and feeling like a significant part of the family. How a child achieves this is predetermined by birth order and by how parents balance love and limits with each child.

Firstborn and only-born children are typically perfectionistic high achievers. They are used to being "first" in everything they do and often cast a discouraging shadow on later-born children. Many of the family's hopes begin with the first or only-born child. These children come into the family during the need for productivity when the family is still new and parents have limited experience or knowledge about raising children. Parents are often more immature, anxious, and likely to fumble about during this time. The parents' first attempts at balancing love and limits occur with the firstborn or only-born child. Consequently, firstborn and only-born children often feel a need to live up to the family's expectations for improvement and productivity.

The firstborn usually gets the best grades in the family and traditionally goes farther academically than do their siblings. Oldest children often become "pseudo-parents" and care for younger children, especially when parents work or one parent is absent from the home. Consequently, they often carry a greater load of responsibilities in the family structure than do other children in the sibling subsystem. But being the first or only-born child also has its disadvantages. Although it appears that they have everything going for them (just look at how many picture albums they have growing up!), they often pay a heavy price due to their neurotic need to "look good" in front of other people. They carry an expectation for high levels of achievement. As a result, they drive themselves unmercifully in every area of their life to conform to the perfectionistic image or role they bear. They tend to be more serious and feel a need to control people and things.

Fortunately, there are some things parents can do to balance love and limits with first and only-born children (Leman, 1985). Perhaps the most important is for parents to be careful about reinforcing first or only-born children's perfectionistic tendencies. Avoid undue criticism that adds to their already high state of internal pressure. Avoid words like "should," "ought," or "must" that place unnecessary emotional demands on them. Parents need to be very clear about what the rules are in the home. Be patient with the first or only-born child and take the time necessary to lay things out so he or she can understand them. The child won't need much prompting once he or she understands what is expected. Spread out the chores among all the children and give greater rewards for larger responsibilities. For example, if firstborn or only-born children are responsible for most of the chores, allow them to stay up a little later or do something one-on-one with a parent. Because they were used to having parents one-on-one before the other children were born, they will enjoy receiving that unique connection. Finally, don't force the first-born to be "instant baby-sitters" without checking with them first or without paying them for their time.

Second- and third-born children, often called middle-born children, are raised in the light and glory of the firstborn child. These children look for significance and belonging in ways that have not already been taken by the first-born. Unfortunately, this often means they find negative ways to get attention. They are born into the family during a time of greater stress and more demands on parents' time (which may mean less time for them) and consequently may get into more trouble at school or home. They may be more likely to hang out with the "wrong crowd," possibly searching for a sense of belonging. But middle-born children also can be excellent peacemakers and negotiators. Stuck between the oldest child and the younger children, they have plenty of practice keeping the peace and negotiating their needs and wants.

Parents of middle-born children can balance love and limits by taking out time to interact with these "neglected" children. Not only do they feel as if they get less time with parents, but they may not be as good at expressing their true feelings about themselves and what is going on in their lives. For example, consider the small child whose older sibling always talks for her and interprets every need. The middle-born child has very little reason to express herself in a verbally assertive manner, given that there is a lot of attention to gain by not doing so and due to the fact that older siblings and parents interpret her needs for her. Consequently, she needs to take the lead and have the opportunity to make choices about where the family goes to dinner or what movie to see on the weekend.

Privacy and personal space are also important when balancing love and limits with middle-born children. They need to feel as if they have something that is exclusively theirs and not the firstborn or younger children's. Parents need to be careful about hand-me-down clothing. While it saves money, it also reminds middle-born children of their less-than-important position in the family. An occasional new item will help balance this out. And don't forget to put their baby pictures into the photo albums, not in a box. The firstborn is more likely to have photographs arranged chronologically in albums. Not doing this for the middle-born child may intensify their feelings of insignificance.

Last-born children are sometimes called the "baby" of the family. This is because the last-born child comes into the family during a time when it is fairly intact. Perhaps mom and dad have decided not to have any more children, or maybe they find out that they can't have more children due to medical reasons. Sometimes the youngest child is a "surprise" after mom and dad thought they were not going to have more children. Regardless of the circumstances, the last-born child has a place of significance in the family rivaled only by the firstborn. This belonging is often expressed in a closer emotional bond with one parent. Older children are often resentful of the special attention and special toys the last-born receives. Most hand-me-down clothes are worn out by this time and "baby" gets all new stuff that middle-born children did not receive. The youngest children are also natural comedians or people pleasers. They were born into a family with plenty of peers and adults and have more practice interacting with others than any of their siblings. Consequently, they may spend more time socializing at home and school than they do staying focused on a task.

Parents of last-born children also need to balance love and limits. They must be careful not to treat the last-born child differently than the older children. For instance, last-born children need chores to do just like the older children. Don't let the older children do all of the jobs around the house, leaving the youngest with no responsibilities. To learn responsibility, they must be given responsibilities. Last-born children are so used to being taken care of by parents and older children that they forget they can take care of themselves. They often are poor decision makers and need opportunities to exercise this ability. Parents will need to help them balance their natural playfulness with responsibility to alleviate problems in school. The youngest children can also make good leaders in a different style than firstborn children. Where the firstborn makes an independent decision without feeling the need for consultation with others, the last-born child may need to create an ad hoc committee to consult before making a decision. Decision making can be an important skill parents can reinforce for the "baby."

Of course not all families consist of three or four children in neat, progressive order. Some families are much larger, others have large gaps of time between births, and some include twins. In the situation where there are large numbers of children or gaps of time between children, the next set of children after number three or four start to repeat the patterns for firstborn and middle-born children. For example, children number 5, 6, and 7 often repeat the patterns for children number 1, 2, and 3. If there are large gaps, the first child who is born after the gap of time often repeats the pattern for the first-born child, and if there are younger siblings, the pattern repeats as number two or three, and so on. Twins also follow this pattern. The first child to be born, however close in time, often repeats the pattern for the firstborn child and the brother or sister then takes on the second-born pattern of behavior. Or the child with the most dominate personality takes on the firstborn characteristics and the twin assumes the middle- or last-born position.

If the oldest child becomes seriously ill, dies, or is extremely passive, the mantle of responsibility is passed on to the next child. In many families, second-born children take on the characteristics usually reserved for the firstborn. The firstborn may in turn adopt the second-born characteristics.

Nontraditional Families and Sibling Birth Order

So far we have discussed sibling birth order from the perspective of the traditional family. In other words, we have not really looked at what happens when a sibling's birth order is displaced by another child. For example, when two families merge into one, as in blended or stepfamilies, some of the children's birth order may be displaced by another child. What happens when the oldest child of one family is displaced by an older child from the other family? What happens when the "baby" of the family is no longer the youngest because of the addition of one or more younger children? What changes when the only child is not the only child any more? In these situations, the oldest and youngest become middle-born by position but not by personality, especially if the oldest and youngest have enjoyed their former positions for some time. The usual result is conflict and difficulty balancing love and limits.

The same displacement occurs in other nontraditional families. Divorced families may split up children and their birth order, making younger children the oldest or only child. Foster families experience a constant merry-go-round of displacement as new children enter and exit the home. Adoptive families go through this adjustment if parents already have children prior to the adoption of new children. In the case of late adoptions of older children, they will be more set in their birth order positions and experience feelings of displacement more strongly than infants who are being adopted.

While it is possible that children may elbow for position in a healthy manner so that everything turns out just fine, it is more likely that children will suffer intense conflict over who is entitled to the birthright. They may feel confused, angry, anxious, and depressed during this adjustment process. The push of separateness will wrestle with the pull of togetherness.

Fortunately, parents of nontraditional families can make this transition easier by balancing love and limits. Perhaps the most important thing nontraditional parents can do is to reinforce the natural bonds and the original birth order positions by creating opportunities for biological parents and children or siblings to be alone together. In addition, do not force children to accept new positions too quickly. Give them the freedom to adjust on their own even if their pace is not as quick as parents would like.

Nontraditional parents should not take sides. This creates a triangle, which may reduce feelings of stress but also prevents children from resolving conflict on their own. We will discuss nontraditional families and triangles in more detail in the chapter on Power Plays. For now, it is wise to let children "elbow" for position on their own, in their own way, without interfering unless the situation becomes abusive or dangerous. In addition, parents should role model appropriate conflict resolution for children to follow.

The reason for examining sibling birth order is to recognize how children learn to relate to others based on one of their earliest experiences with other people. These characteristics result from the social forces created within the family system or structure. These forces will affect how a parent balances love and limits. Not understanding these forces intensifies feelings of family imbalance.

Value Clarification Exercise: That family birth order feeling
Parents can balance love and limits with their own children by reflecting on what it was like to be a first, a middle, or a last-born child. What particular things did you like, hate, or find difficult in your birth position? Look at birth order in your current relationship. What is the birth order of parental partners and how has that affected their teamwork in balancing love and limits?

Boundaries in the Family System

Boundaries are another force that affects a parent's ability to balance love and limits. Boundaries can be defined as a line of demarcation between the family and the outside world, between individual members and the family as a whole, and between subsystems (Minuchen & Fishman, 1981). Boundaries are a normal and healthy part of the family system (Newman, 1994). Boundaries protect and stabilize the family. They determine who is considered an "insider," or part of the family, and who is an "outsider," or not part of the family. Families with clear boundaries find it easier to balance love and limits.

Boundaries can be visible and physical, such as the walls of a room, hallway, screens, or even the furniture in a room. They can be visible and psychological, such as spending the day alone separate from other family members. They can be invisible and physical, such as talking on the telephone or sitting in a regular place around the table. They can be invisible and psychological, such as reading a book or listening to one's favorite music while in the same room as other family members. All of these forms of boundaries can be rigid, giving the message that no one is to bother you when you are in your room or while on the telephone, or they may be loose, allowing others to interrupt to ask a question.

Boundaries also define the permeability of the family system. *Permeability* refers to how easily information and people are allowed to enter or exit the family. Families that allow healthy, appropriate information and outsiders into and out of the home are called *open systems. Closed systems* restrict or refuse to allow outside information in, even if it is healthy. Closed systems include families that are usually heavily insulated and have very rigid rules about who is allowed to know what goes on inside the family and how well larger systems, such as schools, hospitals, and churches, play a role in members' lives. Open systems are more adaptable and willing to learn about new ways to interact and enhance internal relationships. Open systems also allow for honest communication between subsystems. Children are allowed to express themselves without judgment and ridicule, and both positive and negative emotions are encouraged and acceptable. In contrast, closed systems resist change. They have an unbalanced level of responsibility between members, rarely share information, and/or show inappropriate affection between family members. Communication is restricted; for instance children may not be allowed to express themselves or only positive emotions are permitted to be expressed, while negative emotions such as anger, are denied.

Parents in a closed system may punish a child for expressions of anger and force children to hide angry feelings instead of dealing with them in an assertive manner. For example, a child may become angry when told it is time for bed. He may throw a tantrum and argue with the parent. In this situation, two things are occurring simultaneously. On the one hand, the child is feeling angry, which is a valid feeling. On the other hand, expressing himself by arguing is not appropriate. In a closed system, the parent might punish both the feeling and the behavior. The parent might dominate the situation by force through more anger and yelling or hitting the child for his disobedience. This simply increases the very behavior the parent is trying to stop by modeling inappropriate conflict resolution and supplying negative attention to the behavior.

In an open system, the parent might acknowledge the child's anger while setting limits on the argumentive behavior. The parent would not model more aggressive behavior for the child to emulate or reinforce the behavior by negative attention. Parents in closed systems often give mixed or double messages. Children are told to not hit their younger sibling even as the parent strikes the disobedient child. Or children are encouraged to talk about their problems and then are immediately analyzed, judged, or condemned for doing so. The underlying message is "do what I say, not what I do" or "do what I say but only when I get very angry." As a result, children frequently get into power struggles with their parents to gain attention and choose not to come to parents with problems and negative feelings for fear of being punished.

In order for parents to balance love and limits, they must encourage the development of open boundaries in the family system. In terms of love and limits, parents who are inconsistent in the setting of limits demonstrate poor boundaries. Limit setting teaches children where the invisible lines of demarcation are drawn and what the consequences are for stepping over them. One example of this kind of boundary is learning to say "no" and sticking to it. The following parenting tool will assist parents in how to be firm when using limits.

Parenting Tool: Saying "No"

Saying "no" is a communication parenting tool that if used correctly will decrease confusing or mixed messages. When parents say "no," they usually mean "maybe." Some children will interpret "no" to mean "ask me later" or "go ask the other parent." To get respect, a parent's "no" must mean "no."

So how do parents say "no" to their child? Parents must use a firm tone of voice that is slightly above their normal speaking voice but not at the level of screaming. Parenting partners who stick together will be more effective when saying "no." If possible, parents should make decisions together on various issues, such as eating a full dinner before getting dessert or staying up late on a school night. Children will be less likely to manipulate parents when they know they are in agreement.

Some children react to a parent saying "no" by throwing tantrums and verbally abusing the parent. This is most likely the case where the parent has not been consistent in making "no" mean "no" and the child is not used to being frustrated. When this happens, it is important that the (permissive) parent do two things: Stay calm and stay firm. Keeping calm eliminates any negative emotion the child might be seeking, and staying firm communicates to the child that the parent is serious. Let frustrated children vent. If they become abusive, physically or verbally, tell them to take a **time-out** to cool down. Use the **time-in** parenting tool to discuss with them why they took a time-out and discuss their feelings of frustration (see the **reflection** parenting tool).

It is preferable if parents give their child a short, clear reason for saying "no." After they have done so, there is no need to continue discussing the decision. Use the **broken record** parenting tool here.

Saying "Yes"?

Many programs, such as alcohol and drug prevention programs, attempt to teach children how to set boundaries by learning the word "no." So why do children continue to use alcohol and drugs even when they know how to say "no." (Parents know their children know how to say it—ask any parent of a 2-year-old for verification!) Stephen Covey (1989), a popular writer and speaker, contends that although children know how to say "no," they often say "yes" because they do not have a burning "yes" inside to give weight to the word "no" on the outside. Many children know the format, but they do not have the motivation or persistence to stand up to the powerful force of peer pressure. They must be able to say "yes" to health, new social groups, spiritual values, and personal esteem. Perhaps teenagers will be more likely to say "no" to alcohol and drugs if they tell themselves drugs "make people act stupid," or "embarrass themselves," or "get into too much trouble when used," or "If I spend all my money on drugs I won't be able to afford my car." these provide a highly motivational "yes" for many teenagers. Children need to know why they are not using drugs and alcohol. And that why must appeal to their teen natures if they are to set a firm boundary.

Parents also need a burning "yes" when it comes to setting consistent boundaries by saying "no" to their children. Rigid boundaries are formed when parents say "no" with no room for discussion or any reasonable explanation. Doing so sets up a challenge for children to disobey and to lose trust in parents' judgment. Loose boundaries are fashioned when parents say "no" but do not back them up with consequences or reasons. Parents must first analyze why they are saying "no." Perhaps it is not a necessary limit, or they need to find the right words to explain their reasons to their children so they can understand. Of course, children occasionally cross these boundaries even when excellent explanations are given. This too is a way of learning boundaries through consequences. But they are more likely to obey these limits if parents have and give a reason for them.

Systems theory provides parents with a model for understanding how to balance love and limits. Homeostatic feedback mechanisms, family structures, sibling birth order, and boundaries are all ways that parents can feel more balanced. Recognizing how family members interact in a multidimensional manner and bear the responsibility for change can help parents fulfill the roles of the parental subsystem. The next section will take another look at the family system and how it adjusts to developmental changes over time. These changes are called the family life cycle.

The Family Life Cycle

The family life cycle consists of the developmental transitions of the family system as it moves through time (Carter & McGoldrick, 1989). These developmental transitions include the stages of courtship, marriage, birth of the first child, addition of new children, onset of adolescence, children leaving home, coping with middle age, caring for elderly parents, and adjusting to retirement. Time does not stop parents from their role and the responsibilities of balancing love and limits. It only changes the nature of that balance. The choices that parents make during the family life cycle will determine how well the parent is able to balance love and limits.

These transitions can take place in an orderly, gradual manner, or they can occur in a sudden, disruptive event. Both require the family to work together and adjust to change. Of the two, the more sudden, disruptive transition is the more difficult to adjust to and manage. This type of transition involves an unexpected event, such as financial loss, death, divorce, teenage pregnancy, adoption of a child, or the birth of a handicapped child. These changes disrupt the normal flow of the family life cycle and may temporarily create an imbalance in the family structure.

Fortunately, the family has a choice to use these transitions to break out of old coping patterns and develop new, more productive behaviors. An example might include the birth of the first child. Typically, an event of great joy, many families may experience sadness and loss before or after the child is born. Mothers or fathers who are not emotionally ready for parenting may see the birth of the child as a frightening experience and question how they are going to cope. These future moms and dads wrestle with the new roles and responsibilities parenting will bring. This particular transition can be especially difficult if the parent is a teenager. Teenage parents struggle with two developmental transitions at the same time—parenting and achieving adult identity. The teenager is not the only one affected by this event. His or her family of origin must adjust as well. A normal, gradual, developmental transition would be for young adults to leave the nest and go out on their own. This is usually not possible if the teenage parent must remain with his or her family for financial and emotional support to care for the baby. The normal developmental transition of the grandparents is also affected if the teenager chooses not to parent the child and the grandparents must take over this role. Not only are they playing grandparent and parent at the same time, but their traditional transition of moving through the launching of children from the home, and adjustment to retirement cannot be achieved.

Even in older, two-parent homes, parents may not realize the stress that a new baby can bring and how it can affect the amount of time parents have together. Children take a lot of time and attention. Having a new child can affect the level of intimacy and force parents to manage both the child rearing stage along with the marital stage of the family life cycle.

Adjusting to the stage of having young children is also stressful. Families with young children must learn to balance work and family life, cope with the need for quality child care, deal with finances, contend with scheduling problems (family time, couple time, time alone, recreational time, etc.), and most importantly work together to parent children. Parenting becomes more than a straightforward responsibility. It is rocked back and forth by sorting out normal from abnormal developmental issues, coordinating parenting styles, dealing with family of origin issues, clarification of family values, modification of expectations, deciding the best method of discipline, and much, much more.

Families with older children also experience developmental stressors. Roles and responsibilities change in the family, sibling conflicts increase, and school and extracurricular activities impinge on family time. Parental values may conflict with teenage values. Health and substance abuse issues become important, and sexual concerns must be communicated and accepted.

Another difficult stage occurs when parents experience empty nest syndrome. During this stage children decide to leave the home nest and fly out on their own to college or into their own apartment. In addition to adjusting to the lack of children in the home and the drastic change in parental roles, parents must contend with increased financial demands, such as college and care for elderly or ill family members. New career or retirement issues may take center stage along with sexuality and marital concerns if couples are forced to relate to one another anew after they have previously focused on the children rather than the marriage. Grief and loss issues, such as illness and death of aging family members, and personal health problems also must be dealt with.

Nontraditional families also experience sudden, disruptive transitions in their family life cycle. For instance, divorce, which occurs for approximately 50% of all families, has an impact on three different levels of the family life cycle: individual, marital, and family. Post-divorce families must go through additional life cycle stages before they can achieve a new family balance. Parents must cope with the new roles of being a custodial and/or noncustodial single parent. Finding workable visitation schedules, rebuilding financial resources, and searching out new social networks all must be achieved before balance can return. In addition, most divorced parents eventually choose to remarry. Becoming a stepfamily has its own developmental transitions. Recommitting to a new marriage, which might also fail, restructuring financial and emotional attachments to new family members, dealing with loyalty conflicts and unresolved grief issues, and renegotiating parental authority with stepchildren are just some of the adjustments stepparents must make. Researchers estimate that the stepparenting adjustment, sometimes called *blending*, takes 3 to 4 years before a new balance is achieved. One of the strategies, therefore, is patience and mutual support, both inside and outside the new family.

Value-Clarification Exercise: The life cycle line

Take a blank sheet of paper and turn it so the longest direction is horizontal. Draw a straight line, horizontally, down the middle of the sheet of paper. On the far left end of the line write the word "birth." On the far right end of the line write the work "death." This line reflects the parents' life from birth to death. Put a "P" (for present moment) somewhere on the line, however close to birth or death one feels is most appropriate. Indicate along the line the different normal, developmental transitions that have occurred in the family system. If, for example, a parent married at 25 years of age, make a mark on the line where 25 years would be represented. Write "marriage" on that spot and indicate the date. If there is more than one marriage, then continue to mark along the line the different dates that those marriages occurred. Put the other normal developmental transitions on the page as well (e.g., 30 years for first child, 32 years for the second, 35 years for first child in school, 43 years for first child reaching adolescence, etc.) Next, mark the sudden, unexpected transitions on the life cycle line as well. For example, put a mark for divorce, major illness, deaths of family members, etc.

What do parents notice about their life cycle when completing this exercise? How difficult was balancing love and limits, given the various ups and downs that occurred on this life cycle line?

The family life cycle is a way of looking at how developmental transitions create an imbalance in families. How families deal with these transitions will determine whether or not they achieve a balance in their love and limits. Each transition is both a milestone and a crisis point for families, depending on how well they adjust to the transition. Nontraditional families have additional stages to master. For instance, divorced parents must move from being in a two-parent home with most of their emotional and financial resources intact to becoming a single parent with precarious resources. Then they must adjust again emotionally and financially as they remarry and become stepparents. The next chapter will take a look at how power plays between family members create feelings of imbalance in love and limits.

Chapter
4
Power Plays:
The Games Families Play

Another personal and social force that causes family members, especially parenting partners, to feel unbalanced in their love and limits, is *power plays*. Power plays are the games that families engage in to create a feeling of balance. As we have already described, these power plays may actually create an "imbalance that keeps a balance." Although disagreements and tensions are normal in the family system, simply because it *is* a system, they can become unhealthy or imbalanced in and of themselves. They often start out as a way for a family member to get their needs met. Then they turn into dysfunctional and defeating behaviors that occur between two or more members. Most attempts by parents to regain a balance end up only reinforcing these behaviors. They create the very thing they wish to stop. In order to stop the behaviors or power plays parents must first understand the dysfunctional games they play, why they engage in them, and how to untangle themselves. These power plays, in terms of balancing love and limits include: *playing on the seesaw, triangles*, and *tug-of-war*.

Playing On the Seesaw

Parents do not always agree on how to define love and limits. Having different definitions is probably one of the most discouraging aspects of a parenting relationship. Many of today's traditional households have one parent who provides most of the "love" while the other parent provides most of the "limits." Rather than balancing their love and limits *actively* together, they balance in *reaction* to one another. The more limits set by one parent, the more the other parent provides the love. Each parent feels a need to balance the other parent's actions by reacting with more and more love or limits. If this situation continues long enough, the parents will come to resent one another and blame each other for the problems in the family. The reality is that each of them is in some way responsible for the problem, and therefore, each is responsible for its solution.

When two parenting partners takes opposite, extreme parenting positions, this might be called *playing on the seesaw*. The seesaw is a child's playground toy. It consists of a long plank with two seats, one at each end, with a bar or wedge resting under the middle of the plank. One person cannot play on the seesaw alone. It requires two people to play. It is a good metaphor for the game parenting partners play when looking for a way to balance their love and limits.

Each parent takes responsibility for one side of the seesaw, representing either love or limits. Rather than acting in cooperation with one another, both react in competition by pushing down on their side of the seesaw. Each push creates a sense of imbalance which in turn causes the other parent to push harder on the other side of the seesaw. It doesn't take long before the entire family is moving up and down hoping to find a balance somewhere in the continuous motion. Feelings of balance occur for only brief moments, when the seesaw reaches its midpoint, only to have the situation immediately turn to one of imbalance again as one side or the other moves up or down. The results of this game are feelings of anger and resentment toward the other partner. The mistaken belief here is that the other parent is to blame for the imbalances in the family, not me. Efforts for change are concentrated on the other parent and not oneself.

Here is an example of how one family plays on the seesaw:

1. Child misbehaves.
2. Father yells.
3. Child cries/mother intervenes.
4. Mother and father argue/child cries more.
5. Father resumes discipline.
6. Mother withdraws.

What is interesting is that the original problem, child misbehaves, becomes a totally different problem by step 4, mother and father argue. This is why this type of reactive behavior is labeled a game. It doesn't take long for a child to learn how to manipulate her parents. Just divide and conquer. If the child is successful, she will escape the discipline and leave mom and dad to argue.

Value Clarification Exercise: Who sits where on the seesaw?

Is this a familiar game? Assuming every family has some type of seesaw, what kind of seesaw did you observe growing up as a child? What kind of seesaw operates in your home now? To give you greater insight into how the seesaw operates in your home, answer the following questions:

1. Who provides most of the discipline in your home?
2. When the children are hurt or upset, who do they turn to first?
3. Who do the children tend to listen to the most?
4. When you and your partner disagree about how to handle a situation, who tends to win most frequently?
5. Do you parent differently when you are with your partner than when you are alone?

The logical conclusion for a family that continues to play on the seesaw is a relationship full of misery; if continued long enough, it may lead to a total dissolution of the parenting relationship. The game—and the underlying pull of values of each parent in different directions—may be one reason the divorce rate is so high in today's society. To reverse this trend, it may be necessary to understand parents' values when it comes to balancing love and limits. If parents have the same definition of love and limits, then they are more likely to have a feeling of rapport with one another than parents who do not. Consequently, they will be more likely to work together rather than against one another.

While it is true that most parenting partners have many things in common, they frequently get stuck on their differences and forget about the solutions that already exist in the parenting relationship. Parents must also be willing to understand and accept the other parenting partner's need to be a good parent and reframe their actions, however opposite or illogical they may seem, as an attempt to balance love and limits. Stated another way, the other partner is pushing on their side of the seesaw because that is what they believe a good parent should do. Respecting that will help the other parent to stop pushing in reaction to their partner.

For example, most fathers want to be respected. Respect is high on their definitions of love and limits. The mother might support the father's values by making the following changes in her behaviors:

1. Child misbehaves.
2. Father yells.
3. Child cries/mother observes situation.
4. Mother supports father in less abusive manner.
5. Child complies with discipline.
6. Mother models (not lectures) appropriate behavior.
7. Father feels respected (and learns new ways to parent).
8. Parents balance love and limits.

While this is a simplistic example—not all interactions will go this smoothly—the basic premise for getting off the seesaw is the same. Learn what your partner's values are and try to meet him or her without compromising one's own values. In this example, the mother was able to act in unison with the father by observing and acknowledging the situation before she unconsciously reacted. Parents will find that moving closer to their partners, by supporting their values, will result in the partners moving closer to their own values.

Making Unconscious Values Conscious

Parental values are like huge red buttons labeled, "Push Me!" Family members learn to push one anothers' buttons. This is especially true of children who have great experience and skill in pushing a parent's buttons. By making values conscious, parents can prevent children from pushing their buttons, stop themselves from pushing their partners' buttons, and work with their partner in balancing love and limits. In addition, parents can use their partners' values in a way that supports their own values and achieves a true feeling of balance. The difference between balanced parents and unbalanced parents is not having the same or different values of child-rearing, but in seeing these times of disagreement as opportunities to share and learn from one another rather than as contests over who is in control. Parenting partners who manage to stay off the seesaw realize that there are times when one parent will have better insight or at least more patience in dealing with a child's problems than the other. If they cannot agree with the other parent, then parents need to "agree to disagree" (Covey, 1989) in order to stay off the seesaw.

In his book *Getting The Love You Want*, Harville Hendrix (1988) recommends that parenting partners' relationships be more conscious and therefore more balanced and satisfying. One of the exercises he uses with couples to make their relationship more conscious is called, "Your Relationship Vision." He directs parenting partners to take out two sheets of paper and write down a series of short sentences that describe each partner's personal vision of what a deeply satisfying relationship means to them personally. These can include qualities their partners currently have or qualities they wish they had. Examples might include: "We have fun together." "We don't fight." "We agree on the method of discipline of our children." "We share important parenting decisions."

After writing these sentences, partners are asked to share their ideas with each other and note which items they have in common and which items differ. If one partner has written sentences that the other agrees with but did not think of originally, he can add them to his own list. Next, partners are asked to rank each sentence with a number from 1 to 5 according to its importance to the parenting partner, with 1 indicating "very important" and 5 indicating "not so important."

Emphasis is given for what partners feel they can achieve. They are asked to circle the most important items and check off all the items they feel are too difficult to achieve together, at least for now. After this, partners can combine their lists, with the items ranked as 1 at the top of the page on down to the 5s listed at the bottom of the page. Items at the top of the list will be fairly easy to achieve and complete together. Items at the bottom may feel impossible. Partners are urged not to worry about the items on the bottom of the list; they will come in time. Parenting partners can begin to work on each item starting from the top and working down slowly over time. They are advised to put the list where it can be easily seen every day and talk together about how to fulfill each one.

This exercise provides parenting partners with two benefits. The first is that it outlines both the positive qualities along with the negative ones. While it's easy to play the blame game and point fingers at the other partner for the imbalance, it may be more difficult to remember the good things about the relationship especially when there has been a lot of imbalance. The second benefit is that parenting partners do not have to force themselves into reaching consensus on parenting decisions. Forcing a decision can escalate a negotiation between partners into a war. The pressure of having to make a uniform decision can increase power plays rather than decrease them.

Making unconscious values conscious allows parenting partners to get off the seesaw and put their feet on solid ground. Partners give up their game playing (pushing on their side of the seesaw in an attempt to balance the others parents bad parenting example) and work together on balancing love and limits.

Playing Triangles

If parents were to draw a picture of a seesaw on paper they would see that the outline resembles an upside down triangle. Each side of the seesaw and the fulcrum in the middle represents a different point of the triangle. Whenever a triangle exists in a family, conflict and miscommunication are likely to occur.

Murray Bowen (1994), one of the foremost specialists in the field of family therapy, used the concept of triangles to describe how family members attempt to alleviate stress and anxiety in the home. When the level of stress and anxiety is low in a family, members can engage in direct, one-on-one communication of opinions and feelings. But when stress and anxiety are high and the stability of the relationships become threatened, one or both of the parents may pull in a third person to create a triangle, or a three-person interaction. This third person may dilute the stress and anxiety in the family and produce a feeling, however false, of stability and balance. As an example, try to imagine a person sitting on a two-legged stool. What would happen? She would fall over. But add a third leg and the stool is much more stable. This is why family members draw in a third person, to stabilize their feelings of being out of balance.

This action, called *triangulation*, has two primary problems. The first is that vulnerable people, usually children, are unnecessarily drawn into the conflict. Secondly, triangulation may actually increase stress instead of decreasing it. Bowen described four possible outcomes for triangulation: (1) a stable relationship of two people may become unstable by the addition of a third person (for example, the birth of a child brings stress to a stable marital relationship); (2) a stable relationship can become unstable by the removal of a third person (marital conflict arises after a child has left home and is no longer available to stabilize the marital relationship); (3) an unstable relationship can become stable with the addition of a third person (stressful marriage becomes stable with the birth of a child and the refocusing of the relationship of the baby and not one another); (4) an unstable relationship is stabilized by the removal of a third person (marital conflict is reduced by avoiding a third person who consistently took sides and gave fuel to the conflict).

When triangulation creates an unstable situation, this is referred to as complementary communication or relationships (Watlawick, Weakland, & Fisch, 1974). Complementary communication involves a one-up and a one-down position, similar to having a seesaw with one side up in the air and the other resting on the ground. This one-up and one-down positioning of parenting partners is a force of imbalance in their love and limits. But as already mentioned, it may actually reinforce the problem, creating an imbalance that keeps a balance. More specifically, one parent may be assertive while the other is very passive or one parent may be very dominating and the other submissive. Although unhealthy, these parenting relationships frequently exist and complement one another in that the more submissive one parent is, the more the other is free to be domineering and vice-versa. The same is true for love and limits. The more nurturing and permissive one parent is, the more strict and authoritarian the other parent is allowed to be. In this situation, the seesaw rarely moves up and down. Its imbalanced positioning, with one side up in the air and the other side on the ground, is more permanent.

Triangulation is a game played not only by parenting partners, but by children as well. Siblings who continually fight with one another often look to the parent as the referee of the battle and thereby dilute the stressful situation. If parents can maintain positive feelings toward both children and not take sides, the emotional intensity between the two children will diminish. But if parents take sides, they then reinforce the conflict by their attention to it, causing it to continue.

Detriangulation, or How to Break Up a Triangle

Bowen's answer to families who are using triangles in an unhealthy manner is to help each member of the family to differentiate themselves from other family members. *Differentiation* is the process by which family members view themselves as separate intellectual and emotional beings, capable of functioning alone but able to ask for support or give support when necessary. Differentiated individuals use straight lines of communication to deal with stressful, emotional situations, between themselves and other family members. They do not use vulnerable members of the family to form an alliance and gang up on other family members. Instead they strive to maintain direct, one-on-one communication with other family members and refuse to be drawn into family conflicts. It is true that the shortest route between two points is a straight line. It takes longer to get from point A to point B if another point is added to the equation.

Parents can detriangulate themselves by withdrawing from the role of buffer or go-between with their children and not undermining the other parent disciplining a child. Parenting partners can step off the seesaw and ask the other parent to do the same. Once they are on firm, level ground, they can discuss appropriate ways to discipline and work in a more cooperative, rather than a reactive manner.

Adele Faber and Elaine Mazlish in their book, *Siblings Without Rivalry* (1987) offer a three-step model for dealing with fighting children. If children fighting over a toy truck are at the point of disagreement but not physical warfare, a parent's best choice at this time is to not intervene but allow the children to try and work it out on their own. This gives children the opportunity to learn negotiation skills, conflict resolution, and creativity in working out their own problems. Most children will attempt to draw the parent into the fray, but Faber and Mazlish suggest dreaming of your fantasy vacation (or anything other than the fray) instead of getting involved. Simply redirect them to work out the problem themselves and restate their problem by describing the issue: "Both of you want to play with the truck at the same time." If the battle escalates, then the next step is for the parent to physically be present over the confrontation but not yet intervene. The goal is to prevent one child from hitting the other child with the truck, dominating the situation. The parent could further describe the problem by stating each person's viewpoint:

"Tommy, you say you had the truck first, but Stacy believes you put it down to play with something else." This still gives children the opportunity to resolve the situation themselves and keeps the parent from creating a triangle with the children. The final step is to physically intervene if the battle becomes dangerous in words or actions. At this time it may be necessary to remove the truck since it is causing so much trouble or to suggest that both children play separately for a while. After a cooling down period, the parent can suggest the children try again to come up with a solution to the problem. The truck can wait on top of the refrigerator until they reach an agreement.

Parents can use a similar tactic with each other. When one parent is disciplining the child in a way that the other feels is too lax or too harsh, he or she can think of that fantasy vacation and not intervene. Staying out of the situation does not condone the other's discipline. It does convey respect for the other's belief about what a "good" parent would do in that situation. Intervening at that moment would probably backfire anyway, if the other parent becomes defensive about it.

The next step between parenting partners would be to intervene by describing the problem and modeling an alternative method of discipline that might get better results, without attacking the views of the other parents.

A third approach would be to intervene physically, by removing the child, if the other parent becomes physically and verbally abusive. Of course, how one parent defines abuse may drastically differ from the other parent's definition of abuse. By waiting to intervene, the parent will have a better perspective of whether or not the other parent has crossed the line. If the other parent refuses to get off the seesaw and work in a truly balanced manner, professional help, such as individual or marital therapy, may be necessary. And if the situation becomes dangerous for either the intervening parent or child, law enforcement may need to be called to assist in the situation.

Playing Tug-of-War

Another power play is the game of tug-of-war. It is similar to playing on the seesaw in that tug-of-war is a game for two people: a single person cannot play it alone. Like the game of triangles, people can be added to one side and/or the other to increase the odds of winning the game. The difference in tug-of-war versus playing on the seesaw is that balance is sought by power or control.

control. Although pushing down on one side of the seesaw requires strength and is a form of power or control, tug-of-war more clearly illustrates the struggle for power in the parenting relationship. It might be said that tug-of-war more closely resembles a power-struggle game than a power play game.

The object of tug-of-war is to determine who has the greatest strength and, therefore, control. Individuals stand on either side of a marker or line and pull on two ends of a rope. The winner is decided by whoever is able to pull the other person over the line onto their side. Therefore, the more people or the stronger the people that are on one side of the rope, the more likely it is that side will win the power struggle.

Struggles usually occur when there is a convergence of several problems in the family at one time (Carter & McGoldrick, 1989). For example, a family may be having difficulty making a transition in the family life cycle and be faced with an external stressor like a parent losing a job. The more problems that mount against a family the more likely it is that their coping mechanisms will be overloaded. Consequently, family members turn on one another in their frustration and anger. In terms of love and limits, the more out-of-control parenting partners feel, the more they will seek to control the relationship and the discipline of the children. When one partner gives up and lets the other control the situation, a complementary relationship, described in the triangles section above, occurs. But when parenting partners continue to compete, a power struggle, much like the game of tug-of-war ensues.

Communication is the key to setting down the rope and negotiating a mutually satisfying solution. Parenting partners may have difficulty setting the rope down. Tug-of-war does not create feelings of security and trust in the other parent. A parent may fear the other parent will take control as soon as they let go of their end of the rope. Or they may be so competitive that it is unthinkable to ever let go. Letting go may be synonymous with bad parenting or being a victim, so that the act of letting go is psychologically impossible. In these situations, it is necessary to help the resistive parent know that letting go is different than setting down the rope together. It is much easier to reach a mutually satisfying solution if parenting partners are not tugging one another back and forth. In some situations, a marriage or family therapist is required to help the parenting partners set down the rope.

Tug-of-war or power-struggling is also a common experience between parents and children. By the time children reach the age of two they are already playing tug-of-war with their parents. Many parents see this game as a sign of disrespect when, in fact, it is a natural process of childrens' development. Parents label the time period of two to three years of age as the time of the terrible-two's because of the continual power-struggling which takes place between parents and children. The reality is that this is a time of the terrific-two's because of the terrific amount of developmental milestones which must be achieved by the child. By the age of three, most children are expected to master the tasks of talking, walking, eating, and toilet training all at the same time. These tasks are taken for granted by adults. In order to achieve these tasks, children need a high level of independence. A dependent child would expect the parents to continue feeding them, diapering them, and carrying them from place to place. While annoying, these terrible/terrific behaviors are necessary if the child is to reach these milestones.

A bit of advice parents may find helpful during this stressful time is: "Don't fight, but don't give in." When playing "tug-of-war," parents have three options: force the child over the line to their way of doing things, allow the child to pull them over the line to the child's way of doing things, or set down the rope and negotiate a win/win solution. If parents choose the last option, children used to playing this game to get their needs met will do everything in their power to get their parents to pick up the rope. Parents must stand their ground and not pick up the rope. Three parenting tools to assist parents in following this advice are the **choices, broken record,** and **choosing your battles** parenting tools.

Parenting Tools: Choices

One alternative is to provide children with a couple of choices that fall within acceptable parental standards. This option encourages children to make their own decisions and avoids frequent power struggles. As an example, a parent might state: "Which pants do you want to wear to school today, the blue ones or the white ones?" If red pants are not acceptable to you, do not include them in the list of choices. If your child demands the red pants anyway, use the broken record technique. Choices provide children with a feeling of power because they are in control of what they eat, wear, and play. The parent also wins because they have control over the amount and type of choices available to the child. Power struggles are never a win/win proposition. Permissive parents feel so guilty about making children follow the rule, especially when they respond angrily, that they eventually give in, resent the children, and hate themselves for not standing firm. Authoritarian parents rarely give choices to their children and must rely on force to achieve cooperation. Force is on the parent's side as long as the parent is bigger than the child. But children do grow, and by their teenage years many are larger than their parents. What to do then? Reasonable choices are a much more democratic form of cooperation than authoritarian ("do it my way or else") or permissive ("please do it just this once") statements.

Some children will choose the third, unspoken option. When the parents ask them if they want orange juice or milk to drink with lunch, whether they want to do their homework now or after the television program, or if they prefer to fold the clothes or rake the leaves, these children will go for that third option. Parents can respond that the choices are A or B and not C. Firmness and consistency are good balanced parenting practices and provide children with a feeling of security. Children need to know what and where the limits are. Children who do not know what the limits are become anxious and out of control.

Parenting Tool: Broken record

To use the broken record technique, parents repeat to a child the rule, consequence, or expectation they have for the child. Anger and frustration are not communicated in the parent's voice or words when repeating the rule, consequence, or expectation. The parent simply states, "The rule for using dad's tools is to put them back where you found them or they will have to be locked up." Make sure that the child understands the parental standard and agrees to it up-front. If it is not important how dad's tools are treated, then this parenting tool is unnecessary. In response to a child's arguments or excuses, respond by repeating the rule. After three or four broken record statements, take action by making the choice for the child, following through with the consequence for violating the rule, and/or stepping out from the situation. It is not necessary to continue arguing with a child about a rule that is clearly understood. This is another example of a game by children to gain their parents' attention.

This is not the time for negotiation. Tell the child, "We can discuss how fair this rule is later this evening after dinner, but for right now the rule is still _____." This tool may be a real test of parents' patience, but it will help parents become more firm and consistent in their discipline.

Parenting Tool: Choose your battles

Choosing your battles is an important and often forgotten tool. Many of the battles parents get into with their children could be avoided if they would just choose more carefully which battles they wish to fight and which they do not. Not all battles can be won, and some are relatively unimportant. Choose which battles are crucial. If it doesn't matter which pants the child wears to school, then don't fight over it. If it does matter, make sure you are prepared with some balanced parenting tools. Although you may not win all of the battles, you can still win the war of balanced parenting.

All of these parenting tools will allow parents to let go of the rope or not fight and not give in to children's demands. Parents of 2-year-olds and teenagers alike will find these tools useful in creating a win/win outcome in the game of tug-of-war.

The purpose of this chapter is to help parents understand the various forces that can create imbalance in their parenting. We have discussed personal forces, including parents' definitions of love and limits and the perfect parenting standard that cripples parents' balance. Power plays are common between parenting partners and children. The family system and life cycle can create both personal and social imbalances, and nontraditional families must contend with special challenges. Parents must learn to contend with confusing social messages and parenting strategies that may not be effective for them. They must learn that parenting tools are not magic wands. Our next step is to consider the rise of the nontraditional family as a force of imbalance in parents' lives.

Chapter
5

The Rise of the Nontraditional Family

Another force that creates a state of imbalance in families occurs when nontraditional families try to parent their children according to traditional methods of parenting. The nontraditional family of yesterday (the divorced, single, step, foster, and adoptive parents and grandparent parenting their grandchildren) is fast becoming the traditional family of today.

When many of today's parents were children, in the 1950s and early 1960s, the "ideal" traditional family consisted of a father who worked outside the home, a mother who handled most of the homemaker responsibilities, and two or more children. These days, the nontraditional family is more the exception than the rule, for several reasons. Foremost is the need and desire of women to enter the work force. Since the 1950s, the number of women working outside the home has tripled. Thus the dual-career family, in which both mother and father work, out of both desire and need, is much more common. In addition, the divorce rate has risen to an estimated 50% for first marriages and 60% for second and remarriages.

The traditional view from our childhoods holds that one parent provides for the financial needs of the family while the other parent cares for the majority of the emotional and physical needs of the children. Typically, dad was considered to be the provider and mom the homemaker. And so the world of work and home became separate and distinct. Most contemporary parents grew up in this type of home. As a result they have come to feel as if this is the "right" or "only" way for a family to function. Consequently, nontraditional parents who attempt to live according to traditional methods of parenting experience great feelings of guilt and frustration at falling short of this ideal family arrangement. The economic necessity of contemporary families to have both parents work or, in the case of single parents, the only parent to provide for the financial and emotional needs of the family has changed what society considers to be traditional.

Other reasons for the rise of the nontraditional family include the ravages of social ills, such as chemical abuse, or a traumatic experience, such as the unexpected death of one or both parents. In these instances, grandparents and other relatives often take on the parenting role, or the children are placed in foster homes or adopted.

Society's Concept of the Jdeal Family Structure

The traditional family structure has long been considered the ideal family structure. Unfortunately, this belief isolates and reflects unfairly on over half of all American families today. This extreme position handicaps nontraditional parents, who feel they should or must be like other parents. Consequently, they feel they must have a definite family structure to have a balanced family. The reality is that they will never be a "traditional" family, at least not according to the persistent definition. And if they rely on that definition for their self-worth and balance of love and limits, they will suffer.

This brings up the need to redefine societies definition of a "family." Earlier we defined the family as a system, made up of various subsystems, each with specific roles and responsibilities. This definition allows parents to balance love and limits regardless of the composition of the family, traditional or nontraditional. But it is limited in that it relies on the family's structure as its basic premise. A more practical definition, for contemporary parents balancing love and limits, would be based on function rather than structure.

No family structures are all good or all bad. Each has certain strengths and weaknesses. Being a traditional family is no guarantee of marital bliss, parent/child satisfaction, and family harmony. It is possible for all families, regardless of their structure, to become more balanced in their love and limits.

Family Functioning

Rather than define a family in terms of its structure or composition, why not define it in terms of its ability to function? Both traditional and nontraditional families can be fully functioning or non-fully functioning entities. For example, a fully functioning, traditional family may be most comfortable following older social norms in their family life. In this situation, both parents may agree that the father will be the sole provider for the family while mom stays home with the children. To be successful, this family needs to be able to communicate openly and be flexible in its roles and responsibilities. Perhaps dad is comfortable not just at work but at home as well, giving mom time off by cleaning, cooking, and taking care of the children. Or mom may enjoy working part-time to satisfy her need to be out of the house and to help bring income into the family. Either way, neither is threatened by the other person's contribution to family income and nurturing.

Traditional families can also be non-fully functioning families. Typically, these families have unequal roles and responsibilities. Mom's job is to take care of the house and the kids, which entails working 24 hours a day, 7 days a week, while dad's sole responsibility is bringing home the paycheck. The two worlds of work and family remain separate entities, rarely merging. There is no reciprocal sharing of responsibilities, and communication of personal and familial needs is kept to a minimum. Frequent marital conflict and power struggles are common in the non-fully functioning family. Some of these families suffer verbal, physical, and mental abuse. Simply having two parents with absolute roles of work and child care is no guarantee of family happiness. Likewise, having the same two biological parents does not guarantee parents will balance love and limits in an effective manner.

Nontraditional families can be fully functioning or non-fully functioning. The fully functioning nontraditional family does not see parenting in rigid, stereotyped roles. The focus is on individual strengths regardless of whether they are the biological or nonbiological parents. They concentrate on the positive experiences that come out of their new or changing family compositions and not just the difficulties that result from those changes. In contrast, the non-fully functioning family is overcome by the developmental and social transitions that take place in the family life cycle. They are unable to let go of the past and find ways for present relationships and circumstances to work. They allow themselves to continue living under the weight of guilt and consider themselves to be "less than" other parents in society simply because they do not fit the mold. They give up too quickly, before the family has had a chance to heal from past hurts and form new bonds with new, nonbiological family members.

A family's ability to function, either in the traditional or nontraditional structure, takes place along four dimensions (Harway & Wexler, 1996). The first includes daily living tasks, such as obtaining possessions, cooking and cleaning, repairing and improving the home, child care and socialization skills, and caring for one another when sick or injured. The second dimension is leadership. Leadership includes having a democratic or balanced level of power and control, existing primarily in the executive or marital subsystem and shared with all family members. The third dimension is family cohesiveness, the feeling of connection to one another as a family. It can be built over time by the use of family rituals and celebrations, demonstrations of affection, values placed on participation in family events, and endurance through rough times, which provide members with a sense that "we can make it through anything." The fourth dimension is the family value system. This value system governs the family's expectations about behavior, the organization and directions of family activities, and the various goals and rules set up in the home.

The nontraditional family could be considered to be traditional in function as it fulfills these four dimensions. In fact, given these four dimensions, nontraditional families may be more fully functioning than traditional families. Parents must be more conscious in their activities and actions with one another and not do things the way they have always been done. They must put more effort in areas that will make them fully functioning families rather than continuing to do things that don't work, which results only in frustration. These parents must look beyond the composition of the family and rethink the concept of an "ideal" family. Stated another way, they must look at the heart of the family and work from the inside out.

Nontraditional Families and Feelings of Grief

Nontraditional families are quite diverse in structure. They include adults who are divorced, single, step, adoptive, and foster parents and grandparents raising grandchildren. Most of the programs designed to help parents balance love and limits are designed for traditional parents rather than nontraditional parents. In addition, many problems that plague nontraditional parents are often different from those facing traditional parents. One of the differences experienced by nontraditional families includes dealing with feelings of grief.

Grief is caused by a significant loss in one's life. The loss might have been a significant other, such as a mother, father, or child, or it might have been the loss of a dream of how a family "should" have turned out. People make emotional attachments to other people and things, through the passing down of family ideals, values, or beliefs. This attachment occurs on an unconscious level and is central to the identity and life of the individual and the family. Deep in the unconscious reside the individual and family dreams, goals, illusions, and/or projections into the future about who and what they are meant to be and do (Moses, 1989). Although this sounds fairly existential, it is basically about one's self-identity and hopes for the future.

Fortunately, grief has predictable stages of development. These stages are rather discrete and time limited, although they tend to cycle around. As hard as it may be to believe, grief does not last forever, at least not in the same intensity. The fear of most people going through grief at the outset is that feelings of grief will completely overwhelm them. Those feelings are so big and so powerful that they are difficult to cope with. Over time, these feelings diminish in intensity and become easier and easier to adjust to.

Perhaps the best known framework for grief and loss is the work of Elisabeth Kubler-Ross. Elisabeth Kubler-Ross studied patients and their family members who were dying of cancer. Her finished results were published in the now famous book: *On Death and Dying* (1969). In it she described various stages of grieving, that can apply to any form of loss. These stages include: denial, anger, bargaining, depression, and acceptance. All of these stages are ways of coping with loss.

A visual way of understanding grief is to think of it like waves of an ocean. When you are way out in the ocean, the waves are large and frightening. They pull you under and twist you about, creating a sense of hopelessness or fear of your future. This is called the stage of shock or denial. When the waves pass and the ocean feels momentarily calm, this is called the stage of anger or bargaining. During this stage, grieving people must use their energy to swim for shore. The shore represents the stage of acceptance. As they swim for the shore, more waves crash over them, threatening to pull them under and back into the stage of shock and its feelings of hopelessness. But the closer they come to the shore, the less intense the force of the wave. The intensity of feelings of hopelessness decreases. Grieving people now recover more quickly and can continue functioning and swimming to the shore of acceptance. As they reach the shore and can stand on their own two feet, the waves crash against their legs and finally their feet. This, too, feels unstable, but is in no way like being hit by the waves way out in the ocean. Soon, they are on dry ground again. And while they have not forgotten the waves and their effects, they are no longer controlled by them and can accept new realities for their lives.

Nontraditional families can use this illustration to help them balance love and limits. Because they are in the ocean and not on the shore they cannot compare themselves to traditional families. Rather than live up to society's expectation of what an ideal family should look like, nontraditional families need to concentrate their energy on swimming for the shore. Only by working together can all members of the family reach the shore together. Otherwise some members will be left struggling in the waves while others are walking on the shore. This is the first and most important activity of nontraditional families in balancing love and limits.

Divorced Families

Divorce is the process whereby a single family unit separates into two or more parts. It is traumatic even in the most civil of situations. The more conflicts between parents, the more trauma experienced by the child. Studies have shown that children react to the amount of conflict or fighting that goes on between divorcing parents (Garrity & Baris, 1994). The more cooperative the parents are with one another, the more emotionally healthy the child. Children are often the battle ground for mom and dad's war of unresolved issues towards one another. This creates deep feelings of grief for children. Consequently, they fantasize about their parents getting back together, even after their parents have remarried and they have grown up. Additionally, their grief is greater when one parent cuts off involvement with the children, not calling or visiting or acknowledging birthdays. Starting a new family may also be viewed by the child as rejection or abandonment.

Step or Blended Parent Families

Children in a stepfamily experience grief. As strange as it might sound, it is possible for a stepchild to feel both joy and sadness when a parent remarries.

The remarriage signifies both a gain and a loss for the child. It is a gain in that new family members—a new parent and possibly siblings—are added. It is also a loss in that biological parents and siblings are no longer together in a traditional arrangement. Difficulty occurs when family members, usually the children, are less accepting of the new parents and/or siblings. Older children are generally less accepting of new parental figures than are younger children. Older children may have had a longer period of time to attach to a biological parent and therefore feel a greater sense of loss. In accepting a new parent and/or siblings, a child may feel disloyal to the biological parent. Even when biological parents share custody, children experience and re-experience feelings of grief as they move back and forth between mom's house to dad's house.

Parents in a stepfamily also experience grief. There may be unresolved issues of anger or hurt toward the ex-partner that carry over into the new relationship. Fear of making "another mistake" may pop up during times of conflict, creating an experience of grief. Feelings of guilt, of traumatizing one's children or emotionally hurting an ex-partner, may stir up still more grief. Jealousy of the bond between biological children and their parent can create feelings of grief for the nonbiological parent, who may or may not have biological children. Anger may result from having to pay child support and care for the financial needs of one's new family or from never receiving child support and being unable to meet the children's financial needs.

Single Parent Families

Single parents experience grief, too. The biggest source of their grief is the loss of time and money. Single parents seem to never have enough time or money to fulfill all the needs of work, home, and family. Working, single parents are forced to juggle career and family life. At the end of the day, when the next shift begins, they feel exhausted and unable to enjoy time with their children. Some single parents feel guilty for not having enough time for their children or for not having a mother or father for the child. These feelings of guilt can lead to difficulty in setting limits for their children. It can also lead them to deny their own needs for personal socialization and emotional growth in favor of their children. The thought of having a social life to many single parents is simply a joke. These parents need a bill of rights that allows them to take care of their own needs as well as the needs of their children. As we will discuss in the chapter on Permissive Parenting Styles, parents need to take care of themselves before they can take care of others. Single parents may feel that they must remarry in order to adequately provide for their children. Their child needs a father or mother to take care of them. As a result, many single parents remarry too early and end up unhappy and in a worse situation. Unless they are aware of their feelings of grief and take care of themselves, they are doomed to repeat past mistakes. This ends up in more pain and hurt for the whole family.

Adoptive and Foster Parent Families

Adoptive and foster parents deal with feelings of grief. These special parents are faced with the struggle of raising children who may have come from traumatic situations and/or have a different set of genetic traits than themselves. To adopt a child, parents may be forced to accept the reality that they cannot conceive. Not only does the adoptive child not look like the adoptive parent, but special needs, such as attention deficits or learning disabilities, may be present. Adoptive children also know grief. They must contend with the fact that they were "given up" for adoption. They may wind up feeling unwanted and unlovable. In addition, these children may feel different from other children in their family if they are the only nonbiological children present. They may have different color skin, hair, and eyes and thus feel inferior. These children, when older, often search for their biological parents (which can create feelings of grief for the adoptive parents) to answer the question of why they were adopted. Many times the answer they find is unpleasant and painful.

Foster parents are faced with an ongoing series of griefs: accepting into their home a new child, learning to adapt to personalities and needs of that child, developing feelings of affection and love for that child, and then risking loss if the child's parents are able to resume parenting or if someone chooses to adopt him or her. Adoptive and foster parents are not immune to feelings of grief. They struggle with the realization that they are not, and never will be, society's idea of a traditional family. They must also deal with the personal realization that the child they have come to care about is not their own (unless the adoption is finalized) and may be forced to leave their home.

Grandparents Raising Grandchildren

Another nontraditional family that shares feelings of loss are grandparents responsible for the raising of their grandchildren. Grandparents feel grief over a planned retirement gone awry. Instead of having lots of spare time to enjoy the finer things of life, they are faced with the responsibilities of caring for their grandchildren. Many grandparents feel they have failed as parents if their own children are unable or unwilling to care for the grandchildren. And grandparents, like single parents, may have less resources, emotionally and physically, to go through the act of reparenting. Not only are they older and harder pressed to have the energy to take care of the needs of children, but they are also given less financial compensation and legal power to make decisions.

In some situations, grief actually keeps grandparents from taking the necessary legal measures to ensure the safety and well-being of their grandchildren. Because of their own remorse and hope that their child will become more responsible and able to care for their grandchildren, they often fail to take certain legal measures that will ensure the grandchildren's safety and well-being. Errant and irresponsible parents can take their children away from grandparents at any time, unless the grandparents have some legal right to make decisions in the lives of their grandchildren.

Grandchildren must also deal with feelings of grief. These children mourn the loss of their parents and may act out their pain in an aggressive and revengeful manner. Children tend to treat the world around them in the same manner they perceive they have been treated. Therefore, a grieving child may want to hurt himself, others, or property as an expression of his own pain.

If professional help is not enlisted, these children may end up suffering major depression. Many children in this situation already are experiencing depression, but it may be going unnoticed as the symptoms of depression in children differ from those in adults. Adults who are depressed crave sleep, have little energy and may either overeat or starve themselves. In contrast, depressed children may wet the bed, have trouble concentrating in school, get into fights, refuse to cooperate, complain of headaches and stomach aches, or have other symptoms not commonly recognized as depression. Grandparents need the advice of a child counselor or pediatrician to determine if their grandchild is truly depressed and what is the best recourse.

Next, we will discuss the stages of grief. By understanding these stages, parents in nontraditional families will be better able to balance love and limits by better coping with the feelings of grief.

In the Ocean of Grief

Grief is an emotional process by which families must let go of old, shattered dreams and goals and acquire new, more attainable dreams and goals (Moses, 1989). These stages often overlap but gradually decrease in intensity through time allowing the person to reach a new place of acceptance. Although there is no prescribed order to the stages, each stage has a certain order of function. Earlier we described these stages as denial, anger, bargaining, depression, and acceptance (Kubler-Ross, 1969).

Each wave performs a necessary emotional reaction in the life of the grieving individual. This reaction is necessary for the parent or child to adopt new dreams and goals. Most people want to jump straight to the shore bypassing the need to struggle through the waves of the ocean of grief. Unfortunately, this is not possible if true acceptance is to be achieved. Although these waves do not always occur in a universal order, they include: denial, anxiety, fear, guilt, depression, anger, and acceptance.

Denial is sometimes compared to the experience of shock. When a loss is too personal and too painful, parents and children become overloaded and feel a need to distance themselves from the loss in order to deal with it. Denial can be healthy when it allows people to take stock of internal strengths and external resources available to them to cope and accept the loss. Denial becomes unhealthy when they continue to stay in a state of shock and cannot move on to the other stages. Unfortunately, there is no definite time period for how long denial will last. Denial has a time frame all its own and cannot be rushed or completed too quickly.

Kubler-Ross describes denial as the "No, not me" state of mind. Isolation, both physical and emotional, is common during this wave of emotion. This allows the individual to gain some perspective on their loss before moving forward. It is a temporary defense that will be replaced with partial acceptance of the loss. From this point, the individual can begin to utilize less radical defense mechanisms.

The next wave of grief is a feeling of *anxiety*. Anxiety's function is to mobilize and focus a person's energy to begin taking advantage of the internal strengths and external supports identified during the stage of denial. An adult may become very busy, or a child may become hyperactive whenever thinking about the loss or when someone mentions it. Even sights or sounds that are associated with the loss may create feelings of uneasiness or tension. A child who has lost a parent may recognize a certain lady's perfume on another person as one that mom wore and become extremely unruly, apparently for no reason. Adults might get a déjà vu feeling when they go the movie theater or watch a particular Christmas movie that reminds them of the person they lost. This stirring of feeling helps to mobilize their energy to use their resources at a later time.

After a person mobilizes their energies, they may be hit by the wave of *fear*. Fear is a feeling of being vulnerable, at risk, or in danger. On one level it serves to protect us by causing a "fight or flight" reaction. If danger is near, our mind needs to decide, "Do I fight this off or do I flee?" In the process of grief, fear serves to recommit the person to new dreams, relationships, to loving and being loved. But doing so places the person at risk of suffering a loss (being abandoned or hurt) psychologically again. A child may refuse to get close to another adult because they fear being hurt if that person were to leave or die as well. Divorced parents may feel fear at the thought of getting remarried. They don't want to experience the hurt and loss that might occur if they were to remarry and then get divorced again. Grieving people must identify their resources, mobilize their energy, and take a step forward into the jaws of a new dream, goals, or relationship. Fear is a byproduct of taking this step and leads to the shore of acceptance.

Unconsciously, everyone starts out life believing that they are immortal. The newborn child cannot conceptualize that they will ever be alone, separated from their primary caretakers. But as we grow older, we consciously realize that life and relationships are short and temporary. This awakening creates feelings of fear.

This next wave to hit is *guilt*. Parents are all too familiar with guilt. Its function during the process of grief is to resolve basic questions about the meaning of one's relationships and personal existence. These questions must be asked to achieve healthy acceptance. The questions might include: "What meaning does life have, now that I no longer have this dream, goal, or relationship in my life?" and "What do I consider to be of importance, given the impact of the loss on my feelings, way of life, relationships, actions, and beliefs?" To illustrate this state, consider a child who feels that she is somehow responsible for a parent's death or abandoning the family. She is forced to ask herself some very basic life questions about her willingness to love another person and about her own self-worth. With the right support and help, this child will realize she is not to blame although she may continue to feel guilty. Guilt allows people to re-evaluate their lives in a way that denial, anxiety, and fear do not allow. By doing so, they can find their way to new goals and dreams.

After guilt comes the wave of depression. We have already mentioned that this state differs in quality between children and adults, but its function is the same regardless of age or gender. Depression acts as a medium for redefining one's competency, capability, value, and ability. All of these concepts were contaminated by the loss. As people overcome the shock of denial, mobilize the resources of anxiety, face the fear of new dreams and goals, and ask basic existential questions about themselves and their relationships, they are now ready to move on without the person or thing they lost. Doing so creates a feeling of intense sadness. Here they can feel the pain that all the previous states did not allow. They are no longer distant from the loss as in the stage of denial. They are now very close to the full reality of the loss. If they have been able to identify adequate internal and external resources, mobilize their energy and find new dreams to pursue, however frightening they might be, then they are ready to move on toward acceptance. But this cannot occur without feelings of hurt.

Of all the feeling states or waves, this wave is the one most often used to characterize grief. It is often referred to negatively as something that should be avoided. Pills are prescribed daily so that people cannot feel the weight of depression. While medical management of depression is often helpful for chronic sufferers of this state, to use medication unnecessarily during the time of grieving is to work against nature's defense mechanism. It is a false raft on the wave of depression, and the person must sooner or later sink into this ocean of grief if they truly want to reach the shore of acceptance.

This wave and the one that follows are in a different order than the stages described by Elisabeth Kubler-Ross (1969). In her stages of grieving, anger comes before depression. The reason it is used differently here is to more clearly illustrate anger's role in the life of the grieving person. Anger is not commonly expected during grief. This is because so much emphasis is given to depression being the poster child of grieving. If denial is the person's way of saying "No, not me," then anger is the person's way of saying "Why me?"

The last wave in the cycle of grief is anger. Once grieving people have asked basic, existential questions of themselves and of the world around them, they may become angry at what feels like unfairness or a lack of justice in their life. This may be especially true for people who have suffered a loss that has no apparent meaning, when a father walks out on a family, for example, or a person dies in a random and senseless act. Anger fully mobilizes the internal strengths and external supports that were identified during the earlier stage of denial and anxiety. Unfortunately, that sense of violation may turn those resources into weapons that they use on the world around them. They hurt, unfairly so, and they want the world to hurt, too. They want the world to know the irrationality of their loss. Fortunately, anger is a positive state that energizes a grieving person to begin coping, which was impossible during the stages of depression and fear when accepting the total reality of the loss was too overwhelming. Anger also helps develop new skills, perspectives, insights, and attitudes. This is possible because anger holds much more energy than depression. It is hard for people to accomplish new goals when they are depressed. There is no energy and it seems to take action against the injustice. Anger demands that action occur so that the injustice is righted and never occurs again. But like denial, if anger is held onto for too long, it can become unhealthy in the life and relationships of the people who have suffered a loss. Anger can be a force for healing or a force for hurting if militant and abusive.

Many parents and children are relieved when they feel they have gone through all of the waves of grief. They breathe out a sigh, and think, "Now I can go on with my life and not be bothered by all of those uncomfortable feelings I just experienced." Unfortunately, this is not always the case. Remnants of the old, shattered dreams can still pop up in one's memory or thoughts. They may feel frightened many years after the actual event of the loss. Or they may feel depressed long after they have re-entered the stage of acceptance. The process of grief can continue for many years, maybe even the rest of their lives. But it will not arise in the same intensity or feelings that occurred during the time of the loss. Depression may resurface, but not as severely as during the initial loss. Or guilt may reoccur, but for only a passing moment or two, not for days on end. When these times do occur, parents and children simply need to let them have their moment and then let them go. Acknowledge them as important stages in the continued acceptance of a new life and do not attempt to push them out of awareness. This will only frustrate the process and create more problems.

Family and friends are more comfortable dealing with the wave of depression in the grieving person than they are in dealing with the wave of anger. Even professionals who deal with grieving people find anger difficult to cope with (Kubler-Ross, 1969). The reason is that anger can be a random, unpredictable force that is projected indiscriminately on people and objects around the angry person. Nobody likes being a target, even a moving one. It is difficult to be patient and tolerant of a person's anger during the wave of grief, especially if it is irrational and its full force is directed, in a blaming manner, towards them. For example, a child may blame the mother for daddy leaving the family although she was not responsible for the act. This is the child's way of projecting their hurt onto a safe target, whom they do not fear will abandon them, even if they are angry at them. Children are afraid of blaming dad, especially if they have limited visitations, because they fear that he will stop visiting and what little contact they do have will be removed. The mother is a safer, more secure person on which to express their anger.

Of course, nontraditional parents are not the only families to experience grief. Traditional families know grief as well. The point of this section is to illustrate how nontraditional families can feel both joy and sadness, at the same time, in their family. Most traditional parenting classes and books do not incorporate information on grief or even acknowledge that a different type of family structure exists. Society has few, if any, rituals for nontraditional families to deal with grief. If someone passes away, there is a funeral. But what does a divorced family do when all the members of the family are grieving and a biological parent is absent, but still alive? How does a couple cope when they are unable to conceive and choose to adopt instead? Are there ceremonies that ease the pain and reach their stage of acceptance? Unfortunately, there are no formal rituals or ceremonies for nontraditional families. Nontraditional families may need to create their own rituals to ease the passage of grief and make their family transitions easier.

Parenting Tool: Rituals

Rituals are parenting tools that allow nontraditional and traditional families to form collective identities, facilitate healing, celebrate life changes, and pass on expressions of beliefs (Black, 1989). Rituals include daily activities, such as getting ready for bed, eating at the table, and watching a television program. They can also be much more elaborate and sacred, such as a wedding, funeral, bar mitzvah, graduation, or some other religious ceremony. Regardless of their format, rituals are an important aspect of our social lives, and parents can utilize this hidden resource in developing more intimate families. Family therapists have used the concept of rituals to help families that have been hurt by past actions toward one another or by an unexpected trauma. Wedding vows have been restated by stepfamilies, including the parents and children. Letters of anger and sadness have been written to unknown mothers and fathers and then ceremonially burned or destroyed as an act of saying goodbye. Marriage bands have been melted down or thrown into the middle of lakes to break emotional ties and symbolize the need for an emotional divorce, even after families have already been physically divorced. Again, how one performs these valuable tools is not as important as finding a way to signify a gain, a loss, or both, in the lives of families.

While most of our concepts of rituals lie in the realm of the sacred, this book focuses on the more mundane aspects of balancing love and limits in light of the experiences of grief that traditional and nontraditional families go through.

One such ritual, to help parents balance love and limits is the bedtime ritual. For many families, bedtime is a period of conflict and frustration. Parents struggle with getting children into bed and children search for any distraction that will prevent it as long as possible. An example of a bedtime ritual might include:

7:30 p.m. Brush teeth.
7:45 p.m. Read a book together.
8:00 p.m. Sing a short song or talk with lights off.
8:15 p.m. Kiss each other goodnight.

Because rituals are familiar, they reduce feelings of anxiety and decrease power struggles. It is much more difficult to tug-of-war with a parent when there is a set schedule at bedtime.

Mealtimes are parenting tools that many parents take for granted. There is an interesting relationship between families who have trouble communicating and the act of eating meals together on a regular basis. Some research on alcoholic families suggests that these families, which are often chaotic and stressful, rarely spend time at the dinner table together (Jacobs and Wolin, 1989). Severe drinking behaviors disrupt everyday rituals and routines, often eliminating them altogether. As a result the very fabric of the family is unraveled. In order to intervene and create a sense of family identity, parents can reinstate the **mealtime ritual.** A mealtime ritual might involve getting the family together at a regular time in the same location. Important life skills can be taught prior to mealtime by enlisting children's help in meal preparation. Parents may need to break down various aspects of preparing the meal and setting the table and then incorporate them into the children's chores. Discuss the cultural and religious elements of the preparation and meal if appropriate. After the meal is prepared, families can sit down together. Prayers or blessing can be recited to strengthen religious beliefs. Food is shared and table manners observed. Parents should encourage conversation. Some freedom during mealtimes is necessary, although parents may want to maintain some rules of manners to prevent children from getting out of control. Requiring that children ask to be excused from the table and put dishes away in the kitchen can further create family cooperation. How each family performs a mealtime ritual is not as important as the act itself. The purpose is not to create a regimen of behaviors but to foster family identity. Children should come away from the table with the positive feeling that the people around the table are their family.

Value Clarification Exercise: My childhood rituals
Make a list of the rituals you remember growing up with as a child. Do you still have these rituals in your life now? Is there one that you could adopt into your family life, be it traditional or nontraditional? Enlist the aid of the children. What traditions or rituals do they wish to incorporate into the family? What would make their transitions easier?

Chapter

6

The Perfect Parenting Standard

Although parents consciously know there is no such thing as a perfect parent or a perfect child, they continue to compare themselves to other parents or parenting figures who they consider to reflect a "perfect parenting standard." This standard is the primary, underlying force that creates a state of imbalance for contemporary parents who struggle with feelings of guilt, inadequacy, and frustration.

Deep down parents realize there is no one way to parent a child. As we will see later in this book, parents have various styles of parenting, and each of these styles has a strength and a weakness. Even acknowledging this, many parents continue to believe that a good parent should be doing this or a good child ought to be doing that. They impose "shoulds" and "must-isms" or mental demands on themselves and their child that are impossible for anyone to live up to (Ellis, 1975).

These ideals may have come from the examples of parental figures who parents admired for their parenting abilities, or what they consider to be "good" parenting abilities. Parents may have read a book or watched a movie that illustrated what a "good" parent should, must, or ought to be doing. Parents might have observed a neighbor or friend who is a parent and feel that they never seem to have the kinds of problems their family has. All of these things are fantasy that undermine a parent's attempts to balance love and limits.

Parents who subscribe to the perfect parenting standard often have what Albert Ellis, a pioneer in cognitive therapy, calls "I-Can't-Stand-It-Itis" (Ellis, 1975). This malady is an irrational belief that leads to such statements as "I can't stand your irresponsible behavior" or "I can't stand things turning out this way." This belief creates feelings of anger, depression, and anxiety. A parent who can't stand a child's irresponsible behavior is not allowing that child to fail. And like it or not, failing is part of an imperfect world. In fact, failing is a necessary part of learning. Learning by failing is as important as learning by doing. Without acknowledging failure parents and children could never correct their behaviors, and they would be doomed to repeat their mistakes forever. Take, for example, a child learning to walk. If parents are always there to catch the child or assist him as he takes those first steps, the child cannot successfully achieve that milestone in his life. He would come to expect his parent to always be there for him.

Another term coined by Ellis is "damnations." Damnations translate into statements like "Nothing ever works out the way I want it to" or "Life is always unfair to me—as it should not be." The reality is that many situations in life are annoying and irritating, but they are seldom totally unfair or intolerable. When parents believe that nothing they do works out the way they wanted it to, they feel damned. Parents can start to see, hear, or feel why their balance of love and limits is so out of whack. Much of it is due to how they perceive the world in their minds and not simply due to what happens to them in the world on the outside. As the Greek philosopher Epictetus said, "What disturbs men's minds is not events but their judgments of events." In other words, our perceptions of things create our feelings, not the events themselves. Many parents are of the opinion that other people and situations cause their thoughts and feelings, rather than the other way around.

Parents' perceptions act as filters. Negative filters capture and magnify the negative aspects of themselves ("I must be a bad parent"), their children ("They are always getting into trouble"), their partners ("She never sticks to her guns—she always gives in"), or others ("Other parents don't have these problems with their children the way I do"). Negative filtering makes positive characteristics and behaviors difficult to perceive. On the other hand, positive filtering takes a more balanced approach to parenting. It acknowledges negative events and behaviors while concentrating on possible solutions. Changing how adults perceive their parenting situations can improve their feelings of satisfaction and even how others (their children or partners) interact with them.

Value Clarification Exercise: My perfect parenting standard
To become more aware of the perfect parental standards operating in parents' minds and therefore in their lives, complete the following sentences. Make sure to say or write the first thing that comes to mind. Notice how easily the mind comes up with these ideals:

The Perfect Parenting Standard

1. A good parent always . . .
2. Good children should . . .
3. As a parent, I must . . .
4. My children ought to be more . . .
5. If I was more like my own parents, I would be more . . .

Good Parent/Bad Parent

If parents fall short of these perfect parenting standards, and so are not "good" parents, what must they be? Parents are left with the belief that they are "bad" parents. These beliefs are one reason why parents feel imbalanced in their love and limits. Another way of looking at this problem is to say that parents have mistaken beliefs about parenting and are in need of more realistic ones. A realistic belief is more effective and practical when it comes to balancing love and limits. Beliefs are expressions of parents' values about themselves, other people, and the world. Mistaken beliefs create a feeling of demand whereas realistic beliefs create a feeling of balance.

One way to create more realistic beliefs is to evaluate the evidence for a mistaken thought. What law states that children will always listen and be respectful? What evidence suggests that all parents are available to their children at all times? To test whether a standard is realistic, examine it closely, consider what would happen if the opposite were true, and assess whether achieving the standard is even possible.

Another method to be more realistic is to improve one's self-communication. Review the incomplete sentences in the previous exercise. What kinds of feelings do these statements conjure? Frustration? Hopelessness? Anger? Change the wording of each of these sentences to see if the feelings change with it. For instance, complete the exercise again using these incomplete sentences:

1. A responsible parent always . . .
2. Good children sometimes . . .
3. As a parent, I can be . . .
4. I desire my children to be more . . .
5. If I was like my own parents, the positive qualities I would like to have . . .

If parents are to accept the fact that they are imperfect, then they must eliminate "perfection" language from their thoughts and words. Rather than worry about being a good or bad parent, they need to accept the fact that they are acting "good enough." This doesn't mean they shouldn't strive for more from themselves or their children. Excellence is not the same as perfection. Parents simply need to change their mistaken values and beliefs.

"The Courage to Be Imperfect"

It takes courage to be a good enough, or balanced, parent. This is what child psychiatrist Rudolph Driekurs called "the courage to be imperfect" (Driekurs, 1964). There is no such thing as a perfect parent or a perfect child. While there are plenty of accusing (and self-accusing) perfect parenting standards to fall short of, there is no set of rules for being imperfect. Therefore, Dr. Driekurs has come up with a list of principles for developing the "courage to be imperfect." This courage is necessary to balance love and limits.

1. Children should be encouraged, not expected, to seek perfection.
2. Accept who you are rather than try to be more than or as good as other parents.
3. Mistakes are aids to learning. Mistakes are not signs of failure. Anticipating or fearing mistakes will make us more vulnerable to failure.
4. Mistakes are unavoidable and are less important than what the parent does *after* he or she makes a mistake.
5. Set realistic standards for yourself and your child. Don't try to correct or change too many things at one time.
6. Develop a sense of your strengths and your weaknesses.
7. Mutual respect between parent and child starts by valuing yourself. Recognize your own dignity and worth before you try to show your children their dignity and worth.
8. Unhappy parents are frequently discouraged, competitive, unrealistic in their standard for themselves and their children, overambitious, and unbalanced in their love and limits.
9. High standards and expectations are frequently related to parents' feelings of inferiority and lack of adequate parenting resources.
10. Parents need to develop the courage to cope with the challenges of living, which means, they must develop the "courage to be imperfect."

In contrast to the perfect parent standard, these 10 principles of being imperfect could be called real parenting standards. Parents and children learn from mistakes as much, if not more, than their successes. Parents who seek to balance love and limits may be better off role modeling how someone accepts failure. American society appears to emphasize that parents need to teach children how to be successful but de-emphasizes the role of failure in their lives. Parents can admit to making a mistake, not blow up in anger and become depressed over failures, confess to their inadequacies, ask for forgiveness or demonstrate forgiveness for failures, and use past failures as object lessons when disciplining their children.

A common story relates that when Thomas Edison was inventing the light bulb, he failed 999 times before finally getting it to work. When asked how he felt about failing so many times, he reportedly said, "I did not fail 999 times. I eliminated 999 ways that didn't work!" Parents who feel they have failed as a parent in balancing love and limits can take hope. They have not failed as much as they have eliminated many ways that didn't work. Now they can find some that do. The next section will discuss four different styles parents use when seeking a balance of love and limits and how they can create a more balanced parenting style.

Part 2

The Four Styles of Parenting

There are four different styles of parenting: rejecting or neglecting, author-itarian, permissive, and democratic (Baumrind, 1971). Each of these styles correspond to a certain balance of love and limits shown in Figure 3 below. These styles are characterized by either low or high love and low or high limits.

	Low Limits	High Limits
Low Love	Rejecting/ Neglecting	Authoritarian
High Love	Permissive	Democratic

Figure 3   The Four Styles of Parenting Compared to a Balance of Love and Limits.

A parenting style is the manner in which parents express their beliefs about how to be a "good" parent. These beliefs dictate how parents interact with their children, what they feel their role as a parent is supposed to be and what they should expect from their children. Parents' style may vary based on their culture, family history, and the values of the society they live in. Although parents may use aspects of all of the different parenting styles or express different parenting styles at different times, they have one dominant style they use more frequently than others. As parents review each style, they will quickly identify which style they use most often along with the styles used by the parental figures in their own lives. Curiously, parents' styles and their own parental figures' styles tend to be closely related. That is because of the powerful effects of modeling on children. Children learn from and often repeat the parenting styles used by their own parental figures.

Parenting styles are useful in that they give an emotional assessment of the relationship parents have with their children (Darling & Stienberg, 1993). This relationship is highlighted in the strengths and weakness of each parenting style. Parents can also discover the values or system of beliefs that underlie each parenting style. Some of these beliefs may need to be eliminated and new ones added to balance love and limits.

Strengths and Weaknesses of Parenting Styles

Each style of parenting has a particular strength and weakness when balancing love and limits. These strengths and weaknesses are characterized as either low or high love and low and high limits. Of all the styles, only the democratic parenting style allows parents to use both high love and high limits. This is the style that this book advocates for parents. It is described as the *balanced parenting style*.

Only by understanding the strengths and weaknesses of their parenting styles will parents be able to balance love and limits. Parents do not achieve a balance by focusing on weaknesses only. This creates feelings of defensiveness and resentment. In contrast, when parents focus on their strengths and the strengths of their partners, then they can better use their weaknesses as areas for improvement and growth rather than as an excuse for giving up. To illustrate this balance of strengths and weaknesses and its effects on the balance of love and limits, let's compare two extreme stages of the family life cycle: Courtship and divorce.

The family life cycle was one of the personal forces discussed in the earlier chapter on "Balancing Acts." It was defined as the developmental transition that all families must undergo over time. Courtship is the stage in a family's life cycle when two individuals recognize and expect the best from one another. During courtship partners solicit and woo one another in hopes of finding a soul mate or companion to share their dreams, goals, and life. Divorce, on the other hand, is a stage in the family life cycle where two individuals recognize and expect the worst from one another. During divorce partners seek a dissolution of a relationship because they no longer share a common vision or love. Courtship focuses on strengths and is often blind to the weaknesses of oneself and the other. This is why it is often said that love is blind (to one another's weaknesses). Divorce focuses too much on the other's weaknesses and is often blind to the strengths of the relationship. It assumes that because it is bad now, it was always bad and always will be. The word "always" in that sentence indicates a generalization which results in many mistaken beliefs.

The reality is that most relationships are somewhere in the middle of these two stages and include both strengths and weaknesses. If parenting styles are discussed only by what parents "do not do" (i.e., their weaknesses), they will become disillusioned with their own and their partners' parenting abilities. But if parenting styles are discussed in terms of strengths and weaknesses, then parents will feel some hope for the future of their relationship as partners together and their ability to balance love and limits with their children.

Parenting Style Strengths

Parenting style strengths are the tools that make parenting effective. These tools are not magical wands and can be easily added to parents' repertoire of love and limits. Hence, balancing love and limits involves two concepts: identifying and changing one's beliefs, and eliminating old behaviors while adding new, more effective ones.

Parenting style strengths also are the key to changing parents' values and beliefs about what makes a "good" parent and set the tone of the emotional quality of their relationship with their children. Focusing on one's strengths, not one's weaknesses, is the solution to balancing love and limits.

Parenting Style Weaknesses

Parenting style weaknesses can also be defined as a tool. The difference is that weak tools are not as effective or helpful in balancing love and limits as are strong tools. Most of parents' beliefs about what makes up a "good" or "bad" parent come from how effective the tools are that parents are using. Instead of parents being "good" or "bad," perhaps parents are simply using strong or weak tools.

Parents use the tools they know how to use. They learn to use them by the word and example of their own parental figures. Depending on the culture and the situation, these parental figures could be any adult in the child's life, from mom and dad to a relative or a family friend. Unfortunately, because this is all parents know, they persist in using weak tools over and over again, believing that somehow, someway, they might be able to make them work. Perhaps the tools work some of the time for some children. But as P. T. Barnum once said: "You can fool all of the people some of the time. You can even fool some of the people all of the time. But you cannot fool *all* of the people *all* of the time."

Parents continue to use weak parenting styles because they don't know what else to do. In light of this, weaknesses can also be viewed as a potential strength. A potential is the parents' ability to balance love and limits in the future once they have learned what their parenting style is, how it affects the quality of their relationship with their children, and what other tools may be right for the job. Parenting style weaknesses provide a target for what parents need to change to achieve a balance of love and limits. The goal of this section and the chapters that follow will be to equip parents with the right tools to do the job. Existing strengths or tools will be identified and kept in the parenting tool belt. There is no need to throw these tools out. New tools will be added to overcome parents' weaknesses to help them achieve a balance of love and limits. To accomplish this balance, parents must understand the beliefs behind their parenting style and the effects of parenting styles on children and parents.

Effects of Parenting Styles on Children and Parents

Each style of parenting has a particular effect on the attitudes and behaviors of children. How children deal with stressful situations, view themselves, and approach problems can be predicted based on the style used by their parents (Fine & Henry, 1989). This is not to say that parents are solely responsible for the behavior and beliefs of their children. Just as parents inherited the beliefs and behaviors of their parental figures' styles of parenting, they in turn pass on their parenting styles to their children.

These styles may change as they are passed down to the next generation due to social influences and individual decisions, depending on whether or not tomorrow's adults choose to accept or reject their parents' styles. Styles also evolve as parenting partners blend their respective styles of parenting together. This gives the child more than one option to choose from when they become parents: they can keep the strengths of one or both parenting styles and work on changing the weaknesses.

Balancing Parenting Styles

Love and limits represent two different styles of discipline: action and relationship. The authoritarian style of parenting uses action discipline whereas the permissive style of parenting focuses more on relationship discipline. Again, this does not mean that parents have no relationship with their child if they are authoritarian in style. Likewise, permissive parents are certainly not passive instruments in their children's life. But parents will usually be stronger in one form of discipline than the other. Therefore, when love and limits is described as being *high* or *low*, this refers to the relative emphasis or lack of emphasis parents give certain beliefs and behaviors when disciplining their child. *Low love* refers to children's perception of their parents as nonnurturing individuals (Parish & McCluskey, 1994). Love is subjective assessment of the parent/child relationship. It does not refer to the cognitive or factual knowledge that a parent loves a child. In most cases, both parents and children would state that low love parents do love their children, but children would not describe the relationship as warm or highly involved. In the same way, *low limits* would mean that children would not expect firm rules from parents on a consistent basis. Their emotional assessment would be one of over-involvement or warmth without many rules. Or at least they would not expect the parent to follow through on those rules.

Balancing these forms of discipline will be discussed in depth under each style of parenting and particularly in the last chapter on parenting styles, "Democratic or Balanced Parenting." Let's begin with the first parenting style, the "Rejecting/Neglecting Style of Parenting."

Chapter 7

The Rejecting/Neglecting Parenting Style

The rejecting/neglecting style of parenting is low on both love and limits. Generally, this style of parenting is thought of as physically uncaring and unavailable to meet the needs of children, but it could also include parents who are overly critical and condemning of their children. In this way it could be described as the "indifferent parenting style" due to its lack of emotional involvement and supervision of children. Instead, this book will use the terms *rejecting* and *neglecting* to emphasize the many forms of abuse this style can take and its effects on children.

Low limits refers to the lack of adequate supervision and physical care of the child. In these situations, rejecting/neglecting parents allow children to care for themselves and/or leave them with older children to take care of their basic needs. Children below the age of 12 are generally not mature enough, developmentally and socially, to make the kind of decisions that are necessary to guarantee their safety and well-being. And, while asking older siblings for some help with younger siblings and to act independently (dressing themselves, making their own breakfast, etc.) is acceptable, rejecting/neglecting parents put too much responsibility and independence on the children for their own care. Rather than being taught responsibility, they are being physically and emotionally deprived of needed parental care. Low limits also refers to a lack of adequate medical care or improper clothing. Chronic, untreated ear infections, poor dental care, impoverished diet, untreated medical conditions, and lack of adequate clothing in harsh weather conditions are all examples of low limits under the rejecting/neglecting style of parenting.

Low love refers to the lower levels of positive interaction between parent and child in the rejecting/neglecting home. Not only do rejecting/neglecting parents interact less frequently with their child or children, they are also less supportive than more balanced parents. In addition, rejecting/neglecting parents typically engage in less effective, more negative, and more severe physical discipline than balanced parents. In light of this, it is important that rejecting/neglecting parents not be seen as "good" or "bad." The reality is that many parents are using ineffective tools for parenting, passed down from their own parental figures through the process of identification.

Identification and Vicious Cycles of Interaction

Identification is a developmentally normal process through which children pattern their own behavior after significant people in their lives (Sears, Maccoby, & Levin, 1976). This process occurs through modeling of people children most admire, respect, or love and is typically more powerful for same-sex parents and children than opposite-sex parents and children. Researchers have used the concept of identification to explain how children learn sex roles, morality, and aggression. According to Freudian theory, the more children fear the loss or withdrawal of parental love, the more they will identify with and strive to be like the same-sex parent (Freud, 1905). The more uncertain a child is about receiving the love and limits of their parent, as in the rejecting/neglecting style of parenting, the more guilt children will feel when they violate parental standards. Another way of stating this is that children are more highly reinforced by intermittent applications of love and limits because they are less likely to know when they will receive the attention they need and thus must be more on guard. Consequently, this creates feelings of anxiety and frustration for children.

Children also have a part to play in the rejecting/neglecting style of parenting by participating in coercive or vicious cycles of interaction (Uriquiza & McNeil, 1996): 1) In a coercive or vicious cycle the parent begins by attempting to control the behavior of their children by threatening, yelling, and/or hitting them. 2) Children ignore the parent's request or yell and whine in response. 3) The parents often stop threatening, yelling, or hitting the child and/or withdraw from the situation, reinforcing the children's noncompliant behaviors. 4) The children then assume that by acting in that way they can get their parents to stop yelling or hitting without having to perform the task or request made by the parents (such as picking up toys). A feeling of control is imparted to the child, which increases the likelihood that this pattern will be repeated when the parents resume their aggressive discipline. 5) This pattern then replays itself in an ever more dramatic manner, escalating as children attempt to thwart the parents' commands and the parents withdraw even further or become more coercive (threatening in a more angry tone, yelling louder, and hitting more frequently or more severely) to bring the children back into compliance. 6) The children may then respond to the parents' escalated behavior by finally complying with their command, which reinforces the parents' abusive strategies ("this is what it takes to get my child to behave") or the children intensify their own coercive behaviors (more whining, tantrums, yelling, etc.). 7) As the level of confrontation intensifies, many parents will give up on themselves and their children or resort to even more physical and emotional abuse in severe frustration.

Identification and vicious cycles help explain how parents and children perpetuate the rejecting/neglecting style of parenting. Unfortunately, these concepts only explain *what* occurs, it doesn't explain *why*.

Why Abuse a Child? Models of Rejecting/Neglecting Parents

Probably the biggest question of this style of parenting is why a parent would reject or neglect their child. Researchers have looked at many different explanations and have found some underlying causes for child abuse. The different models or explanations for abuse include: personality or psychological defects, social or cultural influences, social situations, and ecological factors (Watkins and Bradford, 1982).

Personality or psychological defects refer to neurotic or psychotic behavior in the individual. This model contends that parents who were abused as children and did not receive love and nurturing behaviors will, in turn, be abusing parents. It also refers to an internal defect that genetically programs parents to be abusive, regardless of the love and nurturing behaviors they received. The **sociological model** refers to the values and effects of society on the individual. These include cultural values, family stress, unemployment, and social isolation, to name a few. The **social situational model** highlights the parent-child interaction as responsible for rejecting and neglecting a child.

These faulty interaction patterns include communication styles and specific environmental stressors.

When grouped together, all of the factors listed in each of these models make up what is called the **ecological model of abuse and neglect.** Each model can explain what causes parents to reject, neglect, or physically abuse their child, to a point. The problem is that there are also examples from each of these models where abuse did not occur. There are examples where parents have lost their jobs, did not receive adequate nurturing from their parental figures, suffer an emotional illness, are socially isolated or have poor communication skills and still have not rejected or neglected their children. While the level of parenting may not be very high in these cases, due to the internal and external stressors parents face, they do not fit into the definition of abuse in which a child's basic needs are not being met. In many cases, parents in these types of situations are adequately meeting the emotional and physical needs of their children. So where does this leave researchers who are looking for THE CAUSE of the rejecting/neglecting parenting style? The answer is that all of the above factors can contribute to this style of parenting, and so the most that can be said is that the more stressors, the more likely the risk of abuse. It also means that each situation must be considered individually and no general explanations ideally define the rejecting/neglecting parent. This is the explanation behind the ecological model of abuse.

The ecological model outlines why a parent might reject or neglect a child when all of the above factors are taken into consideration. A typical scenario might be as follows: A parent lives in a high-risk environment, has very few coping mechanisms, and/or has difficulty communicating feelings and needs, continually faces stressful circumstances (such as being fired or moving frequently in a short time span), has little social support to rely on, and feels hopeless about the future ever moving in a more positive direction. Given this combination, the parent is at high risk of rejecting and neglecting his or her child. Add to that the possibility of a personality or psychological problem, in the parent or the child, and that combination drastically reduces a parents' ability to provide the child with balanced love and limits.

What frightens researchers most about this model is that any parent, given these same conditions, could end up rejecting or neglecting a child. Because there is no sole determinant of abuse, any parent is subject to rejecting or neglecting behavior. The ecological model eliminates the "defective parent" label that society has given many parents. This label makes changing a parent's behavior, if a parent has learned faulty ways of setting limits and demonstrating love to a child, very difficult. If parents believe they are "defective" (that they have a personality characteristic that guarantees they will abuse their children or they were raised under nonnurturing parental figures) then why bother making an effort to change when they are "doomed" to be rejecting/neglecting parents? But if parents believe that their rejecting/neglecting style of parenting is the result of various factors, both within and outside of their control, and not due to a "defect" within themselves, then they will be more motivated to find the tools they need to achieve a balance in parenting. In other words, shame and blame will never motivate a parent to be more balanced. Instead, parents must be educated about what they need to be doing differently and empowered to do those things.

Effects of the Rejecting/Neglecting Style on Children

One of the effects this style of parenting has on children is that they are more likely to repeat the pattern of abuse as parents themselves. This effect can be called the *cycle of abuse*. Children grow up identifying abusive behaviors as the proper way to balance love and limits or, at the very least, rationalize that it is the only way they can manage their children. If not taught an alternative style of parenting, they will simply reenact what they have learned from their parents.

This style can also result in various behavior problems in children. Rejecting/neglecting parents frequently have children who are more *oppositional* (argue, demand attention, act impulsively, are stubborn, and brag), *offensive* (are cruel to people and things, scream, swear, lie, or cheat), *aggressive* (destroy property, attack others, threaten people, or steal), or *delinquent* (set fires, use alcohol and other drugs, skip school, vandalize property, or run away).

These behavioral problems are often referred to as *acting out*. This describes how the child is acting inappropriately toward other people and things. But children can also suffer inwardly and *act in*. Due to their invisible nature, emotional and psychological effects on children can be more devastating than the visible effects of acting out. These visible or physical effects include malnourishment, obvious medical problems, poor hygiene, bruises, welts, and/or broken bones resulting from physical abuse and other more visible problems. The invisible emotional and mental consequences include fears of abandonment, mistrust of others, suicidal thoughts, low sense of self, irrational fears and anxiety, poor social skills, attachment disorders, and more. To heal from this abuse, children may require individual and/or group psychotherapy to assist them in overcoming the effects of this parenting style. Parents, family members, relatives, and foster care providers also may need professional assistance in learning how to work with these children and their problems.

The Chicken or the Egg?

When it comes to abuse, researchers have asked a form of the question, "Which came first, the chicken or the egg?" Do the actions of rejecting/neglecting parents create the children's problems or do those problems create rejecting/neglecting parents? The answer is usually that one reinforces the other. Parents affect children and children affect parents. (For more information on this process, review the chapter on "Family Systems"). Regardless of which came first, the most likely way to end the cycle of abuse is with the parents. It is possible to help children recover from these effects and hopefully prevent them from passing on to the next generation, but parents who wish to find more effective tools to balance love and limits are the primary target for change.

Balancing or Preventing
the Rejecting/Neglecting Parenting Style

It is possible to prevent parents from rejecting or neglecting their children and aid them in achieving a balance of love and limits. Prevention, in its purist form, seeks to eliminate social ills and family problems from ever taking place. This is in direct contrast to the crisis-oriented approach that seeks to pick up the pieces of the problem and try to put them back together. Like Humpty Dumpty after his great fall, all the king's therapists, doctors, and social workers can never put his pieces back together again, at least not as well as preventive efforts can.

This type of prevention is called *primary prevention* because it concentrates on beliefs and behaviors that may head off problems before they occur. Programs that seek to accomplish this type of prevention focus on the ecological factors that increase the risk of abuse and help all parents within a community. Again, focusing on only one type of parent puts them back under a defective parenting label. To avoid this defective labeling, primary prevention considers parents who have the potential for abuse to be *at risk* or *vulnerable* to abuse versus being *abusive parents*. Any parents, under the worst circumstances and factors, are at-risk or vulnerable to abusing their children.

Another type of prevention is called secondary prevention. This refers to rejecting/neglecting parents who are already using this ineffective style of parenting and want to learn more effective methods of balancing love and limits. Here, educators might assist parents along the different factors listed in the ecological model of abuse. Psychological or personality factors might be attended to, such as a father's depression or a mother's history of incest. Sociological factors might be confronted by examining differences in discipline in American culture versus the family's culture of origin, a parent's need for employment, or the need for social support in raising hyperactive children. Social situational factors might be addressed, such as focusing on how a parent is perpetuating a parenting style from her own family of origin and how to use new, more effective tools to do the job of parenting.

Using the ecological model as a guide, the two leading areas of intervention for vulnerable parents include teaching new coping strategies to deal with stressful life situations and assistance in building strong social support networks.

Individual Coping Strategies

There are very few examples of truly good or bad parenting styles. Each style has a strength and a weakness. They are not all good or all bad. This is true even for the rejecting/neglecting style of parenting. While the rejecting/neglecting style of parenting is described as being low on love and limits, this is due to the fact that parents have learned mistaken beliefs about how to achieve a balance in parenting and are using ineffective parenting tools to do the job. In other words, parents who use the rejecting, neglecting style of parenting have poor individual coping strategies.

New coping strategies are needed to balance love and limits. In terms of love or relationship discipline, the rejecting/neglecting style of parenting needs to adopt new ways of communicating and interacting in a positive cycle of interaction with the child. In terms of limits or action discipline, the rejecting/neglecting style of parenting needs to use new behaviors and tools to gain children's cooperation and respect.

Education is the primary means of change for the rejecting/neglecting style of parenting. This education can take the form of audio tapes (for home and car use), books (on general parenting topics or specific problems areas), group parenting classes (offered by local parenting groups and community-based agencies), private parenting consultation (one-on-one with a parent educator or family therapist specializing in parenting issues who can tailor specific solutions to the needs of the parent or family), or family therapy (to address family system dynamics that perpetuate the rejecting/neglecting style). All of these forms of education cover the spectrum of prevention, from more general, primary forms of prevention with the use of books and group parenting classes to more crisis-oriented prevention with the use of a private parenting consultant or family therapist.

Social Support Networks

Social support networks also help parents balance love and limits by shielding them from stressful situations. This shield comes in the form of a network of people parents can turn to for help. In a crisis situation, vulnerable parents feel more capable to handle difficult situations when they feel there is someone to help them cope. This provides another option other than rejecting or neglecting their children in the face of seemingly overwhelming situations.

Social support networks consist of natural or self-created groups of people. Natural social support networks include family, friends, or accessible individuals in a parent's neighborhood, school, or church. Unfortunately, natural networks are not always the best resources for parents. While natural networks are easily accessible, they may not be safe or helpful in preventing parents from rejecting or neglecting their children. Parents who were abused as children cannot use their own parents as sources of support, for parenting advice, or to care for their children. A friend may offer ineffective parenting tools that frustrate parents more because it doesn't work for their children. The friend may advise the parent to give their children a good spanking that might get the parent arrested and result in their children being removed from their custody.

When parents are unable to use natural social support networks, they must turn to self-created support networks. Self-created support networks include professional and paraprofessional helpers, such as social workers, therapists, or members of a support group, like Parents Anonymous or Tough Love. These networks are not natural, in that they do not readily exist in the parents' life and are not readily known to the parents, but may prove to be more helpful once they are contacted and utilized.

In terms of secondary prevention, where parents are already experiencing problems, self-created support networks are helpful because they already understand the issues and difficulties facing parents that natural networks may not understand. Having a group of people who already understand the problems and have found some solutions is more encouraging and safe for the rejecting/neglecting parent. These groups may include parenting in recovery, parenting and emotional illness (in the parents or the child), parents who have been abused as children, parenting and domestic violence, teenage parenting, single parenting, step-parenting, adoptive parenting, foster parenting, and others.

Value Clarification Exercise: Identify your social support network
(This exercise will help you identify helpful resources.) Draw five circles, one inside the other. Make sure the center circle is the smallest with each circle getting gradually larger. In the smallest, center circle, write the word "self." In the next circle, write the word "family." In the third, write the word "friends." In the fourth, write the word "acquaintances." And in the last, write the word "strangers."

When it comes to parenting, some adults have more resources or social support networks than others, some have resources that they did not know existed and some have resources but choose not to use them. This may be due to the fact that the resources have been abusive. Or perhaps parents are uncomfortable talking about certain topics or do not know how to access doctors and other professionals who could help them.

Put a star in the circles listing resources you feel are available to you. Who could you turn to when you need parenting advice? What if you feel overwhelmed and at risk of yelling at or hitting your children? What if you don't have enough money to pay your bills, buy food, or repair the car? Write the words "advice," "risk," and "money" next to the circles you feel most comfortable talking about these problems. Finally, write a list of names that you have identified as belonging to each of these circles. Come up with as many names as you possibly can for each area. The "strangers" circle can also stand for professionals that you may have access to but don't know on a personal level.

Are We All Rejecting/Neglecting Parents?

Although the rejecting/neglecting style of parenting is commonly considered to be abusive toward children, all parents have moments where parenting seems like too much to handle and they want to have their own space. This is natural given the challenges of parenting and the endless work that goes into it. There is no need for guilt just because a parent fantasizes about being on a remote island somewhere, where only adults are allowed to live and children are forbidden. Child-rearing can be difficult and frustrating. There are no magical wands. It is a normal reaction to feel sometimes like rejecting or neglecting children for one's own wants and needs. Parents must remember that they are just feelings and don't have to be acted on in a rejecting/neglecting manner. They can find positive ways to balance their wants and needs with the wants and needs of their children.

Some parents may deny they have these fantasies. But children's "attachment antennas" can pick up the rejecting/neglecting vibes parents unconsciously put out. When parents are tired after a long day of work and caring for children, they put out nonverbal messages of not wanting to be bothered by their child's disliking vegetables with dinner, wanting to stay up late to watch a television special, having monsters under their bed, or needing another drink of water. Picking up on these vibes can make children can feel insecure and restless, resulting in more inappropriate behavior as they do not have words or insight into why mommy and daddy are sending out rejecting/neglecting vibes. It would be better if parents were honest with themselves and their children about their feelings rather than leaving them anxious and confused. Parents can follow up their honest statements with reassurances about their love for the child and the need for all parties to ask for forgiveness and work together through the feelings. In the chapters that follow, parents will discover various insights of their own on how to balance love and limits and tools to find their own personal balance in the process.

Chapter
8
The Authoritarian Parenting Style

The authoritarian style of parenting is high on limits but low on love. This is not to say that authoritarian parents don't love their children. It does mean, however, that their strengths are in setting firm limitations on children rather than offering them affection and warmth.

To the authoritarian parent, obedience is a virtue. As the authority figure, parents' expectations about conduct and order for children are not to be challenged. Punishment is freely used to ensure that this value is maintained. Parents' views on right from wrong are not to be questioned. Strong, negative emotions may be viewed as threats to parental authority and are often suppressed (Gottman and DeClaire, 1997). Younger children must yield and become dependent on parents (Lamb and Baumrind, 1978).

In some situations, society considers this style of parenting to be abusive. This is due to the fact that authoritarian styles of parenting have been the rationale used by many abusive parents. They have taken the weaknesses rather than the strengths of this parenting style and used it to justify harsh parenting practices. Fortunately, there is more to the authoritarian parenting style than just its weaknesses. It does have strengths, which must be considered as well. All of the styles of parenting can be considered abusive if weaknesses are the primary or only focus. To compensate for those weaknesses, parents must recognize and utilize their strengths.

History of the Authoritarian Style of Parenting

At one time, society advocated that parents be authoritarian in their parenting styles. From the early, colonial periods of American history into the late 1950s, parents were advocated to use strict, physical discipline to control their children. America's economy was originally centered around a rural, agricultural lifestyle (most everyone was a farmer) and relied on conformity and obedience for the family to survive.

Because America's economy was centered around a rural, agricultural lifestyle (most everyone was a farmer) conformity and obedience was necessary in order for the family to survive. The reason for this was that size and amount of labor provided by the family determined their economic position. The father was seen as the primary provider and the mother and children were under his direction. Children were not given wages for their labor and so discipline was the means for control. Additionally, the larger the family the more laborers to work the farm. But having such a large family reduced parents' intimacy with each child. Parents did not have time to sit and have long discussions about right and wrong. Therefore, it was believed that corporal punishment was a more efficient form of maintaining order and stability in the home.

Family relationships were different in the past. Marriage often was based on economic necessity rather than romance, and children were treated as "little adults." Children were expected to work a full day and labor on a level close to that of adults. Large families provided more laborers and insured greater production and survival. Family tasks were divided up by gender: boys and men worked primarily in the fields, and girls and women worked in or around the house. Privacy and independence were not highly valued. Most families lived in one or two rooms. Colonial families lived under the motto "one for all" rather than "all for one."

Beliefs about what was a "good" or "bad" parent was also very different in society. Children were expected to be "seen and not heard" and society believed that "bad children must be punished" or "have the devil beaten out of them." "Spare the rod and spoil the child" was the maxim of the day. It embodied the value that obedience to authority was more important than affection or relationship.

Some of these beliefs have carried over to today's authoritarian parent. The authoritarian style of parenting continues to be guided by the beliefs that, "children should not question or disagree with their parents," "too much love and attention will spoil a child," "parents have a right to do anything they want to a child as they are parents' property, " "children are, by nature, wild animals," and "spare the rod spoil the child." Parents may have adopted these beliefs from the parental figures in their lives who balanced their love and limits in a similar manner. This is how they believe a "good" parent behaves. And as has been said before, "everyone wants to be a good parent and no one wants to be a bad one."

It might be said that the authoritarian parenting style is parent-centered versus child-centered (as in the permissive parenting style). The value of respect for God, one's parents, and the laws of the country may be sound, but that doesn't mean that the methods for teaching those values are still valid. As we shall see in the section on permissive parenting styles, society no longer considers these methods as acceptable standards for child-rearing. The belief that parents, as the authority figures, must control a child in order to teach respect is mistaken. Authoritarian parents frequently demand obedience rather than inspire respect. They focus on the punishment of inappropriate behavior and ignore the acknowledgment of appropriate behavior. And they have difficulty modeling right from wrong.

When parents fail to model right from wrong (e.g., "do what I say, not what I do!") they are exhibiting a need for pseudo-perfection. They are acting as if they are infallible, communicating that they are above the law and that children should deny parts of their personal reality (what they feel is right, what makes them feel good, and their ideas and opinions about the world) in favor of what the parents say is right. They find fault in others and refuse to accept responsibility even when they are clearly wrong. They are overly concerned about what others think of them and their child. Children of authoritarian parents often feel they are living a family lie, acting as if they are one thing on the surface and another behind closed doors. Authoritarian parents often push their children into what they believe is "good for them" regardless of what the child wants or likes. Unfortunately, children often do what parents do (i.e., model) rather than what they say. Children are nonverbal long before they learned to talk, and so, they often model their parents' behavior rather than blindly follow parents instructions, especially if there is no wisdom expressed to the child to back it up.

Effects of the Authoritarian Style on Children

The long-term effects of the authoritarian parenting style on children are far from beneficial. Rather than gaining the unquestioned obedience that authoritarian parents desire, children frequently become submissive or retaliate in anger.

Submissive children learn to avoid hostile or threatening situations. They have learned that to survive, it is necessary to do what they are told to do, when they are told to do it, and then do whatever they want when the parent or authority figure is not present. In other words, they learn how not to get caught rather than to do what is right.

Under this style of parenting, children may become revengeful. Revenge is a way of returning hurt for hurt. Children may think, "I won't get mad, I'll get even." In most authoritarian families, anger is not an acceptable emotion. Children are not allowed to express aggressive actions without suffering severe consequences. But aggressive impulses have a way of sneaking out, and so children may act out by lying, cheating, stealing, fighting, or setting fires. They treat the world around them in the same manner in which they perceive they are being treated.

Families with authoritarian styles of parenting often have a pecking order in place. A *pecking order* is a hierarchy of power in which one individual, usually the father, is at the top of the hierarchy and the rest of the family are positioned below. Pecking orders often lead to development of the "kick-the-dog" syndrome, which goes something like this: Dad comes home after a stressful day and yells at mom for not having dinner ready when he arrives. Mom, who has also had a stressful day taking care of the children and the household, resents dad yelling at her and does the only natural thing she can do. She yells at one of the children for making too much noise. Now the child who was making the noise feels as if he has been dumped on and goes off into the other part of the house and does the only natural thing he can do. He hits his younger sister. The girl, having no one smaller or weaker on whom to vent her frustration, goes outside and does the only natural thing she can think to do. She kicks the dog.

Authoritarian parenting styles also affect how children demonstrate affection toward their parents. In families where affection is openly displayed and there are plenty of models of appropriate affection between family members, children feel more comfortable in expressing their own affection. But if parents discourage open displays of affection or act uncomfortable when children hug and kiss them, children withhold their displays of affection. They might even become more clingy or needy with people who they feel are more comfortable with affection. They may feel that since affection is in short supply, they need to stock up on it whenever and wherever they can get it. This problem is prevalent with authoritarian fathers who see affection between father and sons as "mushy" or "wimpy." They want their sons to be "big boys," and they communicate this through their words and their actions. They rationalize that their children know they love them. They don't need to say it or do anything special to demonstrate it. Or they feel that because they provide for their material needs, their emotional one's are being met as well. As the poet Emily Dickenson wrote, "Speech is one symptom of affection, and silence one . . . (1960)."

The authoritarian family is unbalanced in its administration of love and limits. It sets limits on how people show love or emotion. What was once a means of survival in American culture is now an obsolete method of parenting. Just as society has changed, so have accepted methods for disciplining children. That is not to say that the authoritarian style of parenting has no strengths. On the contrary, it has a lot of strengths and is envied for its ability to set firm and consistent limits.

Balancing the Authoritarian Parenting Style

Some parents never question the adequacy of the parenting styles they have inherited. They may argue, "If it was good enough for me, it is good enough for my child." Or they state, "I turned out OK, so it must be the right way to parent a child." On the other hand, some parents state that they will never parent their child the way they were parented. They may feel that their own parental figures were too strict or too lenient in their balance of love and limits, and they would like to find new ways to balance their parenting. The difficulty comes when these parents try to do something different and find themselves at the opposite extreme of the parenting style continuum. For example, an authoritarian parent who learned that style from his parents attempts to change his balance and simply becomes a permissive parent instead. Rather than balancing love and limits, he swaps one extreme for another. The result is that he becomes an authoritarian parent in permissive clothing. He will plead and reason with his children to cooperate, not in a very successful manner, until he becomes frustrated and falls back on spanking the children out of anger. And when a parent is angry that is the worst time to discipline a child.

Other parents may believe that if they were raised under one style of parenting, they cannot change their style and learn new ways to balance love and limits. They feel stuck with the style that comes most naturally, regardless of whether or not they agree with that style. Fortunately, parents can relearn new ways to balance their love and limits. It is simply a matter of keeping the strengths that they have and finding new tools to overcome their weaknesses. This doesn't happen overnight. Parenting styles are learned slowly over time. They may have been learned verbally ("How many times have I told you not to talk back to me!") or nonverbally (being slapped when they talked back to a parental figure). The basic premise for change is that if parents learned one style of parenting, they can learn a new style of parenting.

Value Clarification Exercise: Early recollections

To discover the influence of parenting styles on our attitudes, feelings, and behaviors, answer the following questions:

What is your earliest memory of your parents or some parental figure in your life?
What did it feel like to be a child?
What was the happiest time of your life with your parents?
How does your style of parenting compare to the style your parents or some other parental figure used when you were growing up?

Discipline Versus Punishment

The first step in balancing love and limits is to identify the strengths and weaknesses of a parenting style. The second step is to assimilate aspects of the democratic or balanced parenting style in place of the weaknesses in the authoritarian parenting style.

Authoritarian parents often get the results they seek, at least on the surface. They are very firm and consistent in their rules for children. Although people may not agree with their methods, they cannot deny that they do get results. Many parenting partners have complained that they can't seem to get the children to do anything they ask while the other, more authoritarian parents seem to get them do whatever they ask. Nonauthoritarian parents may appreciate those results even if they don't approve of the methods. This dichotomy occurs because children have learned that authoritarian parents mean what they say and will back up their words with consequences, while the other parents can be more easily manipulated and/or ignored. But appearances can be deceiving. Children do not comply with everything their authoritarian parents say. In truth, they follow whatever the authoritarians say and can enforce. What they cannot enforce (because they are not nearby to do so), the child may choose not to follow.

The weakness of authoritarian parents is their belief that the best way to teach right from wrong is by punishing inappropriate behavior. Authoritarian parents equate discipline with punishment. Discipline internalizes right from wrong through modelling and coaching. Punishment, on the other hand, uses external control to ensure that children choose right from wrong. The goal of discipline is to pass on values to children that they will follow of their own free will. Punishment demands blind obedience from children, not because the parent has done anything to warrant it but simply because they are the parents, the authority figures. Unfortunately, punishment works only so long as the parent is in the room to control the child's behavior or until the child becomes too big to control. Many teenagers with authoritarian parents, run away or hit back when they realize they no longer have to put up with their parents' demands.

Some democratic or balanced beliefs that authoritarian parents can adopt into their parenting styles are that discipline is not the same as punishment and that parents need to model right from wrong by their words and their deeds. These beliefs can be used in place of ineffective ideals, such as "Do what I say, not what I do."

Authoritarian parents need to understand the difference between discipline and punishment. One way to illustrate this difference is by imagining this scenario: You are in a car heading down the highway at 70 miles per hour. You know that the speed limit is 55 mph, so you know that you are violating the law. Suddenly, you see in your rearview mirror a highway patrol car enter the highway behind you. What is your first reaction? YOU SLOW DOWN! Why? Because you are disobeying the law and don't want to be punished for your crime. If you are lucky, you slowed down in time to avoid getting a ticket. After a while, you notice that the highway patrol car is exiting the highway. After you make sure the patrol car is really gone, what do you do? YOU SPEED UP! After all, you have to make up for the time you lost when you had to slow down to the normal speed limit. And this time you go 90 mph.

Consider that scenario for a minute. Did you or did you not know what the speed limit was? If you did know, why didn't you obey it when the highway patrol car wasn't present. If we agree that the highway patrol car represents an authoritarian parenting style, it is easy to see that people do not internalize rules or laws when punishment is the only source of control. Likewise, children only follow authoritarian parents' demands when they are physically present in the room with the child or when their parents might find out about their violation. But if they don't feel they will be caught or there is no one to say "no!" then they will violate the parents' rules.

Flexibility Versus Control

Authoritarian parents believe that in order to be a good parent, one must be consistent and firm. This often translates into an attitude of rigidity when parents refuse to budge on an issue once they have established a limit. After all, to go back on a decision about bedtime, staying over at a friend's house, or using the car would be permissive, right? Not necessarily.

While consistency offers children and their parents security and structure, it may also reflect outdated rules or not match up to a child's developmental needs. Many rules established when children were younger, such as an early bedtime or regular nap times, may no longer be necessary or valid for an older child. Much of children's power struggling is over their need to be increasingly independent and achieve greater freedom. Authoritarian parents often see children's attempts to negotiate their needs as a sign of disrespect. This is because most children are not born with good social skills and so do not know how to appropriately ask for what they need or want. Authoritarian parents may have actually modeled inappropriate ways to get what you need or want. For instance, if children do not do as they are told, they may get spanked for disobedience. As a result, children learn that aggression is an acceptable means of getting what you want. Authoritarian parents who wish to balance love and limits may need to regularly evaluate their rules to see if they are still valid and meets the developmental level of the child.

This can be difficult for the authoritarian parent as they are less likely to understand what is developmentally appropriate for children. This is because they are less attuned to the internal world of the child. Anyone can have a good working knowledge of child development theory and still not clearly relate to the needs of a child. This takes an emotional involvement or relationship with children that authoritarian parents often lack. The more closely parents relate to their children, the more likely they will understand why they are crying, when they are not feeling well, what they find rewarding, who they like to play with, and how they respond to problems. Children who perceive their parents to be "warmer" on the scale of parent/child intimacy are more likely to be socially responsible (Baumrind, 1971). Additionally, most "warm" mothers report that they do not need to use frequent physical punishment with their children, while "cold" mothers report that their uses of physical punishment were not very effective (Sears, Maccoby, and Levin, 1976).

Consequently, authoritarian parents may need to reevaluate their beliefs and behaviors about what and why they are parenting in the manner in which they do. Are they doing it simply because that is how they were parented and they don't know what else to do? Do they believe that their methods of discipline are effective in the long term as well as the short term for their children? Are they aware of social norms and expectations about what is acceptable parental discipline? Are they happy with the outcomes of their parenting style, emotionally and psychologically speaking? Flexibility in thought and action is necessary if the authoritarian parent is to balance love and limits.

Flexibility may be necessary when unforeseen circumstances upset the normal, child-rearing routines. Daily routines help children feel secure. They reduce anxiety and make parenting simpler when there is a outline to follow. For instance, a child may need to follow the bedtime routine of taking a bath, reading a book, brushing her teeth, and going to sleep. Sometimes, unforeseen events prevent this bedtime routine from occurring in the normal manner as when the family gets home from a late visit with relatives. Must parents stick to the routine to show their consistency and ensure security in their children? Parents may need to introduce flexibility into their normal routine by substituting steps in the activity. For example, the parent may choose to just wash up hands and face with a rag instead of going through the full routine of taking a bath. Or there may be just one book instead of three at story time. This way the parent can keep the structure of the routine intact while substituting the activities that allow more flexibility in the situation.

Children readily adapt to these changes in routine and are not traumatized when situations create a need to adjust to them. Authoritarian parents can be more flexible in their parenting styles by following more functional methods of discipline and modifying daily routines.

Authoritarian Versus Authoritative Parenting

One way to balance the authoritarian parenting style is to become authoritative rather than authoritarian. Although the difference sounds minuscule, they are worlds apart. The authoritative parent rules by words and deeds, not by might. They model right and wrong behavior and explain the wisdom behind their actions or decisions. They consider themselves to be practical and moral guides for appropriate behavior. They believe in the wisdom to train up a child when he is young, so he can better tell right from wrong when he becomes older and independent. They view discipline as education rather than control. And they seek a balance of love and limits based on mutual respect, positive expectations, encouragement of effort, and end results.

Authoritative parents have open channels of communication so children can talk about their feelings without blame or shame. They are secure enough in their own authority as parents to consider a child's views and feel that they have a right to be heard. As the executive leader of the family, the authoritative parent allows democratic discussion while maintaining his or her right to veto suggestions that may be unhealthy or harmful for children. The authoritative parent also uses expectations with children rather than demands. Expectations allow parents to stretch children's behaviors and thinking about right from wrong versus pushing them or driving them into rebellion. Expectations may be as simple as modifying how a parent communicates to a child or as complex as altering the family structure. Two practical tools parents can use to modify communication and alter the family structure (and so, become more authoritative versus authoritarian) are **positive expectations** and the **family meeting** parenting tools.

Parenting Tools: Positive expectations
Positive expectations are statements by parents to their children about what is appropriate behavior. The goal of this tool is to teach children what parents want, not what they don't want. For example, telling a child that dirty clothes belong in the laundry basket is different from telling a child to stop leaving their clothes in the middle of the room. Telling a child that feet belong on the

floor is different than telling them to take their feet off the table. State what you want, not what you don't want. This avoids children's complaints that you never told them they couldn't put their feet on a different piece of furniture. This tool also increases the feelings of cooperation and respect. Parents who wish to balance love and limits find that in order to get respect, they must respect their children. Positive expectations decrease defensiveness and increase cooperation. They also eliminate many power struggles between parents and children.

People do not make long-term changes in their lives by being told what not to do. They may do what they are told to do in the short-term to avoid a negative consequence from occurring, but they have no reason to continue to do this when there are no consequences. The human mind simply does not operate on thou-shalt-nots. For example, when parents tell a child: "Don't put your feet on the table," the child registers two thoughts. The conscious part of the child's mind hears the parents say "don't" while the unconscious, more powerful part of the mind hears the words, "put your feet on the furniture." Granted, children know the difference and the mind is complex enough to overrule the latter command in favor of the former, but wouldn't it be much clearer to simply say what you do want (i.e., "put your feet on the floor").

To illustrate this point, try NOT to think of a pink elephant right now. As a matter of fact, try REALLY HARD NOT to think of a pink elephant right now! What immediately comes to mind? A pink elephant, right? The reason for this is that the mind hears two commands: the command "not" and the second command to "think of a pink elephant." Which one will the mind follow? Both of them! You know you don't have to think of a pink elephant just as children know enough to understand what parents mean by their command, but this form of communication is confusing and carries a double message.

Parenting Tools: The family meeting
One of the best tools for an authoritative parent to use is the family meeting. A family meeting is a parenting tool that provides a forum for making group decisions, assigning household chores, sharing positive feelings, and choosing activities for family fun. Family meetings are sometimes called circles, sharing times, group decision making, or huddling. The purpose of the family meeting is to establish a democratic process of communication in the family.

Chapter Eight

Here are some guidelines for establishing a family meeting:

1. Meet on a regular basis (once a week, each night at dinner, etc.).
2. Treat everyone with respect and give everyone equal say, even though parents have veto power.
3. Use reflective listening techniques and "I" messages.
4. Stay with the real issues. Don't get sidetracked.
5. Focus on the strengths of each family member and don't blame.
6. Set the length of time of the meeting and stick to it.
7. Keep a running record of plans, rules, and decisions set by the family and post them where everyone can see them.
8. Remember to have fun.

Although the family meeting is a great way to open communication and respect, there are some potential pitfalls. The first pitfall is when only one parent is interested in participating in the family meeting. Fortunately, decisions can be approved by only one parent. Invite all members to participate, explain the purpose of the family meetings, and hope that they will choose to be a part of the process. The second pitfall is trying to find a time for the family meeting that works for everyone. If a time cannot be found that works for everyone, try rotating the times from week to week to accommodate other members' schedules and/or give them a brief recap of what happened in the meeting. Also, parents can ask for their input on a family decision that will be made at the next meeting if a member cannot be present.

Implement the family meeting as soon as everyone understands its purpose, or explain the purpose at the first meeting. It might also be helpful to establish a few ground rules. For instance, there is to be no blaming or shaming other members of the family, and each person gets a chance to talk. Parents will improve attendance by letting other members know how long the family meeting will last and sticking to the schedule. Many older children may consider family meetings "stupid" or "childish." One democratic method for dealing with this is to allow them to be absent but casually mention that the family will be making some important decisions on the upcoming summer vacation or what movie the family is going to see this weekend. Most children will want to be there to avoid having decisions made without them.

The last pitfall is how to structure the family meeting. Most families will start off by discussing "old business," move on to "new business," and end with *a summary of the meeting. If you aren't having the meeting at a set time, remember to take these steps before everyone is excused. By "old business," we are referring to taking time to review decisions, chores, and fun activities that might have been decided on at the last meeting. Were there any problems? How are the new chores working out? "New business" encompasses how to modify decisions, change the chore list, or make new plans for future family fun. Summarizing is a way for parents to make sure everyone understands what has been decided during the family meeting. Briefly list the high points of the meeting and ask all family members if they understand and are in agreement with the decisions. After this, close the meeting and let everyone know their attendance is appreciated.*

Value Clarification Exercise: Authoritative parenting

1. *Pick one or two statements that can be used as a positive expectation rather than a demand.*
2. *Choose a time and place to have a family meeting.*

Chapter

9

The Permissive Parenting Style

The permissive parenting style is at the opposite extreme from the authoritarian parenting style. It is high on love but low on limits. It provides lots of attention and nurturing to children but is inconsistent in setting clear limits and/or rarely enforces household rules (and there are rules, even though no one is clear on what they are) with appropriate consequences.

Some authoritarian parents who are told they cannot spank their children may become permissive in their style of parenting. Without a clear understanding of what to do differently, parents may inadvertently substitute one weakness for another. They will beg their children to comply with their requests until they can't stand it anymore, explode in frustration, and return to their old discipline method, spanking their children.

Permissive parents prefer to use reason to control the behavior of their children. They frequently consult with children on household policy and negotiate responsibilities and chores. The strength of permissive parents is their ability to form a tight bond with their children, to be accepting and affirming of who their children are, and to use nonpunitive forms of discipline. Their weaknesses include the lack of consistency in delivering consequences for disobedience. They often spend time in drawn out negotiations for even the most trivial situations. They believe that children are capable of regulating their own impulses and that children's impulses should not be frustrated, stifled, or denied expression.

History of the Permissive Parenting Style

Permissive parenting has its historical roots as well. The concept of childhood did not exist as a separate and distinct stage of development until the seventeenth and eighteenth centuries (Hall, Perlmutter, and Lamb, 1982). At that time, a new philosophy about children sprang up, promoting the moral and intellectual development of children through education, protecting children from the corruption and evils of society, and preserving their innocence and goodness. This change of attitude toward children corresponded with the rise of a middle class society in both Europe and North America. The middle class society allowed families to have more leisure time, led to a decrease in infant mortality rates so that more children lived to reach puberty, and established literacy at a much younger age as a result of the rise of capitalism.

Discipline during this time continued to be severe and abusive. Child-rearing techniques relied heavily on beatings to teach children right from wrong. Parents invested little emotional energy in their relationships with their children. And expectations of children continued to be rigid.

Industrialization freed children, particularly adolescents, from participating in physical labor in favor of focusing on their psychological growth. Education, affluence, and new child abuse and labor laws emphasized the need to support adolescents with economic, familial, and institutional resources. Of course, not all children have enjoyed this luxury. Even today, poverty and racial oppression has forced many children, such as those from migrant farm laborer families, to work in defiance of these laws. The principal reason for this is financial need. All members of the family are needed and expected to work to support the family. Children in the inner cities have also received few resources. Although a new era stressing the importance of childhood began a few centuries ago, many children still wait to experience its benefits.

Throughout history, examples of permissive parenting can readily be seen. This style of parenting has been advocated by members of society in reaction to the authoritarian style of parenting. Examples of this advocacy can be seen in the 1940s and 1950s in the writings of Dr. Benjamin Spock, who many parents considered to be the guru of modern parenting (Spock & Rothenberg, 1992). The influx of women into the workplace during World War II, the rise of feminism against the traditional, authoritarian oppression of inequality toward women, and the free love movement of the 1960s with its admonition to question "authority"—all of these have contributed to a more permissive parenting style in society.

In addition, the awareness of child abuse has increased society's restrictions on what constitutes acceptable methods of discipline. The focus has been on whether or not spanking is appropriate for children, whether it be by degrees (did it leave a mark or not?), intensity (was the parent angry when he or she struck the child?), or location (spanking the fleshy area of the upper thighs and buttocks versus other parts of the body?). All of these questions produce endless debate about the abusiveness of spanking or hitting a child. Perhaps what is needed is not more debate, but practical alternatives to corporal punishment. Some contemporary parents, raised under authoritarian parenting styles, have few tools other than spanking in their parenting toolbox. The cookie cutter alternative, time-out, has not lived up to its magical expectations for many parents. They continue to struggle with their children for control. Time-out has served its purpose in allowing parents and children to calm themselves down and not react in angry, abusive ways, but now it is time to add other nonpunitive, parenting tools to our repertoire.

Unfortunately, most contemporary parents were raised by authoritarian parental figures. They learned a different model of parenting than the style now commonly advocated, and they learned a different method of control. Consequently, parents today are attempting to discipline their children with methods they are unschooled on how to use properly. As a result, they have become authoritarian parents in permissive clothing. The danger of this predicament is falling back on old, early parental training from one's own parents during moments of stress and then feeling the pangs of frustration and guilt for doing so.

Adults today are faced with a different set of circumstances and way of life than their own parents. For example, most parents today must balance work and family life, an economic situation that may not have been problematic in one's family of origin.

Balancing Work and Family Life

Today's family is more diverse in structure and outlook than families of decades past. The traditional view of a "nurturing" wife/mother and the "provider" husband/father has become a minority. These changes result from economic pressures on the family. The choice to work or not to work has ceased to be an option for many women. While many mothers may prefer to stay home, they find they cannot due to financial constraints. And with the divorce rate at about 50%, more and more parents are struggling with the role of single parenting, which creates even less choice and more difficulty in balancing work and family life.

For some women, working is a choice. Research has shown that many women experience higher levels of satisfaction personally, and in their relationships, when they work outside the home (Coontz, 1992). The idea of the traditional wife and mother as being the most satisfactory role for women has come under sometimes furious debate. Other studies show that depression and alcohol use were at an all-time high for women during the 1950s, when traditional roles for women were most prevalent. Some of this may have been due to the rigid role definition of women and lack of personal mastery over their lives and future. The only thing many women had to look forward to was endless servitude to house, husband, and children. Emotional well-being was assumed to be natural for a women in this situation. Research has proven that this was not always the case (Coontz, 1992).

The traditional roles of both men and women have changed as well. Many men have chosen to stay home with children, while their wives work. This may be both a financial as well as a personal choice. Many women earn more than their husbands or have better job benefits. Consequently, many couples choose to have dad stay home with the kids rather than mom. Another trend is working at home. The rise of the electronic age has allowed both mom and dad to create more flexible work schedules and work from their home, allowing parents to spend more time with their children.

Balancing work and family life does have its benefits and costs. The benefits include increased social equality, interpersonal power, and enhanced self-esteem for women. Costs include a confusion of role identity ("Am I mother, wife, or worker?") and marital distress. Society still does not know how to respond to the new roles of men and women. Sexual harassment and inequality of salaries are a continuing concern as we approach the next millennium. Because many men are unwilling to share the nurturing role, women continue to bear most of the burden at home in addition to working outside the home. When children are sick, women are more often expected to take off work to care for them. This follows the age-old idea that women are better nurturers than men. Even when both mom and dad work the same number of hours per week, women tend to have more of the household tasks on their chore lists.

The Permissive Parenting Style

There are costs for balancing work and family life as well. While there is a general trend toward shared parenting responsibilities, working parents often express that their children are out of control and while they may be home more often with their children, it is the children that are running the household, not the parents. Clear role definitions, although at times emotionally dissatisfying, do provide clear lines of authority and control. It offers less confusion for parents and children in terms of who does what, when, how, and why.

Transforming the Role of Father as Disciplinarian

Many parents heard their own mothers say, "Wait till your father gets home." Although this was often just an idle threat, used by the mother to regain control of children, fathers were and often continue to be expected to be the primary disciplinarians. The first task for some fathers upon coming home is to spank or reprimand their children. Fathers feel dissatisfied with their role as policemen and the negative tone of their relationship with their children. Additionally, men have not yet completed their own social revolution, from the workplace to home, and so have not fully learned the finer points of child care and the developmental needs of children. Bill Cosby, in his book *Fatherhood* (1986), jokes about how his wife was furious with him for feeding his children cake for breakfast. After all, it did have eggs, flour, and milk as ingredients, and aren't those nutritious things to feed to your children?

Many men believe that women are superior parents, more biologically and psychologically prepared for nurturing and caring for children (Shapiro, 1993). Even with the transformation of parenting roles that has taken place in the 1990s, they do not feel they are as adequate, or as necessary, to children as the mother. This may be one reason many fathers leave the home and their families. After all, the important parent is still in the home. The reality is that while they may be different in style or manner of parenting, fathers are not inferior to mothers or less important to children. But this myth persists, and it explains why many men stick to what they feel is their most important role—being the provider of the home—and leaving the nurturing role to mom.

Familiarity is a powerful force, especially in uncertain times when mothers and fathers are changing their roles. Consequently in times of stress, many parents fall back on old parenting training modeled by their own parental figures. The gender myths of fathers as distant, problem-solving authoritarians and mothers as warm and nurturing, permissive parents is used to alleviate the stress couples feel as they cope with uncertain roles and responsibilities.

Permissive Parenting Values/Beliefs

Although many seemingly permissive parents are acting in reaction to the authoritarian styles of parenting that they or society consider abusive, they are not "true" permissive parents, in the sense that they are acting out a script with no real experience. Proof for this comes in times of stress when they fall back on experience and use the authoritarian style of parenting they learned as a child.

True permissive parents will have learned from the examples of their own permissive parental figures. The basis of their discipline is on talk, not action, in the balance of love and limits. The beliefs that underlie this style of parenting include:

Children should not be allowed to be frustrated or get upset.
Love is all you need to be a good parent.
All punishment is wrong.
Children should be free to express themselves at all times.

The primary value of the permissive parenting style in the family system is that parents and children are equal or that others should be treated as more important than oneself. This leads to beliefs and behaviors that overprotect and overindulge children. Although fairness is important to permissive parents, it frequently has emotional strings attached to it. Permissive parents feel that they are entitled to respect based on "all of the work they do for everybody else" or "members of the family owe them something in return for their selfless labor." The result is a slave or martyr mentality.

Effects of the Permissive Parenting Style on Children

Some of the consequences for children of permissive parents include underachieving and a low frustration tolerance (Lamb and Baumrind, 1978). Because parents take responsibility for their children's actions, children feel they can do whatever they want without severe consequences. Children may also fear new or difficult circumstances. Some risk is necessary to accomplish new behaviors, and experiencing some fear or anxiety in the face of unfamiliar circumstances is normal. To prevent children from experiencing this keeps them dependent on the parent and less responsible.

The strength of the permissive parenting style is in the giving of love. Research indicates that children's self-concepts varied directly with a parent's level of warmth and not their level of restrictiveness (Parish & McCluskey, 1994). Warmth is an important factor in how effective discipline is perceived by the parent. Mothers who are considered to be warm in their parenting style use physical discipline less often, but when they do, they consider it to be more effective than do cold mothers (Sears, Maccoby, and Levin, 1976). This implies that love is a necessary attribute in discipline and a child's self-concept. Most parents feel that discipline is simply a matter of limits and does not require love to be balanced.

However, love is not enough. Without the balance of firm and consistent limits, children are not encouraged to risk or master the difficult stages of life. Instead, overprotective parents encourage their children to take the easy way out. This style, when unbalanced, can be considered abusive to a child as much as the authoritarian style of parenting. As a matter of fact, children of authoritarian and permissive parents are very similar in that they are more dependent on parents, less assertive, and unable to tolerate much frustration. This is due to the fact that both styles tend to shield children from stress, limiting their ability to learn from their mistakes.

Balancing the Permissive Parenting Style

Permissive parents quickly become discouraged with their parenting role. They measure their worth as a parent by their children's actions. They believe, and society often reinforces, that "good" parents must always be in control of their children. Add to that the need to take responsibility for a child's misbehavior and eliminate effective parenting tools on how to regain control of children and what is left is a very discouraged and guilty parent.

The belief that love is all you need begets a martyr role for permissive parents. Parents sacrifice themselves for their children and then feel resentful when the children do not show appreciation for the parents' selfless acts.

Parents frequently tell people around them through their words and their actions, "See how I suffer for my child." They may also communicate: "No one appreciates all of the work I do for my family." The amount of their suffering soon becomes inversely proportional to their feelings of worth as a parent.

To illustrate this martyr role, consider an overdrawn checking account. When someone makes a purchase and writes a check but doesn't have sufficient funds to cover the purchase, they are said to be overdrawn. Parents can become emotionally overdrawn if they write out emotional checks (selfless acts) for their children and their parenting partners without having a sufficient amount of emotional resources within themselves. Permissive parents who feel "overdrawn" also describe feeling "burned out," "depleted," "exhausted," and "resentful."

To prevent becoming overdrawn, parents need to make frequent emotional deposits in themselves, even if in small amounts, before they try to meet all the needs of others. In others words, they can't give what they don't have. Unfortunately, permissive parents continue to try. Another difficulty for permissive parents is that even if they do choose to follow this advice, many parents do not know how to start. They are so used to doing for other people that they fail in the attempt. They may give up even before they have adequately tried or wind up doing something for someone else, in the name of doing for themselves. To balance love and limits, permissive parents need to learn to give to themselves as well as to others.

How permissive parents make a deposit into their own emotional bank account may depend on their personality. Some parents are more extroverted and need the stimulation of other people to get charged up. They like being sociable and need the interaction of friends and family to feel alive. Other parents are more introverted and prefer solitude and quiet, reflective activities. They are overwhelmed by groups of people and would much rather read, take a walk on the beach, or tend to their garden. This doesn't mean that an introverted parent would not like to go to a party—in fact they probably would feel honored by the invitation—but they are quickly drained of energy when in the company of large groups of people. They may prefer socializing with one or two close friends over coffee to mingling in a large group. Likewise, extroverted people also may enjoy sitting quietly and reading a good book, but they may find themselves calling an old friend they haven't seen in a long time, shortly after they start to read. Choosing an activity that goes along with, rather than against, a parent's personality increases the emotional balance in a parent's bank account.

Value Clarification Exercise: Filling up the emotional account
Choose an activity that fits your personality type:

Extroverted: *Go to a party, join a support group or club, go shopping with friends, work out at the gym, invite friends over for dinner, go out to dinner with friends, or join a bowling league or other sports group.*

Introverted: *Go to a movie, have lunch with a close friend, get up early and meditate, read a good book, go for a bike ride, take a walk, go shopping by yourself or with a friend, or spend the day at the park.*

Aggressiveness Versus Assertiveness

Another reason permissive parents have difficulty balancing love and limits is that they do not know how to be assertive with other family members. They may not have had a model of assertive behavior in their own parents and consequently are unable to stand up for themselves and teach right from wrong. All parents have three choices in how they meet their own needs and respond to the needs of others.

The first choice is to aggressively vent or express every feeling and thought that comes into their mind. As an example, a father might tell his daughter how selfish and demanding she is for wanting him to drive her around town without ever saying thank you or please.

The second choice is to passively deny, bury, or hide the feelings and thoughts that come into a parent's head. Using the above example, the permissive parent might continue to drive his daughter around without ever complaining or confessing his frustration. He might make excuses for not being able to drive her around, such as being low on gas or blaming the other parent by saying, "Your mother doesn't want me taking you around so often." He cannot stand the anger of his daughter, so he blames it on her mother.

The third choice is the more balanced or assertive choice. In this choice the father tells his daughter he doesn't mind driving her around but needs to set limits on how much driving he will do. Also, he can suggest that she ask in a more appropriate manner rather than demanding or whining at him to drive her around. This choice offers permissive parents a way to balance their own needs and the needs of the child. It also eliminates the slave or martyr mentality.

Value Clarification Exercise: The assertiveness quiz
Parents can take the following assertiveness quiz. If you answer yes to these questions, you might lean toward the permissive parenting style.

> When grandma and grandpa are visiting and contradict something you have said to your children or if they disagree with your discipline methods, do you back down from your own statements or discipline?
>
> Is it easier for you to just clean up your children's room than to keep pushing them to do it?
>
> If your parenting partner comes home exhausted and does nothing to help with the kids or supper, do you do everything even though you have worked all day too and are also exhausted?
>
> When your children want something in the store and you have already told them "no," do you give in or get into a screaming match when they continue to plead with you for the item?
>
> Do you leave family members' clothes laying all over the house hoping that other members of the family will realize their responsibility and pick up the clothes, only to pick them up yourself at the end of the day?
>
> Do you become angry when the house is a mess and begin yelling at members of the family for how they misuse you and/or don't appreciate you?

Just as authoritarian parents misunderstand the difference between discipline and punishment, permissive parents misunderstand the difference between assertive beliefs and behaviors and aggressive beliefs and behaviors. There is a difference between angry limits and kind but firm limits. When parents let grandparents or children rule the household, they are being wishy-washy and permissive in their parenting styles. They do not have the confidence to stand up for what they believe is right from wrong and consequently are unable to teach these things to their children.

Assertive beliefs and behaviors are very different from aggressive ones. Permissive parents who were raised by aggressive parents may reject this style in adulthood but be left unsure about how to act assertively. Or parents may have had passive parents who let them, as children, rule the household, and so they believe that this is the way to act as a parents. Even more likely is the scenario in which one parent is aggressive and the other is passive. This is another example of playing on the seesaw. One parent's dominating and controlling behavior may have squelched the other parent's authority and dignity.

Parents might even deeply resent the passive parents who would never stand up for themselves and perhaps never protected themselves as children from an abusive (verbally, emotionally, physically, or sexually) and aggressive parent. All of these things make balancing love and limits very difficult.

Fortunately, permissive parents can learn to parent more assertively. Remember, if parents learned one style of parenting, they can learn a different parenting style. This entails learning to be more assertive as well.

Assertive Alternatives

The first place for permissive parents to start is to understand the goal of assertive behavior, which is to find a win/win solution to both their needs or wants and the children's needs or wants. It means both giving and getting respect from children. It means that sometimes compromise is an acceptable solution when neither party can agree on a decision. And it means that parents believe that everyone can get their needs met even if not everyone will get everything they want.

Many of the parenting tools listing in the final section of this book will help permissive parents become more assertive. Perhaps the most important tool for being more assertive with family members are **"I" messages.**

Parenting Tool: "I" messages
"I" messages are one of the most useful and powerful of all parenting tools. So much of parent's communication with children begins with the word you instead of the word I. The word you often results in a defensive reaction. Children are more apt to resist and fight parents when in a defensive mode. This is especially true of teenagers. Parents need to practice using I at the beginning of a statement to their children, especially when asking for a desired behavior.

"I" messages have three parts: 1) feeling/desire, 2) behavior, and 3) consequence. An example of an "I" message for a younger child would be: "I feel angry (feeling/desire) when the bicycle is left in the driveway (behavior) because I nearly ran over it when coming home (consequence)." "I" messages link your feelings to the consequence, not the child. They also communicate value and respect. An example of an "I" message for an older child may go something like this: "I am worried when you do not come home on time and do not call me to

tell me you are going to be late because I am afraid that something has happened to you." "I" messages also communicate ownership of a problem.

Good timing is also important when using this parenting tool. Talking to children during conflict or a dispute may not be the best occasion for an "I" message. It may be necessary for both parent and child to take some time to cool off and then discuss the situation of concern.

Balancing love and limits by being more assertive is hard work. The first place to start is one's values and beliefs. What beliefs do parents have that are sabotaging attempts to be assertive? What misperceptions create feelings of resentment and mistreatment that lead to passive or aggressive behavior?

Permissive parents can use their strengths to adopt these more democratic beliefs. Doing so will allow the permissive parent to become a positive permissive parent. Because of all of the social and personal issues described above, permissive parenting has become synonymous with "wimpy parenting." The commonly accepted picture of the permissive parent is the frantic, disheveled mother with crying children, all of whom are demanding that she buy them something at every store they enter and throwing mega-tantrums when they do not immediately get their way. But permissive parents have strengths as well. For example, naturally using communication-based parenting tools.

Fair Versus Equal

Another problem for permissive parents is confusing fairness with equality. Sibling rivalry, one of the biggest problem permissive parents experience, occurs because parents mistakenly believe that everyone must be treated equally. The reality is that parents cannot treat everyone equally, but they can treat everyone fairly. Fairness implies giving favors in an impartial and consistent manner. Equality, on the other hand, implies giving favors in an exact or identical manner. Very rarely can a parent give all their children love or attention in an equal manner. There are two reasons for this. The first is that children are not the same or equal, developmentally speaking. The second is that love and attention are not as easily divided as a physical material, like crayons or socks. Even with physical materials children will still perceive the other child to have received the "prettier color" or "softer socks" than he or she received. Children often feel that parents give more love and attention to siblings.

There is a cognitive explanation for why children feel they get less love or attention than siblings. Children, especially young children, have a black and white understanding of the world. They see a parent's time and attention like a big pie. When a slice of the pie is removed and given to someone else, they feel that there is less for them. Because they see love and attention as being in limited supply, they feel insecure and anxious. Parents can explain that their love and attention is more like a stack of pancakes than a big pie. Even though parents give one pancake (i.e., time and attention) to one child, they have plenty more in their stack for their other children. In other words, everyone can have some of the parents time and attention.

Another reason children cannot be treated equally is because they are so different in temperament type and level of maturity. Older children are usually better able to handle responsibilities and problems than are younger children. Of course, age is no guarantee of maturity. Some younger children are more responsible than their older siblings. Temperament also plays a role in a child's ability to handle changes in circumstances. Researchers have shown how temperament affects a child's ability to cope with new situations (Thomas, Chess, & Birch, 1968). Some children are easygoing and able to handle whatever life might choose to bring their way, while others react intensely to the slightest change. Temperament is a genetic attribute, inherited from one or both parents and therefore not easily changed. Parents must work with, not against, a child's temperament. To try to treat each child in the same manner, or according to a parent's own temperament, would be to treat most children incorrectly.

Children also differ physically and developmentally. For example, school-age children need less sleep than preschoolers and no longer need to nap during the day or go to bed as early. Younger children question this obvious show of inequality by asking why they have to take a nap when their older siblings do not. These differences can create problems for permissive parents who are confused by the concepts of equality and fairness. Other differences include: Some children are more athletic while others more gifted intellectually or socially, some are quiet and shy, while others are outgoing, some are neat and organized, while others thrive on chaos.

A fair family treats everyone according to individual needs and considers everyone as worthy of love and respect. A parenting tool that permissive parents can utilize to practice fairness is **diagnostic questions.** These diagnostic questions were inspired by the work of Rudolph Driekurs, an Austrian child psychiatrist (1964). They allow parents to diagnose the motives of childrens' misbehavior and interact with them in a more balanced manner. Diagnostic questions allow permissive parents to use their greatest strength—communication—in a more investigative fashion. Interaction refers to how much responsibility a parent takes for the child's behaviors and how to help the child become more responsible.

Parenting Tools: Diagnostic questions

It has been said that children who feel right about themselves will act right (Ginott, 1969). This shows the link that self-esteem plays in a child's behavior. It also demonstrates the importance of love in the balance of love and limits when disciplining a child. Permissive parents are more likely to be tuned into the underlying motives or feelings of the child. Unfortunately, they don't know how to use this knowledge to direct their child's behavior.

Diagnostic questions are parenting tools to help parents determine what the motives are behind their children's behavior and what the best course of action should be in dealing with their child's behavior. A child's misbehavior can be motivated by four needs: Attention, power, revenge, and discouragement. The primary motivation for a child's misbehavior is the need for attention. Attention in and of itself is not bad, but most children seek it any way they can get it. They interrupt their parents when they are on the phone, throw tantrums in the middle of the grocery store, or whine for what they want. When they don't feel they have succeeded in getting their parents' attention, they will get mad and struggle for power with their parents. If that does not succeed, then children will seek revenge. They will follow the old adage: "Don't get mad, get even." Because they feel hurt, they will hurt others. If that does not get them what they want, they will move to the last motive for misbehavior, discouragement. They adopt the attitude, "Why bother? "Nothing I do makes any difference so why should I care?" At this point, children have given up hope. If a child has given up hope, they have come to this attitude over a significant period of time and repeated experiences at failure to gain their parents attention.

Parents can determine their children's motive for misbehavior by asking three diagnostic questions:

1. What emotion am I feeling when my child behaves this way?

2. What happens when I try to correct this problem with my child?

The Permissive Parenting Style

3. *What action do I need to take to help my child get what he or she needs in an appropriate rather than inappropriate manner?*

What emotion am I feeling when my child behaves this way? Parents can determine the answer to this question by listening to their own feelings. If parents recognize that they feel annoyed or irritated by their children's misbehavior, then children are probably seeking attention. Anger is a common emotion for motives of power. Feeling rejected or hurt is typical for revenge motivations. And feeling like giving up (on themselves and their children) is typical of discouragement.

What happens when I try to correct this problem with my child? When children are seeking attention, parents will remind or coax the child to stop their annoying actions. Children respond by stopping momentarily and then starting again with the same behaviors or some new, equally irritating behavior. Power-seeking children defy the parents' attempts to correct behavior. Children continue to act in the same manner and may even try to "one up" the intensity of the struggle. Revenge-seeking children counterattack parents' attempts at correction. They view every action as being out to get them or mistreat them in some way, and so they seek further revenge by intensifying the behaviors or choosing some new weapon to get even. Finally, when children feel defeated, they become discouraged. They act disabled or inadequate to perform any task, such as their chores or school work. Parents' attempts at correction usually end up with passive responses on the children's part or they receive no reaction at all. Parents may hear: "What does it matter if I don't do as you say? I can't please you anyway." "Why go to school, I'm too stupid anyway." or "Why should I get a job? They will just find something wrong with me and then fire me!"

What action do I need to take to help my child ask for what he/she needs in an appropriate rather than inappropriate manner? This diagnostic question recognizes that children are not aware of their motivations for misbehavior. It also recognizes that all misbehavior, even attention getting, stems from discouragement. Children lack the courage to behave in positive, constructive ways. They are simply trying to figure out where they belong in their family, and when their attempts to feel significant are not met with positive responses, they become even more discouraged and try a new or more intense misbehavior. What motive they choose may depend on their interpretation of the situation. But why they choose a particular motive is not as important as understanding that parents can modify their children's misbehavior so that children can get what they feel they need in an appropriate rather than inappropriate manner.

Parents can use the following value clarification exercise to determine your child's motive and then read the next section, learning to take action, to help you determine how to take appropriate action.

Value Clarification Exercise: My child's motive
Review the diagnostic questions parenting tool and ask yourself this question: "Could it be that my child is displaying a motive of _____?" Redirect, not discourage, that motivation by using the Parenting Tools listed in the parenting toolbox section. If you are still uncertain of the answer to this question, ask a friend or professional for an opinion.

Learning to Take Action!

Early in the book we talked about the two sides of discipline: action discipline and relationship discipline. Action discipline is characterized by a balance of limits, seen predominant in the authoritarian style of parenting, whereas relationship discipline is characterized by love, seen predominant in the permissive style of parenting. Permissive parents have a higher balance of love over limits. Their strength is in their ability to form a relationship with their children and in their acceptance of the "childishness" of children (Ginott, 1969). Permissive parents accept that a child's clothes won't stay clean, that they often run more than they walk, or that they may not be able to sit still for an entire church service. But permissive parents also accept their children's misbehavior or rationalize it as simply "childishness." This imbalance leads to over protectiveness and a lack of limitations on inappropriate behavior.

Action is a quality desperately needed by permissive parents. Their form of action often takes place after they feel they have been pushed too far by their children. The parents frustration builds and builds until an explosion results. This leads to feelings of guilt and more permissiveness. Because permissive parents are so verbal, they tend to act by yelling, nagging, or pleading with their children for cooperation. What may result is a vicious communication cycle.

Vicious communication cycles are negative exchanges of communication between two people. A similar form of this was mentioned in the chapter on the Rejecting/Neglecting parenting style. Permissible parents experience vicious cycles in their communication with children. These cycles start small and grow into larger feelings of resentment and anger. Over time, parents and children who are not aware of how they play into these vicious communication cycles feel as if they are in a perpetual downward spin with no hope for relief. Parents often expect children to act negatively toward them, and vice versa, thus creating a self-fulfilling cycle of more hurt.

An example of aversive verbal communication includes (McKay, Rogers, & McKay, 1989): threatening, expletives ("dammit!"), complaining , humiliating statements, put-downs, profanity, sarcasm, accusations, guilt trips, and ultimatums. It can also include verbal noises, such as groaning, sighing, and "tsking" at a parent or child. Other examples include: whining, mumbling, snickering, and using a mocking tone.

Aversive nonverbal communication is not as easily recognized as aversive verbal communication but includes: facial expressions (not looking at children when they are talking, rolling eyes, grimacing, sneering, frowning, tightening lips, raising an eyebrow, and scowling), body movements (shaking head, tapping a finger or foot in annoyance, moving or leaning forward in intimidation, moving or turning away in abandonment, putting hands on hips, kicking or throwing objects, and pushing or grabbing), or gestures (pointing fingers, shaking a fist, folding arms, waving away, and making a chopping motion).

It is useful for parents to be aware of ways in which they are contributing to vicious communication cycles. Prolonged aversive verbal and nonverbal communication can break down the relationship between parent and child. Permissive parents engage in these behaviors, sometimes unknowingly, when they feel overdrawn. While on the surface they seek to engage their children and are often very pleasant with them, under the surface they are hurt and resentful and thus may end up engaging in negative communication on a non-verbal level. Children are very good at picking up body signals regardless of what parents say. In addition to changing their values and beliefs, permissive parents can stop their vicious communicating cycles in a more positive manner and participating in a "caring" communication cycle, made up of positive communication.

A caring communication cycle, in contrast to a vicious communication cycle, begets positive behaviors with more positive behaviors. The trick to establishing a caring communication cycle is to make small efforts toward change rather than attempting to change a problem overnight. Overnight successes rarely happen. Parents must settle for making slow, steady improvements in themselves and in their interactions with their children. Fortunately, these small gains can snowball. One small act of kindness will beget another small act, which will snowball into bigger and bigger acts of kindness and cooperation. Don't let negative feelings rule. Negative feelings reinforce more negative feelings. Parents can stop the vicious communication cycle by taking action through caring communication cycles. Thus, they can take back control of love and limits.

Once permissive parents have taken action through caring communication cycles, they must take action with their children by their behaviors. Natural and logical consequences balance love and limits by setting firm and consistent consequences for children's misbehavior.

Parenting Tools: Natural and logical consequences

Natural and logical consequences are parenting tools that allow children to take responsibility for their actions and learn from their mistakes in a positive manner. Natural and logical consequences have certain advantages in balancing love and limits:

- *They put responsibilities for a child's behavior back in the child's hands.*
- *They allow children to make their own decisions about what is appropriate versus inappropriate behavior.*
- *They permit children to learn from their own actions rather than forcing them to conform to the wishes of parents or society.*

*Natural consequences result directly from our behavior or actions. If a child consistently forgets to take his lunch to school, the natural consequence would be that he would miss lunch and eat an ample dinner that evening. A child who forgets to wear mittens in the winter gets cold hands. A **diagnostic question** to determine a natural consequence would be, "What would happen to my children if they continue in their behaviors without any interference from me?" Say, for example, that a child does not put her dirty clothes in the dirty clothes bin. What would happen if the parent did not interfere by picking up the clothes or nagging the child to do it? The natural consequence would be that she would not have the outfit she wants to wear and is forced to wear some other outfit.*

Sometimes the natural consequence for an action is dangerous or intolerable. For example, if a child refuses to do his homework, the natural consequence would be a failing grade in school. This is usually not tolerable to parents. The answer would be to use logical consequences instead. Logical consequences are established conditions that result from a child's behavior or action. They occur in the social order rather than the natural order of things. If a child did not finish his homework, then he does not get to watch his favorite television program. If a child chooses to not eat dinner then she does not get dessert. A child who doesn't do his chores does not get allowance money or is not allowed to spend the night at a friend's home.

Natural and logical consequences are difficult for permissive parents to employ. They often find them harsh or cruel. This may be due to the fact that they are using natural and logical consequences in a punishing manner. Perhaps, in addition to using a consequence, parents are moralizing or sermonizing to their children (a vicious communication cycle). A father might imply a moral judgment over a child taking a hammer out of the tool box and not returning it. He might preach a sermon on how wrong the child was for taking the hammer without asking or the irresponsibility of not returning it.

Another parent might use natural and logical consequences as a punishment by focusing on past behavior. Parents might complain, "It's after 11 o'clock. You're always late. How many times have I told you to get home by 11 o'clock? Now you can forget about using the car for the rest of the month." Another problem is using logical consequences to threaten or put down a child. A parent might tell disruptive children: "If you don't quiet down, you will go to bed without supper!" or "You're so irresponsible. It's no wonder you never get to stay over at your friends' house with that kind of attitude."

To use natural and logical consequences in a positive manner, parents need to practice talking to their child in a neutral but firm manner (a caring communication cycle). A parent might say to a child, "Before we eat dessert, we need to eat our dinner." Parents can focus on the impersonal aspects of the situation rather than the moral aspects. In the case of the missing hammer, a parent might say, "How are you going to replace the hammer?" If the child has no suggestions, then the parent can suggest using allowance money to pay for it (see the parenting tool of **Restitution**). It is important to leave the problem in the hands of the child. Making all of the decisions on what is the consequence of a child's behavior is taking responsibility again. This impersonal handling of a situation is sometimes called separating the deed from the doer. Focus on the inappropriate behavior and not the child.

Another way to make natural and logical consequences positive is to focus on present and future behavior. The next time a child asks to use the car, the parent can tell the child, "I'm sorry, but I can't let you use the car. I don't feel that you are ready to handle the responsibility of coming home on time on your own. Maybe this weekend you can use it again." Don't dwell on past mistakes. This breeds resentment and anger. Focus on the present and the future. Allow children to experience the consequences of their actions and learn from their mistakes in a positive manner.

Chapter

10

The Democratic or Balanced Parenting Style

The democratic style of parenting is high on both love and limits. It is based on democratic concepts such as equality and trust. Parents and children are equal in terms of their need for dignity and worth but not in terms of responsibility and decision making. When parents first hear that the democratic style of parenting is based on equality, they may think that all members of the family are supposed to have an equal vote in all family decisions. In large families, where there are more children than there are adults, parents would be easily out-voted. If a family were to vote on whether or not they should have ice cream before or after dinner and all members of the family had the same weight in voting, when would the family eat ice cream? Before dinner, of course! What child wants to eat his vegetables, take a bath, or put on clean underwear? Parents under the democratic style of parenting, like the president of a democratic government, have veto power over decisions that may affect the health and well-being of younger family members.

Democratic parents believe that both love and limits are important. Limits, or action discipline, provides the physical security and control children need as they progress from dependency (infancy) to independence (young childhood) and interdependency (later childhood and adulthood). Limits help children understand the boundaries, restraints, and consequences for their actions. They help put a lid on out-of-control behavior, prevent children from harm, and focus behavior in a prosocial, proactive direction. Love, or relationship discipline, provides the emotional security and freedom to move from dependency to independence to interdependence. There are many personal and social forces to unbalance parents as they use both love and limits with their children. Achieving a balance requires many adjustments and modifications along the way as children grow developmentally.

129

Other balanced beliefs include:

Parents need to model right from wrong by their words and their deeds.
Discipline is different than punishment.
Blaming and shaming a child is not acceptable.
Consequences are inevitable and some frustration is O.K.
Children need encouragement in order to try new activities.
Children must be taught how to solve problems.
Discipline is used to teach and guide, not punish, manipulate, or control.

The underlying principle of all of these beliefs are independence and responsibility on the part of the child. Parents present expectations, not demands, to gain a child's cooperation and respect. The golden rule, to treat others as you would have them treat you, is at the heart of the democratic or balanced parenting style. It sets realistic standards of parenting and values humanness over perfection. Too much love and parents will be enmeshed with their children. Too many limits and parents will become rigid in their relationship with their children. Finding a balance of love and limits is a precarious but necessary task.

Effects of the Democratic Parenting Style on Children

Children of democratic or balanced parents are better able to negotiate the rough spots in life. They are more assertive in relationships, have better success in school, and have a higher level of self-esteem. These children tend to be more responsible and are more resilient to stressful situations (Lamb and Baumrind, 1978).

Democratic parenting provides children with high love and high limits. It incorporates the strengths of both the authoritarian and permissive styles of parenting so that children can benefit from the positive aspects of the *authoritative* parenting style and the *positive* permissive parenting style.

Balancing Love and Limits by Teaching Values

In the beginning of this book, we introduced the role that values play in balancing love and limits. Values are the basis for everything else discussed in the book, particularly parenting styles. To teach these values to children, parents must adopt an effective parenting style. Instead of playing the judge and jury of the authoritarian parenting style or the slave and martyr of the permissive parenting style, parents must become a teacher, guide, or model to children about what is right and wrong. Parents are constantly teaching their children. The question is what are parents teaching and are parents satisfied with what children are learning?

Parents are passing down the values of parenting they learned as children under their parental figures. Simply accepting or rejecting their parental figures' styles does not mean the styles have been changed. Parents must ask themselves if this is what they want to do for their children or if they wish to find a new way to balance love and limits. If parents choose this new way, then they must be more conscious about their choice of a parenting style. Balancing love and limits means taking control of parenting styles and teaching the values parents want for their children.

The first step in teaching new values to children is to decide what is not negotiable. The authoritarian style allows little if any discussion on observances, rules, and conduct, and the permissive style allows too much. The democratic or balanced style decides what is open for negotiation and what is not. For some families, religious observance may or may not be negotiable. Going to church or observing religious ceremonies may not be an option, at least when children are young. Other nonnegotiable values may involve family rules, for example, when expressing anger is appropriate. Parents may decide that family members are not allowed to hurt themselves, other people, or property. When angry, children may throw a tantrum, bite others or themselves, hit their parents, or break toys and furniture. Authoritarian parents often feel threatened by children's expression of anger, while permissive parents allow it to go unchecked. A more balanced parenting approach would be to accept the emotion of anger but not its destructive, uncontrolled venting. This gives parents permission to intervene when necessary. Examples of nonnegotiable conduct might also include: "No alcohol or other drug use except medications under parents' supervision, no R- or X-rated movies, or no more than one friend in the car at a time when driving to and from school." The most important part of this first step is that the parents make the decision about what is not negotiable, not the children.

The second step in teaching new values is to participate in community events and services that support parents' chosen beliefs. This might include volunteering at a senior center, delivering meals to shut-ins, or attending a rally on child abuse. A sense of community can help to create a feeling of identity for the family and as an individual. Children are already listening to the values broadcast by society and making choices based on what they see and hear. Parents can take a more active role by aligning their children to what parents believe are more positive values by participating in community events that support those values.

A third way to teach new values is to talk in a clear, open, and preventive manner to children about those values. Prevention refers to how parents talk to their children. How parents talk will determine whether or not children react defensively or listen attentively. The **Parenting Toolbox** section has various talk tools that parents can use to increase their rapport and interaction with their children. Otherwise, these conversations may land literally on deaf ears. Once parents increase their communication skills, they can better teach their children right from wrong. Prevention also refers to *when* parents talk to their children. After the fact is too late. Parents need to talk to their children before problems happen, when they can do so in a calm and open manner.

The fourth way to teach new values is to empower children to make important life decisions on their own and become responsible individuals. Children need more than pat answers to life's questions. They need to understand *why* as well as *what* to make independent, right choices. Authoritarian parents say "do it my way or else" with no explanation on why while permissive parents lecture their children until the children tune them out or stop taking them seriously. Some parents confuse scare tactics with open discussions. Fear is not the most effective method for teaching children values. Showing children horrible tragedies or forcing them to watch the news will only result in traumatizing them. It won't protect them from danger, as some parents might believe.

Finally, and most importantly, parents must model values to children. Children who observe parents practicing what they preach will be more likely to follow that example. Seeing the positive effects parents experience as a result of living out their values and the negative effects that others experience as a result of not following certain values, can be even more reinforcing. Parents with the same gender as their children (father and sons, mother and daughters) who provide positive models by their actions will be the most highly reinforcing model of all (Bandura 1977). Teaching values is not about force or dogma. Parents must be willing to be an example and guide their children into the values they desire them to follow. This is how parents influence what children value for themselves.

Regardless of what parenting style a parent has inherited, he can teach his children a more balanced parenting style through a conscious effort of teaching the who, what, where, why, and when of their values to children.

Balancing Love and Limits by Changing Parenting Beliefs

Parents want to do what they believe a good parent would do and avoid doing what they believe a "bad" parent would do. Therefore, to have high love and high limits, parents must change their ineffective beliefs and adopt more effective ones.

Unfortunately, this cannot be accomplished if parents do not accept responsibility for their thoughts and actions. If parents blame others for the imbalances in the family, then they are forced to wait for them to change before a balance can be achieved. And that could take a long, long time.

Too many parents shoot family members with the "You Gun." The You Gun consists of pointing the finger at everyone around them as responsible for the problems that exist in their lives. Imagine a parent holding out his hand in the shape of a gun, index finger pointing in the direction of a family member, the thumb sticking up in the air, and the other fingers folded tightly against the palm. This image consists of one finger pointed at others, blaming them for the imbalance in the family. The thumb pointing toward heaven, justifying his blaming actions as pure and holy. And three fingers pointing back at himself, hold the accusing parent as three times more responsible for the problem as the child or other parenting partner.

The reason parents use the You Gun is because they feel imbalanced in their love and limits with their children. Imbalance results in feeling overwhelmed, anxious, fearful, or in some type of emotional pain. These feelings occur because parenting is difficult and stressful. When parents experience this imbalance, they often look for someone to blame to alleviate this stress. Blaming acts as a short-term release or defense from the feelings of imbalance. Authoritarian parents tend to blame the child, and permissive parents tend to blame themselves and then get angry or resentful at the child. The reality is that parent and child are responsible together for imbalances in the family. Democratic or balanced parenting is based on mutual responsibility of both parent and child. But parents must come to accept that the only person they have absolute control over is themselves. While authoritarian arm twisting or permissive martyring may work for a while, only balanced parenting can provide lasting and satisfying effects.

There are four principles that parents need for accepting personal responsibility when balancing love and limits (McKay, Rogers, & McKay, 1989):

1. *The only thing you can guarantee to have TOTAL control over is yourself.* You are the only expert on your needs, wants, and desires. Your parenting partner cannot read your mind, and your children do not innately know social rules of conduct. Feeling angry and resentful because family members are not cooperating or working together will not create balance. Having an out-of-control child or unhelpful partner is not an excuse for refusing to accept personal responsibility.

2. *Accepting personal responsibility for oneself models to children how to accept responsibility for their actions.* The preceding section on teaching values focuses on modeling the behavior parents expect from their children. The authoritarian stance of "do what I say and not what I do" models "do what you want to, just don't let me catch you." Blaming others models a lack of personal responsibility and encourages an attitude of entitlement. Under a blaming model, children believe that because they want something very much, they should have it. Because they want their parents' attention, they should always have it. Because they want a certain style of clothing, their parents must buy it for them. They confuse wanting with having. They forget others have the right to say "no." Accepting parents' limits is intolerable. When faced with the temptation to take illegal drugs, commit a crime, or cheat on an exam, they do not know that they too can say "no."

3. *Being balanced does not mean family members will not have conflicts.* Everyone on the planet, in families, organizations, society, and countries wants to get their needs met. Unfortunately, their needs may conflict with the needs of others. A parent who needs a clean house may conflict with a teenager's need to control his own room. A single parent's

need to work often conflicts with the child's need to spent more time with mom or dad. Grandparents raising their grandchildren may have a need to enjoy their later years child-free and traveling the world. This comes in conflict with playing the role of parent all over again.

Conflict over getting one's needs met versus another persons needs is part of everyday life. Blaming others and getting angry at the way things are will not resolve this conflict. It simply begets more frustration and anger, the very thing parents are trying to stop.

Permissive parents struggle with the fact that children may feel some discomfort at not getting their needs met every time they want them met. Teaching responsibility will make it necessary that children experience some delay of gratification. Doing what's right as a parent may conflict with children's desires to do what they want. Authoritarian parents struggle over compromising their need for control and not having instant compliance. *Respect* is not synonymous with unquestioned obedience. Balanced parenting requires negotiation and communication on whose needs get met when. Conflict, when exercised in a democratic atmosphere of mutual respect, often becomes cooperation or, at the very least, compromise.

4. *Balanced parenting depends on the consciousness of one's actions and the effectiveness of the tools used to parent.* Making others responsible for one's actions obscures parents from the warning signs that what they are doing is not working. Inattention to these signs leads parents to doing more of the same and repeating their failures (Weiner-Davis, 1995). Rather than blaming partners and children, parents can accept personal responsibility and find the tools to do the job. Doing this requires that parents understand why they are doing what they do and then doing something different, anything different, to break the vicious cycle.

Four Areas of Beliefs that Cause Family Imbalance

In addition, there are other four major areas of mistaken beliefs that parents often stumble into when balancing love and limits: good-bad dichotomizing, mind reading, magnifying, and global labeling.

Good-bad dichotomizing. This mistaken belief puts the world of parenting into a black and white frame where no middle ground can exist. This type of mental box leads parents and children into power struggles. It places family members at extremes and prevents parents from seeing the strengths in themselves and their children. With this rigid view of the world, parents often miss the loving act of the older brother toward his sister and only see him teasing her. They miss their parenting partners' efforts to discipline children in what they feel a good parent should do and only see them as bad, harsh, or strict. And they fail to thank a child who picked up her dirty dishes for helping and see instead that she forgot to put in the soap and turn on the dishwasher.

Breaking out of this frame requires parents to use coping statements that allow the many shades of gray to exist in relationships. Examples of these coping statements include: "My son doesn't really hate his sister. Some rivalry is normal and healthy." "My partner is doing what he feels a good parent is supposed to do. He is not necessarily wrong, and I am not necessarily right." "My child did help with the dishes, and I can show my appreciation for that effort even though she did not do everything I wanted her to do."

Another balanced strategy is to use percentages. For example, accepting the belief that children are not all bad all of the time—maybe their behavior needs to improve just 10% of the time—will help to eliminate good-bad dichotomizing. If a child disobeys 10% of the time, that means they are obedient the other 90% of the time. Even if the percentages are reversed, with 90% of their behavior disobedient and 10% obedient, they are still not all bad and can be seen in a more flexible and tolerant light.

Mind reading. This mistaken belief makes inferences about what others think and feel. It assumes special insight into family members motivations. And it is so often wrong. For example, a parent believes that a child deliberately got lost in the grocery store just to scare her. Or a child believes that his sibling deliberately bumped into him when getting into the car. Mind reading creates feelings of imbalance because it blames a problem on someone else and infers a deliberate intent. The reality is that the parent or sibling never asked what the other family member intended by their action—because, after all, they already knew, right? Mind reading is a common reason families experience so much imbalance.

For contemporary parents juggling work and family, mind reading can be a kind of emotional shortcut. Stopping to check out another person's thoughts and feelings takes time, perhaps more time than a parent wants to take. But not doing so results in more and more imbalance and in the long run costs more than the few seconds it would have taken to communicate with another member of the family. The parent in the store, for instance, could ask: "When you got lost, I had the feeling you were trying to scare me." If there are facts to back up assumptions, parents can use them as well: "I know that you were angry with me earlier for not letting you get the kind of cereal you wanted." Or they can change the focus of the assumption by talking in the third person to eliminate leading a child's thoughts: "Some children try to get back at their parents by trying to scare them when they are mad at them. Is that what happened to you?" The parent may discover that the child got lost simply because he is a child and a child's attention wanders very easily.

Mind reading is difficult to eliminate. Parents must constantly remind themselves not to assume anything. Stop guessing at the motives of others and ask for information rather than making a judgment. Replacing this habit with a healthier one will improve a parent's relationship with their children (no one likes to have his mind read) and increase a parent's feeling of real control (now you can really find out what the others are intending).

Magnifying. This mistaken belief makes situations worse than they really are. Parents use words like "terrible," "awful," "disgusting," or "horrible." They overgeneralize by using the words "always," "all," "every," and "never." A parent who states that his child "always gets up late for school" or "never goes to bed on time" is magnifying a behavior out of proportion.

The truth is that no child "always gets up late" or "never goes to bed on time." Instead, the parent's frustration at the child and himself makes it feel as if it were true. Even if it were true, making these kinds of statements increases a parent's sense of being victimized and corners a child into only one type of behavior. Magnifying is like throwing gasoline on a fire. It explodes a problematic situation into an uncontrollable crisis.

In order to overcome this mistaken belief, parents must eliminate these magnifying words from their vocabulary. They must commit to describing a situation realistically rather than magnifying it out of proportion. Strive for accuracy. Give the exact number of times the child refuses to get up in the morning. Stay focused on the here-and-now rather than on all the past times a child refused to get up. This prevents past frustrations from building up into an inferno, making it impossible for a parent to deal with the current situation.

Global labeling. This mistaken belief puts a general stamp on a specific behavior. For instance, a parent describes her partner as "lazy" or her child as "selfish" for a specific action and uses the label to describe the whole person. Parents and children are much more complex than this and have many characteristics. "Lazy" and "selfish" are just two provocative labels. Using labels is an excuse to blame someone for a problem and bail out of having any responsibility in the matter, because the other person is "lazy" or "selfish."

The antidote for this mistaken belief is to be more specific. Describe the behavior and leave out the person. Telling a child that he is selfish for taking the last piece of chicken and not asking anyone else if they would like some would be attacking the person. Be more specific and address the behavior to eliminate global labeling. For example, a parent might say: "It is respectful to ask others, if they would like the last piece of chicken before taking it." No where in this sentence is the work "you" or "selfish," and still it makes the parent's point. And, it will get better results.

Value Clarification Exercise: My belief balance sheet
Take a piece of paper and divide it into three columns. In the first column, write down what you are saying to your partner or child. In the second column, across from these statements, jot down which mistaken belief you are using. In a third column, rewrite your original statement in a more balanced manner. Use examples listed in this chapter to identify mistaken belief statements you use and rewrite them into more effective statements.

Balancing Love and Limits by Accepting Different Parenting Styles

The stronger the executive or parental subsystem, the better balance of love and limits parents will experience. An imbalance in how partners approach parenting is probably the most difficult area for parents to resolve. This is especially true when parents are playing on the seesaw and feel that their differences are too great to overcome. For these parents, a strong executive/parental subsystem seems impossible. They forget that it was these differences that originally attracted them to each other. The old saying that "opposites attract" may have a lot of truth when it comes to creating a democratic or balanced parenting relationship. Contrasting styles of parenting may have been what initially attracted two parenting partners to one another.

It is natural for people to want to fill in the gaps of their personality or find a complement to their own skills and abilities. These different styles unconsciously round out their parenting roles. This is why one partner may be more aggressive, more organized, more emotional, or more controlled than the other partner and why together the two personalities seem, at least at first glance, to be a good "team."

Just as values are largely unconscious and tucked away from parents' awareness, certain styles of parenting that were attractive early on in the parenting relationship may have been largely unconscious. Parents may have fallen in love, not just with the other person, but with their ability to make firm decisions or feel passionate about something. Parents may have even fallen in love with characteristics they lacked or felt they never could adequately provide for a child.

The ability of one parent to follow a budget or use common sense may impress another parent whose checkbook is always unbalanced or who feels that finances and life are out of control. The other person creates a sense of balance in life that translates to a feeling of balance of love and limits during child-rearing. After a while, though, these attractive attributes can become annoying. The parenting partner who provided a sense of stability early on in the relationship and could offer common sense when the baby cried all night long comes to be seen as boring, emotionally detached, and too rigid as the relationship progresses.

Parenting changes how people perceive themselves. Setting limits on one's checkbook is different than setting limits on a child. Nurturing oneself is very different from nurturing a totally dependent, often demanding, infant. This evolution from partners in love to partners in parenting creates a feeling of imbalance. Having a child forces partners to merge two sets of cultures, parenting values, and beliefs. It also brings up positive and negative memories of a parent's own childhood. Parents who had abusive parents or whose partner had abusive parents, may fear that their own children will be abused. Adults who idealized their parents may feel incompetent when comparing their own parenting skills to those of their mother and father.

The positive attributes that attracted one partner to another may begin to remind them of negative traits in their own parents. The organizational skills they admired in their partners and in their own parents also remind them of the compulsive, rigid behavior of those people. The spontaneity and attention given by one's partner may remind the other of a parent's smothering over-protection.

Having children also forces partners to make decisions that never had to be made before. It requires them to act cooperatively with one another on such issues as who stays home with the children when they are sick, how to deal with a bad grade on a report card, or how to handle a child with an emotional or behavioral disorder, all of which can result in parental disagreements, arguments, and resentments.

Even the value that parenting partners must act or react in the same manner can be disastrous to a balance of love and limits. Fortunately, these differences can become the groundwork for a fuller relationship if partners are willing to learn from one another rather than continue a vicious cycle of anger and resentment. This is possible only where both parents make an honest attempt at communication and cooperation. In addition, partners can learn from one another's differences and incorporate the other's strengths into their own parenting style.

The first step to learning from the other parenting figure is to accept that differences are acceptable, even necessary, in the parenting relationship. If parents are to develop certain parenting characteristics they never learned from their own parental figures, they must accept and allow their partners to demonstrates these qualities. Believing that the other parent has something valuable to offer the parenting relationship will create cooperation in the difficult task of raising a child rather than resentment.

The second step is to learn new ways to parent from the example of the other parent. Getting out of the way and letting them "do their thing" will not produce growth in one's own parenting skills. Letting the other person have his way is not synonymous with learning. This can become learned helplessness, which results in negative feelings toward oneself and the partner. While one parent may never be quite as good at setting firm rules at bedtime, she can learn to do it more frequently and more consistently than she has in the past, simply by learning from the example of her partner.

The third step is to agree to disagree. Not every parenting decision will be made in total agreement. Nor should every decision be made by one person, regardless of how confident or aggressive he or she is in making decisions. Parenting partners can take turns on how to take care of night-time fears, with one parent singing and holding the child one week and the other parent scaring away the bedtime monsters with a flashlight the next. Or they can compromise by finding a third, equally agreeable solution to getting their child to stay in bed. If an equally agreeable solution does not present itself, partners can always agree to disagree by waiting until a third solution does become possible. Agreeing to disagree is helpful when a discussion becomes heated and partners need to wait until both parties are feeling cooler and better able to see the other person's viewpoint. This behavior is a powerful model to children. It demonstrates that parents can be different and disagree without engaging in a physical or verbal battle. It communicates to children in a very real way how to work things out. Relationships can continue to be satisfying (or balanced) even when an issue is not yet settled.

The fourth step is to recognize that the negative or uncooperative behavior seen in the other parent may be a projection of a characteristic of their parental figures or past experiences. The partner's behavior may not be communicating a particular attitude or personality trait at all. For example, a parent who was abused as a child, may see the behavior of their partner as abusive as well. But, is it really an abusive act or is it a projection from the parent's own past? Take time to reflect on your own past and talk with the other partner about childhood experiences. Insight, not ignorance, will lead to intimacy.

The fifth step is to have a discussion on balancing love and limits free of name-calling, blaming, or shaming one another. Don't make partners feel bad by labeling them as rigid, talking about them in front of friends, or constantly pointing out their flaws. If this is too difficult to master, parenting partners need to find help to deal with these destructive communication styles. Sometimes the old adage, "If you can't say anything nice, don't say anything at all" is true—at least until a qualified professional can be found to help parents communicate. The best time to have this discussion is when everything feels right (balanced) in the parenting partner relationship. Most of the time parents don't want to rock the boat and ruin a rare moment of peace between them and their partner. If this kind of discussion does lead into a vicious cycle of communication, set some structure around it to ensure that it stays positive. Set a time limit or agree to take a time-out if things become elated. Use the positive energy to make lasting changes in the parenting relationship. Not doing so will lead back to a vicious cycle.

> *Value Clarification Exercise: My ideal family*
> *Describe your ideal family? Does it consist of one parent or two? How many children should the ideal family have? What about shared responsibilities between family members, especially the parenting partners? Should both parents work and should children contribute to the financial needs of the family? How does this ideal family differ from contemporary standards for the family? Do you feel society supports or contradicts the values you are attempting to teach your children?*

Balancing Love and Limits by Changing the Parenting Role

A parenting style is the way in which parents express their belief about how to be a good parent and avoid doing what they believe a bad parent does. This is how parents choose what roles to play in the parenting partner relationship and in disciplining their children. The authoritarian parenting style takes the role of police officer, judge, and jury. The permissive parenting style takes the role of martyr and slave. Each role is too extreme or unbalanced.

A balanced role, based on the democratic parenting style, might be one of a teacher or guide. We contrasted the authoritarian style of parenting with the authoritative style of parenting. The difference between these two styles is that one teaches children to be submissive and do what they are told when they are to do it and the other teaches children to be responsible and follow the example of the parents in attitude and action. This is the same basis for the positive permissive parenting style in contrast to the negative permissive style of parenting. The negative style of permissive parenting teaches children to manipulate and ignore parental requests. The positive permissive parenting style teaches mutual respect and natural consequences for their behavior.

The reason that unbalanced parenting styles and the extreme roles that go along with them do not work is that they take a physical, emotional, and spiritual toll on parents. The imbalance discourages both parent and child. Parents quickly tire of playing judge or being ignored by children. They feel hopeless, as if nothing they do works or that everything they do seems to make matters worse. When parents find themselves in this position, it may be time to change their roles. Two such examples of changing the parenting role are "acting as if" and "doing a 180" (Weiner-Davis, 1995).

Acting as if. One way to change parents roles is to challenge their belief systems about what it means to be a good or bad parent. Another way is to change the behaviors that accompany those beliefs. Parents may feel they cannot change their beliefs or are still unable to identify how they approach parenting. Fortunately, these parents will find it easier to change their behaviors by "acting as if."

Parents can change their parenting roles by "acting as if" they are a teacher or guide. Even if they do not feel like they have anything to teach or that they may not be a suitable guide, they can try out the role. The reality is that parents are already teaching their child something whether or not they realize it. The authoritarian style of parenting teaches submission and the permissive style teaches manipulation. "Acting as if" is simply doing what parents are already doing but in a more positive manner. For example, when a teenager gets upset at her mother for establishing a curfew, the parent can "act as if" she is not upset by her daughter's tantrum and act firm and consistent instead of getting into a verbal battle. Likewise, when a 2-year-old throws a tantrum because he does not get a toy he wants in the store, his father can "act as if" the child is not embarrassing him in front of everybody and perform his balanced parenting duties in the way he needs to—with love and limits.

Children will not expect this change in behavior. They will expect parents to act in the familiar ways that they have always acted in the past. They may view their parents much like a robot. Wind mom and dad up and they will respond in the same fashion every time. Right? Not anymore! At least not anymore now that parents can "act as if" things are different. What they will find by doing something different than the child expects the parent to do is that they will change the script they continually play out with their children. By "acting as if," parents can rewrite their roles as well as the sequence of events in the negative scripts they act out with their children. As a result, parents will create a different ending to their parent/child scripts, one that is more positive and balanced.

Value Clarification Exercise: Negative scripts

Consider how you can change your role in the negative scripts you play with your children. What are the issues that create the most negative interactions? On what occasions do negative interactions take place most frequently? What are the places that seem to invite family members to make the most negative interactions? Who are the people most likely to be involved in the negative script? At what times do these problem behaviors occur most often? If you are not the one to start a negative interaction, what role do you play in responding or reacting to your children or partner?

Doing a 180.   Parents who find themselves participating in negative interactions, whether they start it or not, can reverse this trend by "doing a 180." Another way of describing this response is doing the opposite of what parents are currently doing and finding to be ineffective. If, for instance, a parent discovers that he raises his voice with a particular child over a specific issue during a peculiar time of the day, the father can try "doing a 180." He can strive to lower his voice, change the issue, or discuss it at a different time of day. Perhaps, if a mother finds that she tends to be more tired and grumpy at the end of the day while her son is more moody in the morning, she can try to reduce potential conflicts during those times of the day. Use humor by putting up a storm warning sign on the refrigerator or a grumpy person crossing sign in the hallway. Parents can try doing the opposite of what they would normally do in a given situation and break the stronghold that negative scripts have on the family. "Doing a 180" or "acting as if" introduces a novel stimulus to a negative situation and thereby reverses its negative course.

Balancing Love and Limits in the Nontraditional Family

Earlier in the chapter on "Nontraditional Families," we talked about the different definitions of a family and how being a fully functioning family is not inherent in the traditional composition. In this section, we will look at some more ways nontraditional families can balance love and limits.

A common feeling experienced by nontraditional parents is that they are "less than" other types of parents due to their family structure. This results in feelings of guilt and grief. They also may feel isolated and alone. A common mistaken belief is that no one else could possibly feel what they are feeling. The reality is that these feelings are very common. Most nontraditional parents feel that they do not meet society's standard of acceptable parenting. Consider the fairy tale myths of the "wicked stepmother" or the (single) "old woman" who lived in shoe and beat her children and put them to bed. Being a nontraditional parent is often a lonely and thankless job. It is also a job that doesn't have a clear job description.

Same But Different

By using the suggestions and the tools listed in this book, nontraditional parents can begin to develop a clear job description. Perhaps nontraditional parents can use the motto *same but different* to provide a clearer job description.

Nontraditional parents may have the *same* values as traditional parents but the way in which they exercise them may be different. The need to have a strong executive or marital subsystem is the *same* but the makeup of that subsystem may be different. It may be made up of remarried individuals, grandparents instead of parents, nonbiological rather than biological parents, or a single parent instead of mom and dad. Birth order is the *same* in the nontraditional family as in a traditional one but may be more complicated when a firstborn child in a remarried family changes roles due to the inclusion of new siblings after the remarriage and becomes the middle or youngest child. This can lead to a difficult adjustment and the need to continue respecting the child's old position along with the new position. Boundaries are the same as in the traditional family but where and when these are set may be different due to the different structure of the nontraditional family. The perfect parenting standard will be the same in the nontraditional parent but differs as nontraditional parents fall farther from the parenting ideal. Power plays will be the same in the nontraditional family as in the traditional family but detriangulation or differentiation takes place differently. Focusing on nontraditional parenting as the same but different helps normalize parenting for nontraditional families while acknowledging their uniqueness.

Different But the Same

Likewise, focusing on being *different but the same* is also important for nontra-ditional parents, to a point. They need to accept, if they are to move through the states and stages of grief, that they are very different in structure and com-position from traditional families. Therefore, their experiences and feelings will be something traditional parents may not share. To believe that nontradi-tional parents are carbon copies of traditional parents and to attempt to live according to principles established on those terms will result in further failure in balancing love and limits.

Another way for nontraditional families to balance love and limits is to focus not on differences or sameness but on solutions. Finding what works, regardless of the traditional or nontraditional family parents find themselves in, will help achieve a greater balance of love and limits.

Balancing Love and Limits by Seeking Solutions

Most parents don't realize that they already have the basic resources necessary to balance love and limits. Taking a good inventory of one's strengths and weak-nesses will help parents identify the internal and external resources they have already inherited from the parental figures in their lives. True, they have also inherited the weaknesses as well, but at least they have 50% of what they need for more balanced parenting. As in the old question of whether the glass is half empty or half full, parents can see their resources two ways: weak or strong.

Many parents may not be aware of all the resources, internal or external, they can rely on. They see the glass half empty instead of half full. The real problem is that parents do not know how to access their resources and make use of them on a more conscious level. This is referred to as *blocks to finding solutions in parenting.*

Blocks to Finding Solutions in Parenting

All parents have moments, however accidental they might seem, where they feel balanced and in control. Even the parent who claims to have the worst child in history will find times when the child acts respectfully toward another person, puts away dinner dishes without being asked, or walks by a younger sibling without punching him. Parents can usually remember a time when things were going great between them and their children. Even authoritarian parents show moments of nurturing, and permissive parents have moments where they have set firm, consistent limits. The problem is not that good times *never* occur. The problem is that parents don't know how to recreate those good times and make them happen more frequently. Understanding what is different about the good times from the bad times can help parents repeat the good ones and eliminate the bad.

Another block to finding solutions occurs when parents believe that their past controls the present and future. They may have experienced a traumatic past with their own parents or the history between them and their children is so full of mistakes and bad times that they feel they can never balance love and limits or repair the damage. They feel they are doomed to repeat their mistakes or the mistakes of their parents. Parents in this situation block themselves. To overcome this block, many parents will attempt to analyze these problems with professionals, friends, or anybody who will listen. Doing this can sometimes have the opposite effect they desire, especially if the person they are talking to is not trained to deal with that kind of trauma. Talking about a traumatic situation can retraumatize people rather than freeing them from the memory. Although it is true that insight, usually accomplished through verbalizing one's thoughts and feelings, helps make parents more aware of the patterns of behaviors in their lives, it fails to suggest what parents need to be doing differently. Parents can get stuck in the past and never deal with the present or move on to a more successful future. To be truly effective, parents need to balance insight with solutions. To truly overcome this block of past trauma, parents may need to focus not just on the traumas of the past but their successes as well, so that they can change the present and have a more balanced future.

A third block to finding solutions is focusing on other people's weaknesses and not our own. Although this has been said before it is important enough to be said again. Focusing on others eliminates the need to take responsibility for ourselves by placing the power and control for change on others. These other people might include one's partner, children, parent, friends, neighbors, or society in general. Parents who blame others for their imbalance never find that state of balance in their own parenting. Complaining about the husband who never picks up after himself, blaming the wife who coddles the children too much, or identifying the rebellious child as the source of the family's frustration will not, in itself, create change. Instead, it often creates the very thing parents are saying they want to change. Complaining about the husband creates resentment and unwillingness to pick up after himself. Blaming the wife who coddles the children will justify her feelings that the husband is a tyrant. Identifying the rebellious child as the source of the family's frustration will push that child to prove just how much trouble she really can cause. Only by focusing on our own weaknesses and strengths can we begin to find solutions to balancing love and limits.

Balancing Love & Limits by Doing it Your Way!

The best way to create a democratic or balanced parenting relationship, where both love and limits are valued, is to balance love and limits your own way. This means finding a method for discipline that either combines the best of both worlds, of both mother and father, or looking for that third neutral solution.

As an illustration, take Pip's story from the children's book *The Grandma Mix-up* by Emily Arnold. This story reveals how a young boy deals with strong parental figures and conflicting social messages in his life. The story begins with Pip's parents preparing to take a trip by themselves. Unknowingly, his mom and dad had each asked their own mothers, Pip's grandmothers, to watch Pip while they are gone. As you can imagine, Grandma Nan and Grandma Sal arrive at exactly the same time. Pip's parents are confused about what to do, until the grandmothers decide that they both will watch Pip while his mom and dad take their trip. It seems like a good idea at first.

Unfortunately, they get off to a bad start. You see, Grandma Nan believes that they should "get busy" while Grandma Sal thinks they should "just relax." Grandma Nan tells Pip no snacks before dinner. Grandma Sal gives him a bag of Gummy Bears. Grandma Nan wants to inspect Pip's room and clean up the house, while Grandma Sal wants Pip to show her his bike. Grandma Nan makes tuna with sprouts for lunch, and Grandma Sal suggests "an apple, some nuts, a marshmallow, cereal, pretzels, or corned-beef hash." Poor Pip. He decides he is not that hungry.

The situation gets worse and worse. After Pip's nap, Grandma Nan wants to get busy and paint a picture or act out a story. Grandma Sal wants to watch the big game on television. Pip decides to go to his room and write a letter to his mom and dad.

Dear Mom and Dad,

Grandma Nan is too hard, and Grandma Sal is too easy. I want you to come home and do things our way.

Love, Pip

Grandma Nan calls Pip to set the table for dinner. While he is doing so, he notices that his grandmas are making dinner together. Grandma Nan makes stew. Grandma Sal says, "If it stinks, we can send out for pizza." Pip doesn't like stew but he takes a bite to be polite. He asks if he can go outside. Grandma Nan answers, "If you keep clean." Grandma Sal retorts, "Pip can always take a bath." Both grandmas are becoming grumpy.

Grandma Nan wants to do things one way and Grandma Sal wants to do things another way. Pip wants to do things the way that Mom and Dad and Pip always did them. At the window the grandmas are talking. "A child need rules, Sal," says Grandma Nan. "A child needs fun, Nan," says Grandma Sal. "My rule is bed at 8 o'clock," says Grandma Nan. "Oh, loosen up," says Grandma Sal. "A body gets the sleep it needs." Pip runs in and yells, "STOP! I do not want to do everything two ways. I want to do them *our* way, like every day when Mom and Dad are home." The grandmas listens to Pip. They ask him how he does things. He says: "I clean up my room once a week. I make my own lunch every day. I don't take a nap unless I want to, and I never have candy in the morning except at Christmas. No TV on nice days, and I can get dirty when I play. And I don't eat vegetables all mixed up with meat."

And so, the grandmas follow the way that Pip and his mom and dad do things. They put aside their differences and learn to do things Pip's way.

This story is a good illustration of how people can balance the parenting styles they have inherited from parental figures in their own lives. All parents have a certain style they feel makes them a good parent. And they follow this style when parenting their child. When two parenting styles don't agree, they can find their *own* way of doing things. They do not have to continue to parent in the fashion they learned as a child. They do not have to do follow all of the messages that society states they must or should follow. If they are a nontraditional family, they do not have to follow traditional family models of parenting. Instead they can discover their own way of parenting their children. Just as the two grandmas choose to listen to Pip and his way of doing things, parents can use new tools for parenting their children. They can do something different and learn to balance their love and limits by using high love and high limits.

Balancing Love and Limits by Praying for Serenity

All of the suggestions in this chapter and throughout this book can be summed up in a simple prayer. This prayer, made famous by one of the most successful self-help groups in the world, Alcoholics Anonymous, is entitled the *Serenity Prayer*:

> *Lord, grant me the serenity to accept the things I cannot change, the courage to change the things I can, and the wisdom to know the difference.*

Here is a breakdown of some of the essential points of this prayer as they relate to how parents can balance love and limits.

Asking for help. If parents are to balance love and limits and find the serenity they need in parenting, they must be willing to ask for help. Whether that help is from God, a higher power, or other people, parents will need support to help them through the challenge of balancing their parenting. As we discussed the different parenting styles, we found one common denominator in why parents reject or neglect their children: they do not perceive that they have any social support to help them in moments of crisis, or if they do have support, it was either unhealthy or they could not use it. Parents need other parents and professionals who work with parents to get through the rough times. If parents accept the fact that parenting is difficult, they find that it ceases to be so hard because they learn to prevent problems from continuing to rear their ugly head. Asking for help is one way to prevent these problems.

Seeking serenity. Serenity, like balance, is a precarious thing. Parents look for many ways to find this balance—in themselves, in their parental relationships, and in their children. We began this book with a discussion about how balance is related to your own value system. This value system develops and changes over time. Parents behave in a certain manner to be consistent with their beliefs about what it means to be a good or bad parent based on their value systems. In fact, this book is about finding balance, not only of a parent's love and limits, but in the total parenting relationship.

One of the simplest ways to achieve balance and serenity is to find the right tools to do the job of parenting. A common reason parents feel frustrated is that they don't know how to discipline their children. Changing one's beliefs and behaviors makes parents more competent and self-assured in their parenting roles. Knowing they have a toolbox full of tools to balance love and limits will help to create those feelings of peace that balance can bring.

Accepting what can't be changed.   It's appropriate that the Serenity Prayer begins with the request for "the serenity to accept the things I cannot change." Parents are usually focused on what they want to change, regardless of whether it can be changed or not. Sometimes these issues can be changed in the future, but putting them on the back burner to change at a later date is difficult for many parents. Perhaps the best example of this is with teenagers. Many parents are concerned with teenage rebelliousness and feel they need to set limits or change every thing they do when in fact much of what teenagers do can be ignored and let go. The developmental goal of teenagers is to be different from their parents and to seek their own identity in life. Unfortunately, they do not always know what they want to be instead and so will try various styles of dress, haircut, speech, or attitude in an attempt to find out who they are. Parents must ask themselves, does it really matter what color their hair is or what type of pants they want to wear? If they are doing well in school and are basically respectful children, then do I really want to fight over whether their room is picked up or not? If they are not hurting themselves, others, or property, do I really want to get on their case about this thing or the other? Perhaps more peace and balance will come to parents who can clearly decide what is worth fighting over and what is something to accept as is.

Courage to change what can be changed.   Having the courage to change what can be changed is the next part of the Serenity Prayer. What this means for parents is that they must first change themselves before they attempt to change others. Changing oneself takes courage. It takes courage because parents must accept that they, like the parental figures in their own lives, are not perfect.

Having the courage to change things that can be changed also refers to the need of parents to focus on their strengths, not just their weaknesses. It means acknowledging the strengths of the other parenting partner and children, as dim as those strengths might appear to be, instead of only noticing their weaknesses. It means that parents must concentrate on what works and not just what does not work. They must analyze what is different about the times they get their child to cooperate or the times they get their parenting partner to help around the house. Maintaining the status quo leaves parents to live a passive, out-of-control life. They will be like robots, doing what they have been programmed to do, never stopping to look at themselves and figure out new ways to balance love and limits.

The wisdom to know the difference. The most difficult part of the serenity prayer and of balancing love and limits is knowing the difference between what can be changed and what cannot. So many parents use courage to attempt to change what often cannot be changed, such as the family life cycle, developmentally appropriate behavior ("terrible twos"), their parenting partners, and feelings of grief. They fail to attempt to change what can be changed—their parenting styles, beliefs systems, parenting values, and methods or parenting tools.

This last section is about wisdom. It is about how to balance love and limits. It encourages parents to look toward themselves, first of all, as the solution to their parenting problems. Each parent has a set of strengths or resources that they can utilize in achieving a balance of love and limits. Parents should take action rather than simply react to their children and their parenting partners. This prayer advises them to focus on what they can do rather than on what they believe others think they should be doing. It underscores the importance of expectations on children's behavior. Children who are expected to act cooperatively or do well in school generally do exactly that. Parents who expect appropriate behavior can take advantage of one of the most powerful parenting tools inherent in a child, namely the need to please the important parental figures in their lives. Parents can set goals for themselves and their relationships in their family. They can be specific and concrete, realistic, and positive when setting these goals.

This prayer is also about preventive parenting. It suggests that parents can avoid common pitfalls that occur on a regular basis in their lives by focusing on the "differences that make a difference" or the times in which things go well rather than poorly. It is about changing the parents' role in the scripts that occur with parenting partners and children. To balance love and limits, parents need to "act as if" they are already balanced and maybe even "do a 180," the opposite of what they have always done in their family interactions. Finally, these few words are about praying for serenity, asking for help, accepting what cannot be changed, having the courage to change what can, and having the wisdom to know the difference.

If parents will do these things, if they can change how they think and act. If they concentrate on what works, if they use these parenting tools, then they will find the serenity they seek and achieve a balance of love and limits.

Part
3
The Parenting Toolbox

These parenting tools are listed in alphabetical order and can be used interchangeably and simultaneously to fit the discipline needs of each child. Different tools can be used to balance love and limits. At the end of each tool's description is a quick reference that lists how the tool can be best used. The reference will list the recommended age group and its strength as a tool for increasing love or limits. If parents find these tools too overwhelming or have too much trouble implementing them into their daily parenting routine, they may need the assistance of a child or family therapist (see the **family therapy** parenting tool).

All or Nothing: Useful for "acting-out" behaviors, including inappropriate running around the room, aggressive behavior, endless teasing, and practical jokes. Parents can use this tool by giving the child a task or activity that makes the acting-out behavior impossible to perform at the same time as the assigned task or activity. For example, a child who is sitting down coloring a picture cannot be running around the room at the same time. A child who is eating an apple cannot bite other children. A child who is helping mom or dad around the house cannot be picking on a little brother or sister. See the **DR, rewards,** and **structured activity** parenting tools as well.
Ages: 2–5, 6–12; High Limits.

Approach and Withdrawal: Useful with shy, fearful, and cautious children. Often referred to as *slow-to-warm*, these children are hesitant to try new tasks or enter unfamiliar situations. In familiar environments, such as home, these children are the opposite of fearful or shy. But at the park, school, or any public place they tend to cling to the parent. To the child, the parent is a familiar and secure object. To use this tool, you must be extremely patient. Stay with the child and approach a new situation together. Once you have entered the new situation, remain alongside the child until the child is engaged in the new situation. At this time you can slowly withdraw from the new situation allowing the child to inter-act on his/her own. The secret to this parenting tool is to work with the tem-perament of the children and not to push them too quickly into situations that make them feel uncomfortable. Parents may have to go through this cycle of approach and withdrawal repeatedly until their children are comfortable.

Ages: Under 2, 2–5, 6–12; High Love.

Attachment: Uses a parent's emotional interaction with a child to promote healthy self-esteem. This tool doesn't necessarily refer to the amount of phys-ical interaction. While physical interaction may be necessary to develop emo-tional bonding, it is not the essential component .

Attachment is essential during a child's early years. It communicates unconditional love and a deep sense of trust between parent and child. In a practical manner, children form this attachment when parents attend to their needs. When they are wet, they get changed. When they are frightened, par-ents are there to comfort them. When they are hungry, parents feed them. And when they hurt, parents care for them. When parents do not convey this empathy to children's needs, children may carry a sense of mistrust through-out their life. They also do not feel compelled to meet their parents' expecta-tions or try to please them. Attachment is a tool that communicates to a child that their parent or parents are there for them. This promotes a healthy sense of self and ability to master their world.

Ages: 0–2; High Love.

Awards: Rewarding a child's behavior by way of a card, certificate, ribbon, or trophy. Give these awards for spontaneous acts of goodwill or exemplary char-acter traits, such as kindness, charity, generosity, and teamwork. This parent-ing tool assists parents in teaching values to their children. Sincerity and sur-prise make this type of reward highly effective.

Ages: All; High Love.

Baseline: Used to measure the frequency and duration of a child's inappro-priate behavior. This measure must be performed during a time when no intervention or tool is being used with the child, so you can get an accurate estimation of the child's current behavior. Baseline will allow parents to mea-sure the effectiveness of the particular parenting tool you are using. If you discover that a tool is not getting the results you want (i.e., the misbehavior continues at the same level as before or is much worse), then you know to abandon this approach and try another. A baseline can be used to measure how often and how long a behavior occurs. It doesn't discriminate between desirable or undersirable behavior.

To start, you need a few basic materials: a piece of graph paper, pencil, and daily calendar. Next, choose a behavior you wish to increase or decrease (see the **rewards** parenting tool). Along the left side of the paper list the behaviors that are to be increased or decreased. Along the top of the paper write the days of the week. Choose a parenting tool listed in this section and begin implementing that tool only. Monitor the child's behavior on a daily basis. Tally the number of times the behavior occurs (its frequency per day) and the time that it occurred. To see if change has occurred, check to see if there is any difference between the number of occurrences before any intervention is made and after an intervention is made. For behaviors you want to increase, there should be more occurrences of that behavior per day or week. If you want to decrease a behavior, there should be fewer behaviors per day or week. If there are not any dramatic changes or if the changes are in the wrong direction (desirable behaviors decrease and undesirable behaviors increase), then review the parenting tool to see if it is being implemented properly and/or choose a new parenting tool to test. Don't worry if the change doesn't occur immediately. Children test their parents to see if they will be consistent with these new interventions or if parents are going to fall back to old, inconsistent ways of disciplining. One to two weeks may be needed to witness any real results.

Remember to include appropriate rewards to maintain the behavior changes over time. Choose a relatively easy behavior to change the first time. Do not try to change too many behaviors at one time. The value of this parenting tool is in its ability to get a baseline measure of a child's behavior and to test the validity of the parenting tools you are using. It may also be helpful to notice what happens just before the behavior starts to gain an insight into what is already reinforcing a child's behavior in order to stop that from occurring. See the **point-reward chart** for more information.

Ages: All; High Limits.

Bedtime Ritual: For many families, bedtime is a period of conflict and frustration. Parents struggle with getting children into bed, and children search for any distraction that will prevent it as long as possible. An example of a bed-time ritual might include:

7:30 P.M. Brush teeth.
7:45 P.M. Read a book together.
8:00 P.M. Sing a short song or talk with lights off.
8:15 P.M. Kiss each other goodnight.

These kind of rituals are familiar, and familiarity reduces feelings of anxiety and lessen power struggles. It is much easier to tug-of-war with a parent when there is not a set schedule at bedtime.
Ages: Under 2, 2–5, 6–12; High Limits.

Behavior Penalties: Used for decreasing disturbing or dangerous behaviors, such as hitting, swearing, temper tantrums, property destruction, running into the street, stealing, or lying. Behavior penalties penalize children for undesirable behaviors. Time-out is one form of a behavior penalty. It penalizes children's behavior by isolating them for short periods of time. Other behavior penalties include imposing a monetary fine for each undesirable behavior, such as a dollar for every swear word uttered. Another penalty is to take away privileges for undesirable behaviors, such as taking away a television privilege for lying or fighting.

This tool has a few weaknesses. Most parents fail to reward their children's positive behavior at the same time they are using behavior penalties to decrease undesirable behaviors. Children get discouraged and resentful at being punished without some type of positive reinforcement. Some children may even seek revenge on a parent or sibling to return "hurt for hurt." If they feel hurt by a behavioral penalty, they may lash out at another person, usually someone weaker or more vulnerable (it is difficult to hurt someone bigger and stronger). This tool also uses external force to gain a child's compliance and does not teach the child what is appropriate behavior. Parents should not assume that children know what is expected of them even if parents have said it a million times. Another weakness is that the penalty may not be important to the child. For example, a child who gets lots of spending money from grandparents will think nothing of dropping a dollar into a jar for swearing. Or a child who likes to play computer games will not feel punished for being sent to their room—and their PC. Identify a behavioral penalty that will make an impact on the child.

The strength of this parenting tool is its ability to make quick, short-term changes in behavior. To guarantee longer term solutions, slowly but consistently eliminate the use of behavior penalties and begin applying more positive, unconditional rewards. Use the **baseline, behavior contracts, DR's,** and **point reward** systems listed here to begin and then gradually increase the amount of internal, unconditional rewards used. Try using the **positive expectation** and **describing** parenting tools listed as well. Monitor the frequency of the undesired behavior while rewarding more desirable behaviors to measure the amount and type of change that occurs. In addition, use the **choices** parenting tool listed below to ask children what their preferences would be: "Lose a privilege or clean the room." Remember, firmness and consistency tempered with positive rewards are necessary to make this or any other tool work.

Ages: All; High Limits.

Broken Record: Technique in which the parent repeats to a child the rule, consequence, or expectation the parent has for the child. Anger and frustration should not be communicated in your voice or words when repeating the rule, consequence, or expectation. Simply state, "The rule for using dad's tools is to put them back where you found them or they will have to be locked up." Make sure the child understand the standard and agrees to it. If it is not important how dad's tools are treated, then this parenting tool is unnecessary. In response to a child's arguments or excuses about behavior, respond by repeating the rule. After three or four broken record statements, take action by making the choice for the child, follow through with the consequence for violating the rule, and/or remove yourself from the situation. It is not necessary to continue arguing with a child about a rule that is clearly understood and mutually agreed upon.

This is not the time for negotiation. Tell the child, "We can discuss how fair this rule is later this evening after dinner, but for right now the rule is still _____." This tool may be a real test of your patience and will help you become more firm and consistent in your discipline.

Ages: 6–12, teenagers; High Limits.

Call the Police: For children who are acting violently or threatening violence toward parents. While this tool may appear extreme, it is often a better solution than engaging in a physical confrontation. When parents feel they can no longer cope with or contain the situation, they should call the police and state that their son or daughter is out of control and acting violently. The police will try to calm the child down or neutralize the violent situation and may not have to arrest the child. In the long run, this may be the best choice available to parents to help themselves help their children.

Ages: teenagers; High Limits.

Cheerleading: Increases children's feeling of resourcefulness. When a child makes something creative or solves a problem, act as a cheerleader. Say, "Wow!" or "Bravo!" Ask an inquiring question, such as: "How did you come up with that?" The child will be happy to describe how he came up with his solution. Avoid making suggestions to the child on how to improve the solution. This will rob the child of the joy of discovering it on his own. If the child asks about another way to solve a problem, then you can offer some new suggestions.

Ages: 2–5, 6–12; High Love.

Choices: Providing children with a couple of choices that fall within acceptable parental standards. This tool also encourages children to make their own decisions and heads off frequent power struggles. As an example, a parent might state: "Which pants do you want to wear to school today, the blue ones or the white ones?" If red pants are not acceptable to you, do not include them in the list of choices. If your child demands the red pants anyway, use the **broken record** technique. Choices provide children with a feeling of power because they are in control of what they eat, wear, or play. You win because you have control over the amount and type of choices available to your children. Power struggles are never a win/win proposition.

Permissive parents feel so guilty about making their children follow rules, especially when the children respond angrily, that they eventually give in. Consequently they end up resenting their children and become angry at themselves for not standing firm. Authoritarian parents rarely give choices to their children and must rely on force to get their cooperation. Their version of using choices is to tell their children: "Get to bed or else." This is not really a choice. Force might work while the parents are bigger and stronger than the children. But eventually children will grow up, and many end up larger and stronger than their parents. What will parents do then? Reasonable choices are a much more democratic form of cooperation than authoritarian ("do it my way or else") or permissive ("please do it just this once") statements.

Some children will choose the third, unspoken option. Parents ask their children if they want milk or orange juice to drink and they say soda pop. Take your bath now or after the television program and they say in the morning. Rake the leaves or fold the clothes and they say go play. When your children go for that third option, simply tell them that the choices are A or B and not C. Review the **broken record** technique for support here. Firmness and consistency are good balanced parenting practices and provide the child with a feeling of security. Children need to know what and where the limits are. Children who do not know where to find the limits become anxious and out of control.

Ages: All; High Love, High Limits.

Choose Your Battles: An important and often forgotten tool. You can avoid many battles with your children if you choose more carefully which battles you wish to fight and which you do not. Not all battles can be won. Some don't even matter in light of the big picture. So parents must choose which battles are really important. If it doesn't matter which pants your child wears to school, then don't fight over it. If it does matter, make sure you are prepared to stand firm on what you expect from your child.

Ages: All; High Limits.

Chores: Helps increase children's self-esteem and responsibility. Chores are little tasks that children routinely engage in to help with the upkeep of the house, care for pets and animals, and meet their own personal needs, such as dressing or bathing themselves. These "little tasks" can become big fights if parents do not handle them properly and/or children stubbornly refuse to cooperate. The first step toward increasing cooperation is to teach children how to perform their chore. Young children may have seen the task performed countless times but still not understand what is needed to complete it properly. Demonstrate the task or complete it together for the first couple times to illustrate how it should be done. Don't expect perfection. Remember to encourage the child, not discourage him or her. Give small amounts of praise for each effort and redirect the child back to the next part of the task if her attention wanders or she becomes bored with the job. Rotate the chores for each child to eliminate boredom but don't do this too frequently as it can confuse younger children on what they should be doing. Use chore charts to list the jobs for the week and to measure a "job well done." Make the chores reasonable for the age and ability of each child. And don't make them impossibly long, even if the child is capable of completing a huge list. The object of this tool is to teach responsibility and increase self-esteem, not create a group of little employees. Reward the end result, tangibly through money or treats and/or socially, through parental appreciation (see the **Rewards** parenting tool).

Ages: 2–5, 6–12; High Love, High Limits.

Consistency: The foundation for balancing of love and limits. When parents' actions follow their words, the whole family benefits from consistency. This tool teaches children that parents mean what they say and say what they mean. Children are secure in the knowledge that parents will act in a certain manner because they had said that they would and because they have demonstrated proof through their actions. Without this tool, children feel insecure and anxious. They mistrust parents' words because they do not back up what they say. They are unsure of whether a parent really will come tuck them in for the night, even if they said they would. Parents who inconsistently enforce rules have children who inconsistently obey them. A child who is told he will not get to watch television until his homework is done will fight with the parent over doing the homework because he does not believe the consequences will be imposed based on past examples of inconsistency. The only way to prove to children that parents will be consistent is to be consistent.

Ages: All; High Love, High Limits.

Conversation Extenders: Encourage children to converse with their parents. For instance, if a child says, "I like Billy," then the parent might respond by saying, "Tell me about what you like about Billy." The child, because of lack of good social skills and development, may only give one-word answers to parents' questions. When this happens, the parent can help extend the conversation by asking more questions that elicit more information. It is important to use the child's own words and this sounds less robotic. It too reassures children that parents are listening to them and value their thoughts. See the **open-ended questions** and **reflections** parenting tools for more information on extending children's conversations.

Ages: 6–12, teenagers; High Love.

Deed from the Doer: Separates children's actions from their identity as worthy people. The underlying premise is that a child is still loved although parents may not love what he or she has done. The action does not determine the value of the child in the parent's eyes. If a child misbehaves, parents do not shame or blame the child but state how that particular action was inappropriate or how disappointed they are with that behavior. Parents can also remind the child of the rule that was violated. In addition, parents should communicate a need to solve the problem created by the child's action. See the **fix-up** or **restitution** parenting tool. Children need unconditional love based on who they are, not based on what they do or don't do.

Ages: All; High Love, High Limits.

Describing: Parents explain a problem they have, without blaming or attacking the child. To use this tool, parents must accept the fact that they, not their children, own the problem. It may not be a problem to the child that he has a messy room or has not combed his hair. If children were bothered by such things, they would not have to be corrected or reminded in the first place because they would have already taken care of it. Children, if left to their own devices, would rarely change their underwear, fold the laundry, or eat their vegetables. Is this because children are "uncivilized animals" as some authoritarian parents might believe? No! Children must be taught to change their underwear, fold the laundry, or eat their vegetables. Balanced or democratic parents not only teach their children right from wrong but how and when to care for themselves. The most effective method for doing this is to model those behaviors. Children are more likely to do what a parent does rather than what a parent says. Accepting ownership of a problem reduces the parents' frustration at the child and allows the parent to take a more educational approach to discipline.

Describing is one way to model and own a problem and still teach a child to take responsibility for its solution. Instead of yelling at a child, describe the problem to her. You might say, "I noticed wet towels all over the bathroom floor." This gets the message across more effectively as saying, "How many times have I told you not to leave your wet towels on the bathroom floor?" You can also describe a problem that needs solving by using only one word. Using the example of the wet towel, a parent might firmly say, "Towel," indicating the need to pick it up and put it away. The child will know exactly what you mean since she's heard it so many times before. In the event that this tool does not work with children right away, parents can try using the **natural consequences** or **behavior penalties** tools in conjunction with the **description** parenting tool. Also see **post-it notes** for the written version of this tool.

Ages: All; High Limits.

Diagnostic Questions: Help parents determine what the motives are behind a child's behavior. Children's misbehavior can be motivated by the need for attention, power, revenge, or because of discouragement. Most of children's misbehavior is due to the need for attention. Attention in and of itself is not bad, but most children seek it inappropriately. They bug their parents when they are on the phone, interrupt conversations, and whine to get their parents' attention. When they don't feel they have succeeded in getting their parents' attention, they will begin a power struggle. If that does not succeed, then children may seek revenge, adhering to the old adage: "Don't get mad. Get even." Because they feel hurt, they will hurt others. If that does not get them what they feel they need from their parents, they will move to the last motive for misbehavior, discouragement. They will adopt the attitude, "Why bother? Nothing I do makes any difference so why should I care?" At this point, children have given up hope. Parents can determine their child's motive for misbehavior by considering three diagnostic questions:

1. *What happens when I try to correct this problem with my child?* Parents can determine the answer to this question by recognizing their own feelings. Parents usually feel annoyed or irritated when children are seeking attention. Anger is a common emotion for motives of power. Feeling rejected or hurt is typical for revenge motivations. And feeling like giving up (on themselves and their children) is typical of discouragement motivations.

2. *What happens when I try to correct this problem with my child?* When children are seeking attention, parents will remind or coax them to

stop their annoying actions. Children respond by stopping momentarily and then starting up again, with the same behaviors or some new, equally irritating behavior. Power-seeking children defy parents' attempts to correct their behavior. Children continue to act in the same manner and may even increase the intensity of the struggle. Revenge-seeking children counterattack parents' attempts at correction. They view every action as being "out to get them" or mistreat them in some way. And so they seek further revenge by intensifying the behaviors or choosing some new weapon. Finally, when children feel defeated, they become discouraged. They act disabled or inadequate to perform any task, such as their chores or school work. Parents' attempts at correction usually end up with passive responses on the child's part, or they receive no reaction at all. "What does it matter if I don't do as you say? I can't please you anyway." "Why go to school? I'm too stupid." "Why should I get a try out for the team? I'll just embarrass myself, and they won't want me to play!" These are some of the mistaken beliefs children may hold.

3.   *What action do I need to help my children ask for what they need in an appropriate rather than inappropriate manner?* This diagnostic question recognizes that children are not aware of their motivations for misbehavior. It also recognizes that all misbehavior, even attention getting, stems from discouragement. Children lack the courage to behave in positive, constructive ways. They are simply trying to figure out where they belong in their family. When their attempts to feel significant are not met with positive responses, they become even more discouraged and try a new or more intense misbehavior. What motive they choose may also depend on their interpretation of the situation. But why they choose a particular motive is not as important as understanding what parents can do to modify their child's misbehavior so that they can get what they feel they need in an appropriate rather than inappropriate manner. For example, if a child is seeking attention inappropriately, what action can a parent take that would provide appropriate attention to the child? Or if a child is seeking power, what can make her feel powerful without resulting in a power struggle? If a child is using revenge, how can a parent not return hurt for hurt or reinforce a child's forgiving behavior to turn this motive around? And

finally, if a child is feeling discouraged, what can a parent do to encourage his efforts, however small they may be?
Ages: All; High Love.

DRs: Differential reinforcement, a behavioral management term for scheduling when and what parents reinforce in a child's behavior to increase desirable behavior and decrease undesirable behavior. DR parenting tools will be discussed in four separate parts, including differential reinforcement of other behavior, differential reinforcement of incompatible behavior, differential reinforcement of alternative behavior, and differential reinforcement of low rates of responding.

Differential reinforcement of other behavior specifies which behavior will not be reinforced. Consequently, all other behaviors are then open for reinforcement to decrease the likelihood of the one targeted behavior. A parent might target any number of undesirable behaviors, including thumb sucking, whining, spitting, hitting, taking toys from other children without asking, or walking around during meal times. A parent might state, "When you don't do this, you will get this." Be consistent in providing that reward for the other behavior. It is important that parents do not reward other undesirable behavior. Limit the reinforcement to other positive behaviors.
Ages: All; High Limits.

Differential reinforcement of incompatible behavior reinforces behavior that is not compatible with the targeted, undesirable behavior. For example, a parent might reinforce a child who is sitting down quietly rather than running around the room. Or a parent might reinforce when a child uses a normal tone of voice instead of a whiny tone. The more physically incompatible a behavior to the targeted behavior, the better choice it is for reinforcement.
Ages: All; High Limits.

Differential reinforcement of alternative behavior reinforces more socially acceptable behaviors than the targeted, undesirable behavior. Children often do not have a wide range of socially acceptable behaviors to draw upon in a given situation. Parents can teach these skills to their children or reinforce an appropriate behavior when it does occur, even if it was by chance. Reinforcing alternative, more socially acceptable behaviors increase children's "vocabulary" of behavior that they can rely on in social situations. This tool differs from the other DR tools in that a specific, desirable behavior is taught and reinforced.

For instance, an adolescent who is overly aggressive with his peers may be displaying a lack of socially assertive skills to make friends or be liked. A parent can teach more assertive behavior to make friends or be liked and reinforce efforts toward that goal. This will decrease the aggressive behavior while increasing the assertive, desirable behavior.

Ages: All; High Limits.

Differential reinforcement of low rates of responding is designed for use with children who display high rates of undesirable behavior. Because the undesirable behavior occurs so frequently, it may be difficult to utilize the above DR tools. The most realistic way of decreasing these behaviors is to reinforce lower rates of responding in an undesirable manner versus an alternative or no rate of response. This tool takes a more gradual approach to changing the behavior until it is at a rate that is more manageable for the parent.

The parent might choose to use the **baseline** parenting tool to establish how often the undesirable behavior occurs. Once this has been established, a criteria is set on what is the next, lower level of frequency to be rewarded. Once that level has been reached, another lower level is set, and so on until the behavior is down to a manageable level.

A child who interrupts a parent 20 times per day might be reinforced for 15 or fewer interruptions from the child per day as a next level. The next week, 10 or fewer interruptions are reinforced, and so on, until only five interruptions occur per day for a period of 1 to 2 weeks (this makes sure that the behavior has been permanently decreased and doesn't revert back to higher levels). Five interruptions per day may be tolerable to the parent and considered "normal" for a young child with limited ability to delay gratification.

Parents need to be careful how they reinforce a child using this tool. Children should be reinforced as they meet the lower criteria but not soon after an inappropriate behavior has occurred. This tends to reinforce that specific, inappropriate behavior rather than the lower rate of behaviors. Pick a neutral occasion to give the reward. Parents may also want to set a fixed interval to reinforce a child to simplify this procedure. A parent could reinforce a child twice a day or every two hours on a fixed schedule for the prescribed low rate of responding for that time period. For example, if a child spits 40 times per day, the parent might reinforce the child, every 2 hours, for only spitting four times, assuming a 10-hour day. No reinforcement is given during the remaining portion of the day and never immediately following the child spitting.

Lastly, this form of reinforcement will reduce but not eliminate an undesirable behavior. After it has been reduced, the parent can use one of the other DR parenting tools to eliminate it completely.

Ages: All; High Limits.

Dirty Words: Eliminating the bad habit of swearing. Regardless of whether children "swear like a sailor" or say a single expletive, parents need to realize that children don't invent dirty words on their own. They often mimic what they hear others around them say. This can be especially embarrassing if children hear their parents saying these words and are repeating them in public. While parents can't control children's natural tendency to mimic their world, they can control their own language, set limits about the types of media entertainment their children watch, and establish some family rules on the consequences of using swear words. The underlying message of this parenting tool for children is that dirty words are not acceptable regardless of who says them or where they heard them.

When establishing family rules, parents need to model acceptable language. They need to also make it clear that what happens outside the home is different from what is acceptable inside the home. You might even need to ignore dirty words when spoken by young children, who do not know the meaning, to avoid unnecessary reinforcement by your shock or disapproval. Sometimes when you attempt to discipline a child who uses a dirty word, you only reinforce its use. By **selectively ignoring** the use of a swear word and reinforcing the use of more appropriate language, you will increase acceptable language and decrease inappropriate language.

This parenting tool also encourages parents to consider the underlying motive for using swear words. Are the children feeling frustrated or angry, or are they simply trying to get an adult's attention? Answer the underlying need by offering alternative ways to deal with frustration and anger and spend more time engaged in **quality time** with them. Parents may need to ignore the overt behavior and focus on the inner need rather than the other way around.

Ages: All; High Love, High Limits.

Discussion: A familiar communication tool often used in the wrong manner. Many parents use this tool to lecture or reason with their children, which virtually guarantees that their children are mentally checking out. Discussion is more of a two-way conversation in which different opinions and ideas can be stated without negative consequences. The goal of this tool is to engage in a conversation with children about important subjects that they are or someday will face, such as drugs, alcohol, premarital sex, and gangs. Because most parents are not equipped with all the answers to these life issues, they can use a number of helpful workbooks, videos, magazines, and texts that will facilitate a healthy discussion. You can use the materials directly in the discussion with children by reading or watching them together. Or you can review the materials ahead of time and then discuss them with your children.

Timing and approach are important elements to a successful discussion with children. Timing refers to when a parent brings up the topic to discuss. When the child's friend is spending the night or the child is engaged in a favorite activity is not the best timing. The former will embarrass the child and the latter will not gain his full attention. Find a quiet moment to talk with your child, maybe at the end of the day. Or set up an appointment with the child to have a discussion. In terms of approach, be persistent don't pressure her into a discussion. The more natural a parent is, the less resistance the child will likely give. And don't let "it slide." It may be awkward for both parties at first but will prove rewarding in the end.

Ages: 6–12, teenagers; High Love.

Distraction: For parents dealing with a "spacey" or "dawdling" child. Dawdling children are often those who, due to temperament or a need to assert their independence, move through life at their own pace. This type of behavior can be frustrating to parents. Additionally, young children don't understand what all the rush is about or why it's important to leave at a certain time. By forcing children to move or fighting with them to get ready, parents are creating an environment ripe for power struggles. Distraction allows parents to work *with* children rather than *against* them. For example, if a child has found a number of stones or interesting leaves while at the park, parents can suggest that they go home to polish the stones or glue the leaves on a poster board. The intent is "to go home." By suggesting a fun activity, the parent distracts the child from wanting to stay indefinitely at the park.

Another suggestion is to try playing a game. Enticing children to get dressed by reciting a rhyme, such as "one, two, buckle my shoe," or using humor to make the boring activity more fun can distract the children and get them to cooperate with the parent.

Choices are another form of distraction. Ask your child if she wants to ride in the front seat or the back seat when it's time to go home. The message is that it's time to go home, but you allow the child to assert her independence by choosing where to sit.

Patience, ingenuity, and humor make up the essential ingredients of this parenting tool. See **time cushion** and **verbal warnings** for additional help.

Ages: 2–5, 6–12; High Love, High Limits.

Doing the Unexpected: Parents act in an unexpected manner to catch children off guard and so gain their attention. For example, a parent might stand on top of a chair and make a dramatic, nonverbal scream to show her frustration at a child's behavior. Whispering can catch the attention of a child who is not listening (or acts as if he is not listening). Walking out of a room instead of playing referee for a fight is another example of doing the unexpected. Acting silly or using humor may also change a child's behavior when other methods appear ineffective. Doing the unexpected breaks parents out of ineffective, repetitive patterns of behavior. Children participate equally in "more of the same" patterns of behavior. They expect parents to act in a predictable manner. It is as if the parent and child are following a script. This parenting tool changes the cycle by surprising a child, reducing negative attention, and decreasing stressful home situations.

Ages: All; High Love.

Doing Nothing: Useful for overprotective or controlling parents. These parents have difficulty letting their children experience life on their own. They feel they must oversee their children's life and become a "hovering parent" always assisting or helping their children. They have difficulty letting children make decisions on their own and want to protect them from failure. Unfortunately, failure is an important means of learning about life. When failure is not part of life, children will be more likely to repeat a misbehavior because they did not have the opportunity to learn when mom or dad stepped in. Instead of hovering over children, parents can learn to "do nothing." Doing nothing allows children to do something on their part. While they will fail at times, they will also have the opportunity to learn from their mistakes. This is how children achieve responsibility and control. The sense of accomplishment that results from overcoming their mistakes is inestimable.

Believe it or not, this tool may be more difficult on children than on parents. Children are not used to being frustrated or trying new tasks solo. This independence may cause some feelings of anxiety and may even lead to a power struggle if children interpret the parents' behavior (or lack of it) as uncaring. But the power struggle is simply another tactic by children to get attention from the parents or rescue them from their fear of failure. If you keep getting stuck in that "hovering" mode ask yourself, "Why do I intervene?" and "What makes it so difficult to let my children learn from their mistakes?"

Ages: Under 2, 2–5, 6–12; High Limits.

Dramatic Play: Comes naturally to children, but can be fun for parents too. All children love to dress up in their parents' clothes and play house, doctor, or cowboys and Indians. Parents can use this natural language of children to teach values or build a neglected relationship with young children. When invited to play, parents can pretend they are sad when a child won't share with them, dramatize being selfish, or have two children act out a scene that portrays a common problem and solution. Be especially careful to not overdo it or appear preachy. Later, parents can talk to their children about how they felt (see **conversation extenders, open questions,** and **reflections** parenting tools) during the dramatic play. Dramatic play may also include the use of puppets, dolls, or expressive materials such as paints, crayons, clay, and sand. See **expressive arts** for more information on using these materials.

Ages: 2–5, 6–12; High Love.

Encouragement: Rewards a child's little efforts rather than their end results. Sometimes, children may misbehave because they are discouraged about their place in the family and their value to their parents. When children question this fundamental source of identity, they act in ways that quickly reestablish their feeling of belonging, even if it means belonging as the family troublemaker. Encouragement provides discouraged children with the steps necessary to lift themselves out of their feelings of hopelessness and despair.

Most parents confuse encouragement with praise, but encouragement is different. Praise tells children how "good" they are for their accomplishments rather than their efforts. Parents often tell their children how "big" they are getting or how "smart" they are when they perform a task well. While this type of praise appears beneficial, it can be harmful. Young children have a immature view of the world. They do not completely understand how the world operates. They confuse fantasy with reality and may take what parents say literally. When parents tell their children how "big" they are getting, children misconstrue this to mean literal size, not how independent or self-sufficient they are becoming. Consequently, children compare themselves to other children to determine who is the biggest, smartest, fastest, or funniest. In life, there will always be someone bigger, smarter, faster, and funnier than they are. This is why the innocent statement of being "big" can be so discouraging. In contrast, encouragement lets children know how much parents appreciate their cooperation, how excited parents feel about their teamwork, or how pleasantly surprised they were at the children's volunteering to help when they weren't even asked. Most importantly, encouragement communicates how pleased the parent is that their child tried regardless of how well they have done. See also the parenting tool **deed and the doer**.

Ages: 2–5, 6–12; High Love.

Expressive Arts: Similar to the **dramatic play** parenting tool in that it uses the natural language of children to teach values and skills. Expressive arts differ from dramatic play in that it uses a variety of materials as a medium. These materials consist of paint, crayons, felt and glue, modeling clay, sand, water, or other such media. Many old household items, such as paper towel tubes, egg cartons, empty plastic milk cartons, old bits of material, and buttons, can be used as expressive arts materials as well. Parents can use this tool with little or no expressive arts skills. Simply go to the library and pick out a craft book that fits the age of your child and follow the directions, or join a parenting club that teaches these skills. Regardless of how you learn to use expressive arts, it is important that you use these skills to their full advantage. Children who are overrun by their feelings, be they anxiety, anger, sadness, or joy, can use this tool to express those feelings. When children draw, paint, or mold clay, they give form to their feelings and so feel a greater sense of control over these emotions. Parents can facilitate this process by labeling these feelings for their children. Don't worry if you get it wrong the first time, the child will let you know and you can correct yourself to meet his needs. Sometimes, no feelings are stated and still the child appears more relaxed or in better spirits. If that is the case, don't worry about making some profound interpretation of his feelings. The child doesn't need it. At the very least, parent and child can enjoy the time spent together. That always feels good.

Ages: 2–5, 6–12; High Love.

Faith Building: Use this tool to state your belief in a child's ability to accomplish a task the child feels inadequate in performing. You might urge your daughter on with a hearty "You can do it!" if she seems to doubt her ability to accomplish a new task. Faith has been defined as believing in what cannot be immediately seen. Most children cannot picture themselves succeeding in a particular area of life. This may due to their development (they are not mature enough to perform such abstract tasks) and/or their experience (they feel they have failed in the past or they have never tried it before so they don't believe). They require adults, who have both of these capacities, to encourage them and inspire them to try a new activity.

Faith building is what psychologists call a self-fulfilling prophecy. If a child is told he is lazy, he may believe it is true and start acting lazy. Whether or not he was really lazy in the beginning is irrelevant. That seed would never have grown into a full plant had not other people begun to water it and nurture it by labeling it and providing negative attention. Anything that parents pay attention to will increase. In some instances, negative attention is a more powerful reinforcer than positive attention. Consequently, children will live up to their parents' expectations. They will create a self-fulfilling prophecy in which they act in the very manner they and others have described for them.

Parents must be willing to let children try new tasks on their own. Doing a task for them or constantly helping them out communicates a lack of belief in their abilities. Even more importantly, parents must be willing to let children

decline to perform a task without shaming them for it. Children are not good or bad because they don't perform a task. Their decision simply means that they are not yet ready to attempt it, either physically or psychologically. Parents must keep inspiring children with faith until they are ready.
Ages: All; High Love, High Limits.

Family Meetings: Provide a forum for making group decisions, assigning household chores, sharing positive feelings, and choosing activities for family fun. Family meetings are sometimes called family circles, sharing times, or group decision making. The purpose of the family meeting is to establish a democratic process of communication in the family.

Here are some guidelines for establishing a family meeting:

1. Meet on a regular basis (once a week, each night at dinner, etc.).
2. Make sure everyone gets treated with respect and has an equal say (but don't forget parents have veto power).
3. Use reflective listening techniques and "I" messages.
4. Stay with the real issues. Don't get sidetracked.
5. Focus on the strengths of each family member and don't blame.
6. Set the length of time of the meeting and stick to it.
7. Keep a running record of plans, rules, and decisions set by the family and post them where everyone can see them (maybe on the refrigerator).
8. Remember to have fun.

Although the family meeting is a great way to open communication and respect, there are some potential pitfalls. The first pitfall is when only one parent is interested in participating. Fortunately decisions can be approved by only one parent. Invite all members to participate, explain the purpose of the family meetings and hope that they will choose to be a part of the process. The second pitfall is trying to find a time for the family meeting that works for everyone. If a time cannot be found, try rotating the times from week to week to accommodate other members' schedules and/or give them a brief recap of what happened in the meeting. Also, parents can ask for their input on a family decision that will be made at the next meeting if a member cannot be present.

Implement the family meeting as soon as everyone understands its purpose. The purpose can be explained in the first meeting. It might also be helpful to establish a few ground rules. For instance, there is to be no blaming or shaming other members of the family, and each person gets a chance to talk. Parents will increase attendance by letting other members know how long the family meeting will last and sticking to the schedule. Older children may consider family meetings "stupid" or "childish." One democratic method for dealing with this is to allow them to be absent but casually mention that the family will be making some important decisions on the upcoming summer vacation or what movie we are going to see this weekend. Most children will want to be there to avoid having decisions made without them.

The last pitfall is how to structure the family meeting. Most families will start off by discussing "old business," move on to "new business," and end with a summary of the meeting. If you aren't having the meeting at a set time, remember to do these before everyone is excused. By "old business," we are referring to taking time to review decisions, chores, and fun activities that were decided at the last family meeting. Were there any problems? How are the new chores working out? And so on. "New business" is concerned with how to modify decisions, change the chore list, or make new plans for future family fun. By summarizing, parents can make sure everyone understands what has been decided during the family meeting. Briefly list the high points of the meeting and ask all family members if they understand and agree with the decisions. After this, close the meeting and let everyone know your appreciation for attending.

Ages: All; High Limits.

Family Therapy: Use this if you feel "stuck" in your attempts to balance love and limits. If after several tries, a family is unable to talk peacefully, share feelings, and work things out, then a professional trained in family therapy may be the appropriate choice. These professionals might include Marriage, Family and Child Therapists, Licensed Clinical Social Workers, and Psychologists who are trained in a variety of disciplines to help families become stronger and healthier. They can help families deal with parent/child conflicts, divorce, and child behavior problems. Not all family therapists are the same; it is advisable to shop around until you find one that has the right experience and meets your financial needs. Also, make sure you feel comfortable discussing your problems with this therapist. Family therapists are listed in the Yellow Pages with local resource and referral agencies, and parenting hot lines. Word of mouth is another way to narrow the search.

Ages: All; High Love, High Limits.

Fear Busters: Tackle the monsters that haunt children's bedrooms and their imaginations. Fears are a normal part of childhood. Children ages 2 to 6 are especially prone to fears of separation, the neighborhood dog, or the monster that lives under the bed. Children at this age have an active imagination and fantasy life and only have working knowledge of the world around them. For instance, the 4-year-old child knows that the vacuum can suck up dirt, but not that it can't suck him up. The 5-year-old child sees ghosts on the television and in her closet. Two-year-olds know mom or dad has to leave for work in the morning, but they are not 100 percent sure the parent will return in the evening.

Fears can also be a symptom of other problems in the family. Children who overhear fighting parents may use monsters under the bed to redirect uncomfortable feelings that stem from family problems such as mom and dad fighting. Other traumatic incidents—death, divorce, moving, losing a good friend, starting at a day-care center—in children's lives can cause fears. Each child will respond to events in different ways, some in a traumatic fashion and others in a more resilient manner.

A child's fears may be considered abnormal when they linger too long or get worse over time instead of better, when they interfere with the child's ability to function in areas that previously posed no problems (peer relationships, diet, sleeping, schoolwork, etc.), and when children panic frequently for no apparent reason.

Children may attempt to cope with these fears by masking them so as not to appear silly or foolish. These masks only change the symptoms. They do not eliminate the fear. For example, a child may develop chronic eating and sleeping problems or headaches and stomach aches without a medical cause. They may become extremely anxious and develop obsessive or compulsive behaviors, such as washing her hands every 10 minutes or repeatedly locking all the doors in the house. Another child might regress in behavior to a younger, more comforting age or develop a strong avoidance of particular places and objects, such as buses, bathtubs, or animals.

Parents can bust these fears by taking a number of preventative steps. For 2- to 3-year-old children who fear separation from their parents, you can help to provide a sense of security and reassure children that you love them and will return to pick them. At the same time encourage their independence and individuality.

For 4- to 6-year-olds who fear monsters, you should monitor what the child watches and reads that might breed unrealistic fears. Remain patient with a child who is already haunted by these fears. Not overreacting or giving undue attention will help to reduce them by preventing negative attention from developing. When children fear the dark, parents can use bedtime rituals to alleviate nighttime anxiety and use a night light or soft music to ease the transition to sleep.

For children who fear dentists or doctors, you can encourage them to express their fears safely without brushing them off. Don't tell a child that a shot won't hurt when it probably will. In addition, you can role play or bring along a favorite toy to comfort your child during a visit to the dentist or doctor.

For school phobias, parents need to determine if the fear is of the school or separation from the parent. If the fear is really about the school, you may need to determine the source of the fear. Is it the teacher, other children, difficult school work, failure, tests, or making friends? Remove secondary gains for staying home, such as getting to play with mom and dad, and spend some time at school assisting the child in overcoming school fears.

For children who fear the water, go slow and do not push them, literally or figuratively, into the water. Start with a little water, such as a small tub or sprinkler and work up to larger pools of water, such as a wading pool and the shallow end of the pool. Place children in swimming classes to build confidence in their abilities and use water rings or other safety devices as needed.

When children fear animals or insects, you again need to go slow. Do not force children to interact with the object of their fear. Let them interact at their own pace. Emphasize that they are bigger than the animal or insect and point out that the animal appears more afraid of children than they are of the animal. Teach children how to handle animals. Most dogs will bite when their tails are pulled, and cats will scratch when hugged too tightly.

Ages: 2–5, 6–12; High Love.

Fix-Up or Restitution: Teaches children to be accountable for their actions. If a child takes a toy from another child's hands, then that child is asked to "fix or make up" the situation by handing back the toy and apologizing. Restitution is made when a child damages or destroys someone's property and must either repair the damage or pay for it with their own money. For very expensive items, reasonable restitution must be negotiated. For example, the child must work in the neighbor's garden for a set number of days to make restitution for damaging or breaking an expensive item. Don't forget to provide unconditional rewards for the child's ability to be responsible during and after damage has been fixed up or restitution made. Parents can also use the **mutual problem solving** tool to enlist children's ideas in how to make a reasonable restitution.

Ages: All; High Limits.

Follow the Leader: Can be used as a game and as a redirection tool. When using this tool as a game, parents can invite their children to play "follow the leader." This game is fun on family trips or vacations. Families with more than one child can have each child take turns leading the family hike or singing a song. The leader has the *power* to choose which forest path to take or which song to sing. Each child (and parent) gets the opportunity to be the leader, thereby encouraging equality and fairness. When used as a redirection tool, children who are being controlling can be directed to take charge of a particular task, such as getting the family together for dinner or organizing a wood gathering party for the campfire. Children who frequently power-struggle with their parents can benefit from this latter application.

Ages: All; High Love.

Freeze Play: Variation of the **time-out** parenting tool. Time-out is usually conducted by isolating or excluding a child from the rest of the family or classroom. In this form, children would be sent to their room, a chair in the kitchen, outside the classroom door, or facing a wall. Time-out has a number of disadvantages. It involves the use of punishment that may seem harsh to some parents and children, so harsh that many children will become emotionally upset or physically aggressive when put in isolation or exclusion time-out. Fortunately, parents have an option, the nonexclusion time-out or freeze play.

Nonexclusion time-out or freeze play, eliminates reinforcers (interaction with others) from a child who is acting inappropriately. It does this by freezing the moment of interaction with the child for a very brief, but poignant amount of time. For example, if a child starts whining when told she must wait for dinner to eat, you can firmly, but evenly, say, "Stop!" Avoid eye contact for a few seconds, and the child is prohibited from communicating during this time. Then you can nonchalantly carry on the task at hand or use the **time-in** parenting tool. Be careful not to place too much emphasis on talking about the misbehavior later as it might inadvertently reinforce the child to misbehave again to gain attention.

You should tell the child what is going to happen during freeze play and the expectation that there will be no communication or eye contact during that time, so that the child knows why the parent is acting this way. In addition, the old rule of thumb for time-out, 1 minute for every year of life, can be used in **freeze play** by substituting seconds for minutes (e.g., one frozen second for every year of life.)

Ages: 2–5, 6–12, teenagers; High Limits.

Grocery List: A preventative measure to keep shopping with children from becoming a frustrating experience for parents. One of the reasons it is so frustrating is that children get the "gimmes" ("Gimme that candy." "Gimme that toy."). They want everything in sight. The grocery list tool can be used to deal with this problem *before* it happens. Before going to the store, explain to your children what you need to purchase and then ask the children what they would like to get. You may have to put a price limit on their choices, but at least children know that they can get something. In fact, this alone may decrease the gimmes. To make absolutely sure, remind children on the way to the store what you need to purchase and what they have chosen to buy. Also, remind children just before entering the store of the choices they have already made. Once in the store, make your purchase and then tell children that now they can get their purchasing choice.

Children get the gimmes because they get so wrapped up in their emotions that they can't control themselves. This parenting tool prepares children long before, just before, in the store, and after a short wait. Children who are impulsive may have difficulty using this tool. It may also teach them to delay gratification, a necessary life skill. As a backup, review the **choices** and **broken record** parenting tools as well.

Ages: 2–5, 6–12; High Limits.

Growing Pains: Helps children make the physical, emotional, and psychological adjustments to growing up. Most young children can't wait to grow up, to experience the world of the adult, and to feel mature and in charge. But some children find that growing up is not all it's cracked up to be. Just as children may feel physical pain when their bones and muscles grow, they also feel emotional and psychological pain at maturing.

Youngsters who mature earlier than their peers need help in dealing with changing bodies and emotions. When physical development outdistances social and emotional development in young girls, for instance, they can become targets of sexual interest by older boys before they are ready to deal with it. It gains them new, unexpected attention, but can lead to situations that may not be desirable. Boys may pressure them to go out on dates or act sexually. They may also be targets of inappropriate teasing and jokes by both boys and girls.

Boys who mature early experience different problems. They may be at risk of becoming involved with delinquent groups of older boys or being treated rougher or more adult-like than they are inwardly able to handle. Overall, it appears boys tend to adjust better to early maturity than do girls, especially if they are involved in sports. Their early development becomes an asset and gains them positive attention.

Parents can use the growing pains parenting tool by being aware of the discrepancies in physical development and other areas of development. Remember that the level of judgment and control is still at the same age level as their peers, regardless of their appearance of being more self-controlled. You should initiate calm, open discussions about these differences and how to cope with them. Conversations may need to include sexual education so your children don't learn this information on the street or through trial and error. You may need to help children express their anxiety, fears, and confusions. To do so, use some of the talk tools listed in this section. Ultimately, children will need goals and values that will steer them safely through their school age and teenage years, because this developmental stage is the testing ground for making good decisions.

Ages: 6–12, teenagers; High Love, High Limits.

Habits: Teach children positive behaviors. Children and parents are creatures of habit. How they behave and interact is based on very simple, daily routines. For example, what people eat, when they eat, and how they eat is based on daily repetition. If a behavior has been learned, it can be unlearned. However, some habits may be hard to break or change. Going on a diet can be difficult because people do not view eating as a habit that has been learned but as a force that is much more undefined and immeasurable. New habits can be learned to replace old ones and create more appropriate behaviors in parents and children. For example, parents and children habitually engage in the same arguments over doing chores. Parents will often ask, "How many times have I told you to do your chores?" This quickly becomes a dysfunctional game where parents get angry and children resist and selectively forget to do their chores. A new habit might include setting up a chore chart and reinforcing children for doing chores without being reminded and giving no rewards for chores undone or forced. Each day you reinforce chores completed without argument and on the child's own initiative without being negatively reinforced by yelling, coaxing, or reminding. If you must yell, coax, or remind, then no rewards are given. Children will soon adapt to the new system of rewards for chores completed and so adopt a new habit that is satisfying to both parents and children. The same procedure can be used for improving study skills, displaying desirable social skills, or any other behavior than can be defined in habitual terms. See the **DR** parenting tools for more specific information.

Ages: All; High Limits.

Helping Others: Increases children's empathy and spiritual development. By the time children have reached the age of 5 or 6, they are fully able to understand the hurts, needs, and problems experienced by others. Parents can reinforce helpful behavior and decrease self-centeredness by planning ways to help others. This plan does not necessarily mean writing a check to a charity. While this is helpful, it requires no tangible effort from children. Plan something that will involve a physical activity and cognitive awareness on an important social issue, such as poverty, AIDs, the elderly, or homelessness. Allow children to have input into what they would like to do and what they think would be a good way to help. Parents will be surprised how creative and sensitive children can be. Use the family meeting parenting tool to discuss what the family will do together to help others.

Ages: All; High Love.

High Fives: A nonverbal parenting tool that complements or reinforces young children. Parents can reward children for desirable behavior by getting excited and saying, "Give me five!" and holding out their hand to be slapped. Young children gain a sense of accomplishment by this simple action. This is a nonverbal equivalent of the cheerleading parenting tool.

Ages: 2–5, 6–12; High Love.

Homework Helper: Parents of school-age children will need this at one time or another. Both parents and children can come to dread homework. Fortunately you can use these general guidelines to overcome the homework hassle. First, consider what is the underlying problem behind not doing the homework. While on the surface it may appear that children are unmotivated or just plain lazy, the real problem may be much bigger than that. Some children may have to contend with a hyperactive or restless nature; they have difficulty concentrating for long periods of time. Other children may have a learning disability that makes reading, writing, and arithmetic laborious. Or parents may have their own personal issues, such as resentment of the teacher for giving so much homework, a need for perfectionism, or negative memories of their own parents attempting to help them with their homework as children. You can teach children good study skills and self-discipline. Homework is really about knowing how to study. Help your child find a quiet place to work, furnished with all the needed materials (paper, pencil, eraser, glass of water, etc.) for studying and outline what must get done. Prioritize work by what is due first or will take the most amount of work to finish. Schedule tasks over the number of necessary days until the work is due. Break down homework tasks into smaller, more manageable pieces. And reward the child for completing each piece by allowing a 10-minute break or supplying a cookie and milk or a pat on the back. See **school daze** parenting tool.

Ages: 5–12, teenagers; High Limits.

Huddling: Similar in function to the **family meeting** parenting tool but different in form. Huddling is a quick, informal, type of family meeting that any number of family members can have together. It can occur at any time or place. Football players do this before every play to make sure the team knows what the plan is and to make clear everyone's job. Rather that set an agenda and have a formal meeting, family members can stop whatever they are doing to have a quick meeting about a specific problem or task. Parents can play the captain by telling the family to "huddle together." Put arms around one another for support or just gather together in a circle, face in. Talk about the problem or task and assign jobs or ask for quick input. Decide on a plan of action, and then say "Let's go!" Parents can use this tool at the zoo to decide what they are going to go see first, at the restaurant to decide what everyone wants to eat, and at home to decide what toys need to be gathered before going to the park.

Ages: All; High Love, High Limits.

Humor: A parenting tool that has saved many potentially abusive situations. Humor acts as a release valve for the stress that accumulates during the day with children. Raising children is a challenge during the best of times. During the worst of times, it can be discouraging.

Humor can take many forms. During a stressful situation, parents can laugh at themselves. We all make mistakes and chuckling at ourselves during these dangerous moments can both relieve the tension in the room and teach your child that life shouldn't be treated so seriously. By laughing at yourself, you can show your children that one's self-esteem is not based on what you do (a conditional attitude) but on who you are (an unconditional attitude).

Parents can also make a *soft* joke of their children's mistake. These jokes should be in good taste and take into consideration children's sensitivity. Some children are crushed by what others would consider a harmless jest. Remember, the object of this parenting tool is to decrease stress, not increase bad feelings. This second application of humor also teaches children that life shouldn't be taken too seriously. It encourages children to pick themselves up, dust themselves off, and go on after making a mistake.

An example of this tool in action might be the stressful situation of getting everyone ready for work and school in the morning. If on the way to school you sense a dark cloud in the car, try injecting a little humor. Change the mood by singing a funny lyric or telling a knock-knock joke to keep the mood affable. Children will get into the spirit of the humor by telling their own jokes, even if they are made up on the spot. If children do not respond to this tool, try using the **storytelling** or **wishes** parenting tools.

Ages: All; High Love.

"I" Messages: A common and powerful parenting tool. So much of parents' communication with children begins with the word "you" instead of "I." This habit may create a defensive reaction in the child. Children are more apt to resist and fight parents when in a defensive mode. This is especially true for teenagers. Practice using "I" at the beginning of a statement to your child, especially when asking for a desired behavior.

"I" messages have three parts: feeling/desire, behavior, and consequence. An example of an "I" message to a younger child would be: "I feel angry (feeling/ desire) when the bicycle is left in the driveway (behavior) because I nearly ran over it when coming home (consequence)". "I" messages link your feelings to the consequence, not the child. They also communicate value and respect. An example of an "I" message for an older child may go something like this: "I am worried when you do not come home on time and do not call me to tell me you are going to be late because I am afraid that something has happened to you".

Good timing is also important in using this parenting tool. Talking to children during conflict or a dispute may not be the best occasion for an "I" message. Both parents and children may need to take some time to cool off and discuss the situation of concern. "I" messages also communicate ownership of a problem. For a more detailed look at ownership, see the **mutual problem solving** parenting tool.

Ages: All; High Limits, High Love.

Job Description: Ensures that children understand what is expected of them when performing a chore or job at home. Just as in the office, parents write out a job description that details what is expected of them, this parenting tool reduces power struggles and conflicts during and after the chore is done. Don't be condescending to children, especially older children, when writing these job descriptions. More detail or steps may be necessary for younger children than older children. A thorough job description states who is to do the job, when it is to be done, how it is to be done, and where it should be done.

Ages: All; High Love, High Limits.

Journaling: For parents who feel overwhelmed, confused, or flooded with a host of emotions that get in the way of balanced parenting. Journaling requires that parents write down their thoughts, dreams, and feelings about themselves and their parenting experiences. Most parents keep these feeling private and/or share them reluctantly for fear of ridicule. Journaling has a way of clarifying your thoughts and feelings, which often get jumbled up and confuse you even more about how to balance love and limits. Keeping a journal can help you determine which values and beliefs you hold about yourself as a parent, what makes you feel like a good or bad parent, and how accurate those values and beliefs really are. You do not have to write every day, just when you feel inspired to do so. Journaling is also useful with the application of other parenting tools. Record when you start to use a parenting tool. How do you feel about the results? What worked or didn't work? What other tools could you try instead?

Ages: All; High Love.

Manners: A subject of great parental frustration. Manners are the socially acceptable way of doing things, such as eating politely at the table, entering a conversation, and asking for things. Teaching manners is really about discipline as manners are about internalizing what is considered right and wrong. They describe the rules of how to behave in social situations. Good manners in children create feelings of pride in a parent, just as bad manners can produce embarrassment.

One way of teaching manners is to establish a good example. If parents eat broccoli with their fingers, then their children will, too. If parents eat in the living room in front of the television while the children sit at the table, then the children will eat their broccoli any way they want because they have no supervision. The earlier a parent starts teaching manners, the better. Parents who think it's cute when toddlers put spaghetti on their head will find it difficult to correct inappropriate table manners when they are older. Parents need to reinforce or show verbal appreciation for good manners. When a child says "excuse me" before interrupting or "thank you" to another person, you must let the child know how you appreciate the use of manners.

Manners also comunicate respect. Saying "hello" and "how are you" are ways of expressing respect and concern for another person. Knowing how to use the telephone properly communicates respect. It is very irritating for callers when children scream in their ear, play jokes, refuse to get the parent, or set the phone down and forget to inform the parent of a caller.

Manners also can reflect the value of cooperation. Teaching children how not to argue over who cheated who in a game or telling another person, "You are not my friend anymore" when upset teaches children cooperation. Sometimes a gentle reminder can model appropriate manners. For instance, reminding your child that "Johnny is your guest; be polite" can help him learn how to relate to others in a social situation. Older children may prefer to be reminded or corrected in private, if possible. Either way, teaching manners is not easy or fun but a necessary part of balancing love of limits.

Ages: All; High Limits.

Mealtimes: A parenting tool many parents take for granted. There is an interesting relationship between families who have trouble communicating and the act of eating meals together on a regular basis. Some research on alcoholic families suggests that these families, which are often chaotic and stressful, rarely spend time at the dinner table together. Severe drinking behaviors disrupt everyday rituals and routines, often eliminating them altogether. As a result the very fabric of the family is unraveled. To intervene and create a sense of family identity, parents can reinstate the **mealtime ritual.** A mealtime ritual might involve getting the family together at a regular time in the same location. Important life skills can be taught by enlisting the help of the children in preparing meals. Parents may need to break down various aspects of preparing the meal and setting the table and then incorporate them into the children's chores. Discuss the cultural and religious elements of the preparation and meal, if appropriate. After the meal is prepared, families can sit down together. Prayers or blessings can be recited to strengthen religious beliefs. Families should share food politely and practice table manners. Parents should encourage conversation. Some freedom during mealtimes is necessary, although parents may want to maintain some element of control to prevent children from getting out of control. Asking to be excused from the table and putting dishes away in the kitchen can further create family cooperation. How each family performs a mealtime ritual is not as important as the act itself. The purpose is not to create a regimen of behaviors but to foster family identity.

Children should come away from dinner with the positive feeling that the people around the table are "my family!"
Ages: All; High Limits, High Love.

Medical Checkup: Often suggested by helping professionals when working with a parent or child. A family therapist might suggest that parents have their child checked out by a doctor simply to rule out organic or medically related problems. It doesn't mean that something is organically or medically wrong with a child, but many problems children experience can be related to diet, allergies, hearing abilities, or a chemical imbalance. Many parents do not take their children in for a checkup because they fear looking silly for doing so or for fear that the doctor will prescribe drugs for their child. If you question a doctor's recommendations, you should seek a second opinion. The best scenario is that nothing is wrong and parents and helping professionals can concentrate on behavior or emotions that might be creating family problems. Parents and helping professionals might create a bigger problem if they approach a problem that is not the result of behavior and emotions and instead must be treated medically.
Ages: All; High Love.

Momentum: Uses the force of a readily exhibited desirable behavior to reduce the likelihood of a readily exhibited undesirable behavior. Children who will not perform a task or behavior suggested by a parent may to willing to engage in another task or behavior that will increase their momentum toward the desirable behavior. For instance, a child who will not readily open his mouth to take a medication or brush his teeth will stand up and sit down in a chair. Ask him to stand up and sit down for a few repetitions and then immediately ask him to open his mouth. The momentum of standing up and sitting down can spontaneously lead to the child opening his mouth. A child who will not pick up a towel on the floor will catch a ball and throw it back to the parent. Throw the ball back and forth a few times and then ask the child to pick up the towel. If an older child will not take her plate to the kitchen but will get up to get some dessert, ask her to get the dessert and bring it to the table and take her plate to the kitchen on the way. Identify what your children will do that is close in action to the behavior they will not do, and then do them in that order. This sequence will increase the likelihood of compliance from the child.

Ages: All; High Love, High Limits.

Monitoring: Use periodically to check on children to ensure that they are safe, acting appropriately, and following through with responsibilities. It communicates the values of consistency and structure to children. In its most ideal form, monitoring is a "hands off" activity. Simply allowing children to see that they are in fact being monitored reinforces their security and the need to behave appropriately. Without words, parents can look outside to see if their children are safe, observe their social skills when playing with other children, or peek into their room to check on their progress in cleaning it up. Parents use words if their children are not safe, not using appropriate social skills, or not cleaning their room. Once parents use words, they are no longer just monitoring, they are now interacting. At this time, parents interact (with the least amount of verbal action possible to communicate their faith in the child's ability to act safely and appropriately and to follow through) and then return to monitoring. Monitoring provides parents with a balance between "hovering" or smothering their children all the time (communicating a mistrust of their abilities) and no supervision whatsoever (communicating a lack of concern or importance of the child to the parent). When parents must interact, use various tools such as, **describing, faith building,** or **mutual problem solving.**

Ages: All; High Love, High Limits.

Monkey See, Monkey Do: Uses the power of modeling to teach children how to behave by their parents' example. Parents behavior often communicates the contradictory message of "do what I say and not what I do!" Children usually do the opposite. They do what their parents do, not just what they say. Parents will be more effective in getting children to exhibit appropriate behavior, obey rules, and make good decisions by doing these things themselves. Parents who tell their children not to misuse drugs and follow that admonition themselves will increase the likelihood of their children following their advice. Of course, this doesn't mean that parents have to be perfect. In fact, modeling imperfection and coping with frustration and failure can be excellent learning opportunities for parents and children. Do parents model temper tantrums when they do not get the promotion they feel they deserved, or do they deal with their feelings in an appropriate manner? When Dad tells little Johnny not to hit sister Susie, does he contradict his words by hitting mommy or Johnny when he is angry at them? Words alone are not enough to balance love and limits. Parents need to practice what they preach. Words, when combined with action, make the best teacher of right and wrong. See **dirty words** parenting tool.

Ages: All; High Love, High Limits.

Moving the Furniture: Controls the environment to control children's behavior. Sometimes the easiest way to decrease inappropriate behavior is to manipulate the environment, thereby decreasing the child's opportunities to engage in unwanted behavior. For instance, turning off the television or moving it to another part of the room or house during dinner time will eliminate children's ability to watch television instead of eating their dinner. As silly as it sounds, many parents will go on yelling or scolding children for watching television during dinner, never considering the option of turning it off or moving it out the room. Another example of using this parenting tool during dinner time is to change sitting arrangements. Putting brother and sister on either side of mom or dad may eliminate elbowing and teasing during dinner. Other examples include taking out the bathroom mirror or covering it up if children persist in making faces in it instead of brushing teeth, removing distracting toys from their room when it's time to clean it up, putting the computer into another room if it frustrates mom when children play it in the living room while she tries to read or work, giving older children their own room (if it is available) instead of rooming with younger children, or rearranging the kitchen to allow the child better work space to do their homework under mom's supervision and with fewer distractions.

Ages: All; High Limits.

Mutual Problem Solving: Used to negotiate win/win solutions. The goal of this method is to find a mutually acceptable agreement that both parent and child are happy with and will follow through on. The mutual problem solving parenting tool has six steps:

♦ Step one: Approach the child in a nondefensive manner. Parents can do this by stating, "There is something that I would like to talk to you about. Is this a good time?" Although the child may be a little suspicious, he will usually say, "yeah." If the child refuse to talk simply approach him in a nondefensive but assertive manner and leave off the, "Is this a good time?"

♦ Step two: Talk about the child's feelings and needs. If the child is chronically late for dinner, state, "I know it must be hard to leave your friends when you are playing," or "It makes you mad when I call you to come home right in the middle of a game."

♦ Step three: Talk about your feelings and needs: "On the other hand, I am waiting for you to come in for dinner," or "I feel angry when you don't come home at the time we agreed on."

♦ Step four: Brainstorm a few mutually agreeable solutions to the problem. Try saying, "Let's come up with a few ideas that would be good for both of us."

♦ Step five: Write all of these ideas down without judging or criticizing any of the ideas (eliminating bad ideas is reserved for the next step). Prime the pump by offering a couple of suggestions yourself. If the child refuses to offer any suggestions, tell her you will proceed to use your ideas but that she may not like them.

♦ Step six: Decide which suggestions you like, which suggestions you don't, and on which you plan to follow through. Both the parent and the child should be included in this step. Make sure that the final solution is agreeable to both sides.

Ages: 6–12, teenagers; High Love, High Limits.

Natural and Logical Consequences: Allow children to take responsibility for their actions and learn from their mistakes in a positive manner. Natural and logical consequences have certain advantages in balancing love and limits:

♦ It puts responsibility for children's behavior in their hands.

♦ It allows children to make their own decisions about what is appropriate versus inappropriate behavior.

♦ It permits children to learn from their own actions rather than forcing them to conform to the wishes of parents or society.

Natural consequences are the natural results of our behavior or actions. If a child consistently forgets to take his/her lunch to school, the natural consequence would be that he or she would miss lunch and eat an ample sized dinner that evening. A child who forgets to wear mittens in the winter gets cold hands. A **diagnostic question** to determine a natural consequence would be, "What would happen to my child if he continues in his behaviors without any interference by me?" Say, for example, that a child does not put their dirty clothes in the dirty clothes bin. What would happen if the parent did not interfere by picking up the clothes or nagging the child to do it? The natural consequence would be that the child would not have the outfit they wanted to wear and is forced to wear some other, perhaps older outfit.

Sometimes the natural consequence for an action is dangerous or intolerable. For example, if a child refuses to do her homework, the natural consequence would be a failing grade in school. This is usually not tolerable to parents. The answer would be to use logical consequences instead. Logical consequences are established conditions that result from a child's behavior or action. They occur in the social order rather than the natural order of things. If a child did not finish her homework, she would not get to watch her favorite television program. If a child chooses to not eat dinner, he would not get dessert. A child who doesn't do chores doesn't get allowance money or is not allowed to spend the night at a friend's home.

Natural and logical consequences are difficult for permissive parents to employ. They often find them harsh or cruel. This may be due to the fact that they are using natural and logical consequences in a punishing manner. Perhaps, in addition to using a consequence, parents are moralizing or sermonizing to their children. Parents might imply a moral judgment over a child taking a hammer out of the tool box and not returning it. They might preach a sermon on how wrong the child was for taking the hammer without asking or the irresponsibility of not returning it. The parent might also use natural and logical consequences as a punishment by focusing on past behavior. Many parents will retort, "It's after 11 o'clock. You're always late. How many times have I told you to get home by 11 o'clock? Now you can forget about using the car for the rest of the month." Parents might also use logical consequences to threaten or put down a child. A parent might tell disruptive children: "If you don't quiet down, you will go to bed without supper!" or "You're so irresponsible. It's no wonder you never get to stay over at your friends with that kind of attitude."

To use natural and logical consequences in a positive manner, parents need to practice talking to their child in a neutral but firm manner. A parent might say to a child, "Before we eat dessert, we need to eat our dinner." Parents can focus on the impersonal aspects of the situation rather than the moral aspects. In the case of the missing hammer, a parent might say, "How are you going to replace the hammer?" If the child has no suggestions, then the parent can mention that he will have to use his allowance money to pay for it (see **restitution**). It is important to leave the problem in the hands of the child. Making all of the decisions on what is the consequence of a child's behavior is taking responsibility again. This impersonal handling of a situation is sometimes called separating the **deed from the doer.** Focus on the inappropriate behavior, not the child.

Another way to make natural and logical consequences positive is to focus on present and future behavior. The next time a child asks to use the car, the parent can tell the child, "I'm sorry, but I can't let you use the car. I don't feel that you are ready to handle the responsibility of coming home on time on your own. Maybe this weekend you can use it again." Don't dwell on past mistakes and wrongs. This breeds resentment and anger. Focus on the present and the future instead. Allow children to experience the consequences of their actions and learn from their mistakes in a positive manner.

Ages: All; High Love, High Limits.

Negative Reinforcement: Usually works against parents rather than for them. Understanding how this tool works will help parents in preventing it from sabotaging their balance of love and limits. Negative reinforcement is when children are reinforced or rewarded, sometimes unknowingly, for inappropriate behavior. Parents rarely do this consciously. Why would a parent reinforce the very problem they want to eliminate? Primarily because they underestimate a child's need for attention, even if it is negative. When parents yell or scream at children for not picking up toys or for coming home after curfew, they may be unwittingly reinforcing their children by dramatic displays to continue this behavior. In addition, when permissive parents sit and overdiscuss or negotiate issues with children, they are positively reinforced for their behaviors by the time and attention supplied by parents. This is especially true when parents fail to give ample positive reinforcement for good behavior. Children often feel emotionally starved for attention and realize that they can get it quicker and easier by their inappropriate behavior than by their appropriate behavior. Working parents and single parents experience this irony due to the demands on their time and energy to responsibilities other than their children. Children feel this lack of attention on them and may demand it by acting out. Working parents and single parents may have very little energy by the end of the day and feel that all they can manage is to put out "fires" and deal with the basic responsibilities of home. The solution is to identify what is reinforcing the undesirable behavior and consciously work on reducing that reinforcer and then provide more positive social rewards for appropriate behaviors. (See **triggers** parenting tool).

Ages: All; High Limits.

Negotiation: A powerful parenting tool for older children. Although some parents will need to use this tool earlier than others, depending on the personality of their children, all parents will find this tool valuable in their interactions with their children. Negotiation is a tool that allows for a win/win situation to occur between two parties who do not already mutually agree. It incorporates several steps:

- ◆ *Know what is negotiable and not negotiable.* Specifying what is negotiable and what is not negotiable is helpful when working out a compromise. This firmly establishes a parent's bottom line, or limit on a subject. Parents must make sure to be realistic as well as firm.
- ◆ *Be open-minded.* Be willing to listen and consider the other person's viewpoint. If the child feels you have already made up your mind, then the negotiation is just a charade and the child will be rightfully angry and resentful.
- ◆ *Set a time limit.* Keeping it short will prevent the discussion from wandering down a "rabbit trail" or going in circles. Keep things on the topic at hand and to the point.
- ◆ *Keep it private.* Don't embarrass an older child by negotiating in a public place. They will be more likely to react to what they think others are thinking about them. Also, keeping it one-on-one will prevent power plays from developing by having other people joining in the negotiations either for or against one side or the other.
- ◆ *Stay calm and cool.* Don't try to negotiate when angry, tired, or preoccupied with other things. It is difficult to stay rational when other

thoughts and feelings are crowding for attention. If the situation gets heated, take a time-out to cool down and then resume talks. Set this up as a ground rule beforehand if a heated discussion is likely.

♦ *Acknowledge the others' points.* Even if they are totally off base, acknowledge your children's feeling. They are obviously important to them even if they are irrational. This will also encourage positive relations and cooperation when the final solution is reached rather than back stabbing and sabotage.

♦ *Restate the final solution.* Reiterating the solution to the negotiation will make sure that everyone involved is clear on what was agreed upon. It will eliminate the possibility of not following the solution because of miscommunication.

Ages: 6–12, teenagers; High Love, High Limits.

Open Ended Questions: Encourages children to talk to their parents. Open-ended questions require that the child respond with more than a one word answer. Questions that require only a one word answer are called closed questions. Examples of closed questions include: "How old are you?" or "What grade did you get on your spelling test?". Both of these questions can be answered with one word. To get children to expand their conversation, use an open ended question, such as, "What did you like about school today?" or "What happened on your spelling test?" It is possible for a child to answer "nothing!" in response to these open questions. If that happens, there are usually two approaches. First, leave the child alone. He may not be ready to talk about his day. Second, use other parenting tools, such as **conversation extenders** and **reflective listening** parenting tools. Some children have difficulty expressing their thoughts and feelings. Using various tools together may be more efficient, and less mechanical, in getting a child to talk.

Generally, older children have better communication skills than do younger children. But parents can use this parenting tool with preschoolers as a way of developing their new language abilities. In fact, communication skills can decrease aggressive actions, like biting, when the problem underlying the aggressive behavior is frustration over not being able to communicate a need or want. Open-ended questions provide young children with new, safer outlets for their frustration and teach them how to get more of their needs met!

Ages: 2–5, 6–12, teenagers; High Love.

Organization Opportunities: Assist older children in organizing themselves and their activities. By the time children reach the age of 8 years, they are developmentally able to master organizational skills. They are also more social creatures and enjoy team sports. They will start to look at what their peers are doing and want to be more like them. They like to make their own decisions and select their own activities and projects to be involved in. Parents can assist older children by helping them manage this new developmental milestone and steer them away from choices that are unhealthy, unfeasible, or even dangerous.

This age should not be a time for more power struggling. Instead it should be a time for modeling responsibility and appropriate decision making. Children will need to know how to set a schedule, practice for competency, and achieve goals. While their genetic programming creates a desire for mastery in these things, modeling by parental figures will help them know how to achieve it safely and prosocially.

When providing organizational opportunities, avoid the extremes. At one extreme parents can provide too many opportunities. While having a full social calendar, including sports, projects, church activities, and social functions, can be enriching, too much of a good thing can lead to burnout and tension. Having too few opportunities by discouraging or not encouraging children to try new things can lead to underdeveloped organizational skills.

Balancing love and limits here refers to trying a few new things and helping children to prioritize their commitments. Foster the need to finish a commitment before starting a new one. Activities can be like a small child in a candy store—so much to choose from and everything looks good, but there are only a few cents to spend.

In addition, some families have more discretionary income to spend on activities. Some families can pay for music lessons, while others must learn on their own. Some families can afford to buy athletic uniforms and equipment, and others must borrow. Time may be limited for parents juggling work and family life. Here again is the need to prioritize and help children understand financial realities.

Pressure is another crucial issue. Children should never be forced into an activity. While all children get tired of practice or bored with a new group after a short time and need to be encouraged to continue, don't push and shove them into an activity. Keep in mind the child's abilities. Is the activity designed to fit her ability levels? How will the activity benefit the child? How does it affect the rest of the family? What are the expectations on the child and the parents? Who is in charge of the activity and what kind of leadership ability and philosophy do they hold? Don't be afraid to ask these questions. People may look at a parent strangely, but the whole family will benefit by learning more about the different organizational opportunities available and make a better decision for it.

Ages: 6–12, teenagers; High Love, High Limits.

Overcorrection: Requires a child to eliminate an inappropriate behavior and practice its opposite, more appropriate behavior through the imposition of work. A child who writes on the wall with crayons is required to not only clean his mess but all the walls in his room. Not only does this reduce the likelihood of the inappropriate behavior from occuring again but it makes for a really clean room.

The first part of this parenting tool incorporates **fix-up** or **restitution.** The second part improves the environment but does not include a positive reinforcer to increase the inappropriate behavior. Instead, the heavy work decreases the behavior.

There are various applications for this parenting tool. Parents can use it increase social skills. Children who will not share can be asked to repeat two or three trials of practice sharing in which one child asks for a toy and the other child responds appropriately. It can also be used for homework problems, such as misspelled words and incorrect arithmetic problems. Parents can have children write misspelled words 5 times each or do 10 extra division problems. Or parents can use it with aggressive displays, such as door slamming. Children can be asked to shut the door 10 times in the correct manner. Regardless of the application, overcorrection is an efficient tool for decreasing unwanted behaviors.

Ages: 2–5, 6–12, teenagers; High Limits.

Parent/Child Contract: An agreement between a parent and child (note the singular tense) that sets up an exchange of desired behaviors for desired rewards. The agreement should include not only what the child will do, but what he or she can expect to receive in return. Make the behavioral exchanges simple and easy to achieve. Write up a summary of who does what, when, where, and how and place it where the child can see it. Sign it to make it official and then modify it on a weekly basis to fine-tune the agreement. Was it too difficult? Do you need to change when or where it occurs? Do you need to teach the child how to accomplish the expected task? In the event that you have more than one child, write up a separate contract for each child as each child's abilities and personality are unique. The democratic style of parenting views each member of the family as equal in terms of their right for respect and dignity, but not in terms of their responsibilities and functions. Use the **baseline** parenting tool before starting and the **problem solving** parenting tool to steer clear of any negotiation difficulties.

Ages: 6–12, teenagers; High Limits.

Parental Disappointment: A simple statement to express a parent's disappointment in a child's behavior. This communication-based parenting tool teaches children to be more aware of other people's feelings about how it feels to be interrupted on the phone, for example, or to have a personal item taken without asking. You might say, "I am disappointed by the way you acted in the store." Make the comments behavior specific. Don't criticize the child. Just comment on the behavior. Parents who state: "I am disappointed in you" end up shaming the child and lowering self-esteem. You may have noticed that the parental disappointment parenting tool is closely related to **"I" messages** and **deed from the doer.** Interchange and use these tools together. To ensure greater effectiveness, follow this tool up with the **positive expectation** parenting tool.

Ages: 2–5, 6–12, teenagers; High Love.

Peer Grading: Grading your children's friends to protect them from negative influences. As children mature, they become more other-centered than parent-centered. They are as heavily influenced by the peer group and its culture as that of their parents. They may believe parents cannot understand what they are experiencing as teens and preteens. In some ways this is true. Adolescents today experience more adultlike influences and decisions than most parents did when they were that age. Adolescents today are faced with making decisions about sex, drugs, and antisocial behavior much earlier than ever before. On the other hand, parents also have a better perspective on right and wrong than do their children, regardless of what their children might believe.

This tool is used primarily to protect children. It is not meant to be a judgmental instrument to widen the parent-child gap. You may not want to not disclose this tool to your children simply because they might misconstrue what you are trying to do. The goal is to assess how powerful and how positive or negative an influence your child's friends have. An A grade would include peers who demonstrate behavior consistent with your own set of values and behaviors. You know them well and have observed their behavior in a lot of diverse situations. They have shown that they do well in school, respect adults, participate in their community, and resist negative influences. Consequently, they are peers with whom you allow your child to have a lot of freedom and less supervision. B grade peers are children about whom you have less knowledge. They appear to be solid children with good social values and appropriate behavior, but you have not observed them acting in many different situations. Consequently, you allow less freedom and provide more supervision than with A grade friends. C grade peers are even more unknown; you are a little unsure about their type of influence on your child. More interaction under parental supervision is necessary. D grade peers have demonstrated a negative influence on your child; thus your child is allowed little, if any, interaction, unless closely supervised. F grade peers have openly displayed antisocial behavior and are engaging in behavior that is not consistent with your values. They are off limits to your child.

It is important to remember that these grades are not lifelong brands. A child's peers can change grades after they have demonstrated more appropriate social behavior. They can also drop in grades based on their decisions and actions. The higher the grade, the less supervision and more freedom you allow your child with those friends. It may be insightful to ask yourself: "How would other parents grade my child as a peer?" Peer grading has nothing to do with a friend's race or economic background. These demographic issues might affect opportunities, but they have nothing to do with values or behaviors. Grading is simply a tool to help you protect your child from negative influences by controlling the amount and type of interaction with other children who may have a negative impact. Use the various talk tools listed here to communicate your decision about your child's peers.

Ages: 6–12, teenagers; High Love, High Limits.

Physical Space: A useful tool for parents of older children. As children get older, they require more privacy and control over their physical space. Allowing children their space is a form of respect. Parents are quick to state that children "have no respect" for their authority, but few parents can say how they communicate that respect to their children. Knocking before entering children's rooms is a way of communicating respect for their space, as is asking permission for hugging or kissing an older child. Some older children are deeply embarrassed by any public display. While they want this kind of affection at home, in private, in front of their friends is a different manner. Check with them first. Just ask: "Can I give you a hug?" And then respect the answer. Parents can also respect children's physical space by letting them take care of their own property. If they have a pet, allow them the responsibility of caring for it. Let them launder their own clothes. Parents can respect them and teach responsibility at the same time. If you choose to care for the pet or wash your children's clothes, communicate this to them and let them know that you respect their stuff and will wash their clothes so long as they respect you by putting it into the hamper and not the bathroom floor. Physical space can be a win/win situation for parent and child.

Ages: teenagers; High Love, High Limits.

Planned Transitions: For use with children who have a hard time making changes. Some children have a tendency to dawdle in the mornings when parents need to rush off to work or throw a fit whenever the parent tries to leave the playground or the store. These children do not handle changes well. Parents can make changes a little easier with planned transitions, verbal announcements or physical devices to let children know that a change is coming up, giving them time to prepare.

As an example of a verbal announcement, you might let your child know how much longer until it is time to leave for school or get ready for dinner. Count down your announcements, for example, "10 minutes til it's time to go . . . 5 minutes . . . 1 minute . . . It's time to go." In the case of physical devices, parents can use egg timers or clocks to plan these difficult transitions. Let your child know that when the timer goes off or the big hand is on the twelve, then it will be time to go. Even if children are too young to tell or understand time, they understand the need to get mentally ready for the actual physical event.

Ages: 2–5, 6–12; High Limits.

Point-Reward Chart: Use in conjunction with the **parent/child contract.** A point-reward chart consists of a daily or weekly calendar or some sheet of paper with a number of boxes. These boxes or calendars are used to tabulate the number of times a desired or undesired behavior occurs. These are behaviors listed in the parent/child contract. After the child has completed a specific number of desired behaviors or check marks, the parent gives the child a reward.

This tool allows children to observe their progress and understand how much is expected of them. Instead of check marks, you can buy some stickers and let them place a "star" or "happy face" on each box. Young children are reinforced simply by the placement of checks or stickers in the boxes. Parents can increase ownership of the procedure by letting children check off or place their own sticker on the point-reward chart. To guarantee success, start off with low expectations and build up to more difficult tasks. For example, you might start off with the expectation that "toys will be put away 3 out of 7 days per week without being reminded by mom or dad." Later you may want to up the ante by stating the "toys must be put away 5 out of 7 days per week." To determine what a child is capable of doing, use the **baseline** parenting tool. Don't forget to reward effort as well as end result. See the **encouragement and rewards** parenting tools.

Ages: 6–12, teenagers; High Limits.

Positive Expectations: Statements by parents to their children about what is appropriate behavior. The goal of this tool is to teach children what parents want, not what they don't want. For example, telling children that dirty clothes belong in the laundry basket is different from telling children to stop leaving their clothes in the middle of the room. Telling a child that feet belong on the floor is different than telling them to take their feet of the table. State what you want, not what you don't want. This heads off children's complaints that you never told them they couldn't put their feet on a different piece of furniture. This tool also increases the feelings of cooperation and respect. Parents who wish to balance love and limits find that to get respect, they have to respect their children. Positive expectations decrease defensiveness and increase cooperation. They also allienate power struggles between parents and children.

Ages: 6–12, teenagers; High Love, High Limits.

Positive Labeling: Use to reinforce behaviors that you consider valuable. Labels in general are something parents want to avoid. They create self-fulfilling prophecies that allow children little room to move and become who they desire to be. For more information on labels, see the **reframing** and faith-building parenting tools. Positive labels focus on character traits, not people. Instead of saying your child is an artist, acknowledge his artistic ability. This allows the child the freedom to decide for himself if he wants to be an artist or not. Children can be artistic in many areas of life. When two children are picking up a box together to move it out of the way from where they want to play, parents can positively label this behavior as "nice teamwork." The children would never dream of acting as a team, but they often display "teamwork." It is your job to give appropriate behavior a positive label if you want to see more of it in the future. Children will give themselves the label of a "team" if they so desire and change their attitudes about being a "team player."

Ages: All; High Love, High Limits.

Post-It Notes: A written version of the **describing** tool. Instead of using words to describe a problem, try posting it on a note. Leave a note on the refrigerator that says "Cake is for after dinner, fruit for before." Or post a note on a child's door that reminds her to clean her room or feed the dog. For the more adventurous parent, try writing a note on a piece of paper, fold it into a paper airplane, and toss it into a child's lap from another room. Short poems and lyrics are another creative variation on this theme. This tool gains children's attention and reminds them of their responsibilities without blaming or nagging. Even young children who can't read get a kick out of this tool. Parents can draw sad face and talk about how they feel when people leave their wet towels on the floor.

Ages: 6–12, teenagers; High Love, High Limits.

Privileges: A common parenting tool of many parents. Privileges refers to the granting of a reward for an earned behavior. If a child cleans his room, he earns the privilege of renting a video. If she does her homework without arguing, she gets to go to the party on the weekend. This tool is very similar to the **rewards** parenting tool. The difference is that rewards are more widely applied whereas privileges are special rewards a child can earn. Many parents confuse privileges and rewards. Parents misunderstand privileges as childrens' rights. A right means you do not have to earn it. When children demand to go to the weekend party, parents can tell them that is a privilege for which they must behave in a certain manner or perform a certain task to earn it. It is not a right! In fact, most things can be considered a privilege. Rights constitute the basic care, supervision, and nurturing of a child. They do not refer to special activities, events, objects, or projects. These fall into the category of privileges. Of course, parents shouldn't be rude or controlling when telling children that these things are privileges and not rights. Stating them in a matter-of-fact way and positively expecting them to follow through is all that is needed.

Ages: All; High Love, High Limits.

Public Recognition: Announces a desirable action on the part of a child. This tool is best utilized in a subtle, off-handed manner. Parents can mention an action or trait they found desirable to another adult while in the presence of the child. An example might be, "Do you know what Johnny did today? He picked up all his clothes and put them in the dirty clothes hamper without having to be asked once." Watch the child beam with pride. Public recognition is an internal reward (see the **rewards** parenting tool) that can be used for young and old children alike.

Ages: All; High Love.

Puberty Preparedness Training: For parents of preadolesents, typically between the ages of 8 and 12. Parents of "tweenagers" should prepare themselves as much as possible for the many changes their children will experience. These changes involve the physical, cognitive, social, emotional, and spiritual self of the child. While some children mature sooner than others and girls quicker than boys, all children experience these changes at some point in their transition from childhood to adulthood. This transition is commonly known as *puberty*.

One way to prepare for puberty is to find information on the developmental changes your child will experience. A good book, article, television special, or internet site will be helpful in explaining what is to come. Of particular importance is obtaining information and courage to talk to your child about sex. As their reproductive organs develop and their hormones begin to rage, children will be naturally curious about sexual behavior. Parents who are prepared to talk to their children about these things will find that they sleep better at night knowing that their children are not getting information from some other, inappropriate source. As difficult as this may be for some parents, the more openly and simply sexual behavior is communicated, the easier the experience. Another good tool for puberty preparedness training is patience. Puberty is a trying stage of development for both the child and the parent. Patience is a virtue in dealing with mood swings, social embarrassments, attitude changes, and identity crisis. See the **growing pains** and **swinging to the mood music** parenting tool for more information on preparing for puberty.

Ages: 6–12, teenagers; High Love, High Limits.

Quality Time: Emphasizes *how* parents spend time with children rather than how much time they spend. What makes the time "quality" is that parents are available to their children. While communication is an important element in quality time, it doesn't necessarily mean that parent and child must always talk. In some situations quality time may not involve "doing" anything at all. Parent and child could simply be working on separate activities in the same room. Or it could involve watching an old movie together or talking a walk around the block. Regardless of the activity, during quality time parents are available to listen to their children if they wish to ask a question, share something important, or discuss some newly discovered bit of knowledge. Many families spend a lot of time in the car traveling to and from school or day care. This is an excellent opportunity for some quality time. For other parents, setting aside blocks of quality time will be vitally important to the parent-child relationship. Parents must make their children and time with them a priority in what may otherwise be a hectic life.

Ages: All; High Love.

Redirection: Used most often with young children. When children are getting into trouble, stop them, explain why you are stopping them, and redirect them into a more appropriate activity. This tool works well with young children because of their short attention spans. Five minutes after leaving an intense argument over who had the toy first, they have forgotten why they were angry. This tool is also effective because it does not require parents to lecture, scold, or nag at their children. They just have to get them involved in some other fun, and more importantly, desirable activity.

Ages: Under 2, 2–5, 6–12; High Love, High Limits.

Reflections: A powerful talk tool, because it focuses on the child as person. Contrary to what most parents might believe, children want their parents' approval, especially at an early age. A child's self-concept is determined to a large degree by what a parent says and what a parent does. A child who is valued in word and deed will have a good self-concept while a child who is mistreated and ignored will not. Reflections are an excellent way for parents to ensure that their children have a good self-concept.

Reflections operate in a similar fashion to a mirror. Just as a mirror reflects your physical image, a parent can reflect a child's emotional image. Knowing what you look like is difficult unless you have some reflection to determine shape, color, and form. Similarly, children do not know how to feel about themselves without some feedback and description. But children are not looking for physical descriptions. They are in need of emotional descriptions. Parents can use the reflecting parenting tool to provide this description.

The reflections parenting tool validates children's feelings about themselves and the situations they experience every day. Parents make these statements about the emotional world of the child. You must demonstrate that you are open to hearing what the child has to say, on the surface (the story) as well as deeper down (the emotional feelings). The goal is to communicate to the child that "I am listening" or "I understand what you are experiencing." Interrupting, interrogating, and psychoanalyzing will not produce this effect. You can probably remember a situation, talking to a supervisor, friend, or loved one, in which your feelings were disregarded or the problem analyzed rather than simply understood. Those kind of responses hurt old and young alike.

The actual procedure for this parenting tool is quite simple. There are only three steps: *remove distractions, communicate attention,* and *reflect the child's feelings.* The first step is to remove distractions, so you can give the child your full attention. You cannot pay attention by listening to your child and watching television or cooking dinner at the same time. Turn off the TV or take the pot off the stove. If it is not possible to remove the distractions, then try to minimize them as much as possible or ask the child to wait until you can give him or her your full attention. It is better to wait than to try to compete with some other activity.

The second step is to communicate your attention. Give your child a physical and a verbal acknowledgment that he or she is being listened to. Children have a way of knowing when parents are not really interested in what they have to say. Turn and face your child. Let your child know you are ready to listen, "Tell me more about what happened" or "How did that make you feel when that happened?" As your child answers the question, inject short statements that convey the message, "I'm still with you and I'm still listening." Examples might be: "I see." "Wow." "Yeah." "Oh!" "Uh-huh."

The third step is to actually reflect the child's feelings. Up until now, you have succeeded in making a connection with your child. This is not reflection but the act of preparing to reflect. So far the picture is warm but still fuzzy. Make it clearer by using the format: "You feel (*child's emotion*) because of (*situation that caused the feeling*)." An additional piece to this would be to clarify the child's values by including the statement, "and it is really important to you that (*value that child is expressing*). As an example, let's imagine that a parent is faced with a child who did poorly on a test because other children were pestering him. The parent would reflect this by stating, "You are angry at those kids for pestering you and making you get a bad grade at school." Anger is the feeling word not overtly expressed by the child and reflected back by the parent. If the parent wants to clarify the value as well, she might state: ". . . and it is important to you to do well in school."

Another example of reflections might be a child telling her parents, in a very animated manner, about an upcoming field trip. A parent could reflect, "You are excited about your upcoming field trip." Most children will take as much as 20 minutes to relate the same information a parent reflects back in just a few seconds. This is called *paraphrasing.* Paraphrasing summarizes the child's story by listing the main points of the story and labeling the child's feeling about it. Sometimes parent must listen very closely to capture the feeling behind the words. Don't worry if the child's feelings are not captured the first time around; most children are willing to give the parent a second chance. After all, reflections feel pretty good and most kids are willing to let you try again. They might even tell you the feeling word you missed. Simply restate the correct feeling word and go on with the reflections.

Some parents may be having trouble reflecting a child's feelings when the child is talking about something with which the parent does not agree. It is possible to reflect feelings about the situation without agreeing with the behavior. Reflection of a feeling is not the same as condoning a behavior or a belief. Parents can discuss that after they have made a connection and reflected the child's feelings. At that point, the child will be in a better place to receive parents' advice about what it is right or wrong about a situation or behavior.

Experience has shown that children who feel right about themselves act right. Children who feel hurt or angry act hurt or angry to those around them. This is fitting given that children are egocentric ("the world revolves around me") by nature. Therefore, children are more likely to listen to parents when they feel that their parents are listening to them. Hence are two cautions. The first: Don't be a parrot. Many parents try to reflect a child's feelings by repeating their exact words. If parents continue along this path without capturing the essence of the child's communication, the children will be annoyed and/or stop communicating altogether. Second: Don't give up. It is normal to feel awkward at first. But with practice, parents become fairly accomplished at using this tool. After witnessing the dramatic changes in their children's self-esteem and behavior, parents will question why they didn't use this powerful talk tool sooner.

Ages: All; High Love.

Reframing: Allows parents to avoid negative labeling and see children in a new light. When parents typecast their children, they assign labels that turn into self-fulfilling prophecies. Labels that parents give to children can include:

bookworm	hell on wheels	princess	good
Mr. Fix-It	jock	stupid	bad
lazy	artist	difficult	

The worst labels are those that compare one sibling to another and place children in opposing roles, so that one child is the "smart one" and the other is said to be the "athletic one." This restricts the smart one from being athletic or even sports-minded, if he so desires, because the other sibling is already athletic. And the athletic child believes she is stupid, because mom and dad already said her brother was the smart one. While the reality is that some children are more gifted in certain areas, due to heredity, temperament, or the child's own choosing, it may also have a lot to do with parental projections of their own wishes and desires placed on their children's shoulders. Parents who wish they had done better in school may pick an academically gifted child and bestow on him the unconscious responsibility to achieve what his parents didn't achieve in life. This is an unfair burden. Parents need to reframe their view of their child as unique and having the ability to be multigifted if they so choose. This eliminates the one-sided labels with which children must cope.

Another form of reframing puts a child's negative behavior into a more positive, more tolerable light. For example, a whining child might be seen as spoiled and annoying or as having a difficult time expressing a problem. A child who is failing in school could be called unmotivated and lazy, or she might have a reading disability or be emotionally distracted. A child who runs away can be seen as a juvenile delinquent or as attempting to deal with a difficult home life. More commonly, a passive and withdrawn child could simply be a cautious or slow-to-warm child. It all depends on the view that a parent takes. Reframing is not intended to make excuses for a child or for a parent to live in denial about a child's misbehavior. It is intended to help parents be more emotionally resourceful when dealing with a particularly difficult behavior.

Ages: All; High Love.

Removing Yourself from the Situation: For parents who have reached their maximum frustration tolerance. Think of this tool as a time-out for parents. Taking care of children is a stressful job in the best of circumstances. Taking care of more than one child or having a child with a special developmental or medical need makes it even tougher. In addition, many parents just need a short break after spending 24 hours a day, 7 days a week with their children. A few minutes alone or talking to someone over 3 feet tall seems like the most glamorous of vacations. When parents feel their blood pressure rising, they should tell their children what they are feeling (nicely, of course) and excuse themselves from the situation. Let your child know what you are doing so that he doesn't become anxious about being abandoned. Then retreat to another location, free of children, for a few moments to regroup. This tool works especially well when there is more than one caregiver in the home. This application of the parenting tool is called "Tag Team" parenting. Tell your partner you need a break and ask him or her (nicely, of course) to take over for a while.

This tool may be difficult for some parents to embrace. Permissive parents believe that to be good parents, they must always be available to their children. They are afraid to express negative emotions around the child, fearing that they will damage their child emotionally. Just the opposite is true. By expressing your emotions, positive and negative, children learn how to appropriately express their feelings. Negative emotions that are pushed out of awareness have a habit of popping up where you least expect. Verbal abuse and physical ailments (ulcers, headaches, muscle tension, etc.) are a couple of ways that these emotions sometimes surface. Better that parents express themselves in a healthy manner. Authoritarian parents have a difficult time with this tool because they believe that they must be in charge and in control at all times. Unfortunately no parent can be in charge or in control at all times. Everyone needs a break or feels out of control of certain situations. Controlling behaviors may be negatively reinforcing an already stressful situation.

For clingy or anxious children, this tool may increase their fears of being alone. Parents can reassure them that they are not leaving for good and that they will be close by. They just need a few moments to themselves. Try setting a timer or put on an educational video and tell the child you will be in the other room, by yourself, and you will do something together after the timer rings or the video is over. If children interrupt this time or begin to fight with each other (an attention-getting *mis*behavior), assertively inform the children what your intentions are again and reassure them that they will be OK. Then reset the video or timer to the beginning. They will soon get the message that you mean what you say and that they are just fine by themselves watching the video. For added strength review the **broken record** parenting tool.

Ages: 2–5, 6–12, teenagers; High Limits.

Reasoning: Useful with older children. Reasoning can replace lecturing and nagging children. It serves to explain to children why they are being disciplined or cannot perform a particular activity. Make the reason simple. You need not defend your decision; just state the reason for your actions. This tool decreases children's resentment and mistrust in parents. Authoritarian parents state: "Do what I say, and don't question my authority." Children who understand why do not need to question their parents' authority. Permissive parents overuse this tool. They talk and talk but do not back up their decisions with action. After a while children will tune permissive parents out, so use this tool sparingly.

Ages: 6–12, teenagers; High Love.

Rewards: Reinforcers of children's behavior. It does not matter if the behavior is good or bad. Rewards reinforce behavior—as simple as that. In other words, rewards are a neutral tool that parents can use to change their child's behavior. It is up to parents to choose which behaviors they want to change and why.

In making your decision about which behaviors to change, try these suggestions:

♦ Choose one or two behaviors to start.
♦ Choose the most frustrating but easiest behaviors to change. Frustrating behaviors have a way of demanding a parent's attention. But choosing a behavior that is too complex will not work. Complex behaviors have a way of reinforcing themselves. In other words, the child is getting a reward from the action itself or from some unknown variable. A frustrating, easy behavior would be something that the child does fairly often without too much intervention from the parent.
♦ After you are successful with the frustrating but easy behaviors, move to harder, more persistent behaviors.
♦ Chart your success and failures. This information gives you ammunition for better strategies and more creative interventions. See the **baseline** and **point-reward charts** parenting tools.

You can choose to use external or internal rewards. External rewards are sometimes described as "bribes." They involve an exchange of a physical item, such as toys, sweets, or money, on the part of the parent for a desirable behavior on the part of the child. Internal rewards, on the other hand, offer intangible rewards for the child, such as a word of appreciation or a job well done. These rewards focus on the child's need for approval and significance by helping out, volunteering, or cooperating with a parent. An internal reward can be given through a smile, touch, and/or words.

Rewards can also be conditional or unconditional. Conditional rewards are given only when a specific condition or task has been completed. Conditional rewards can be external or internal in nature. For example, parents may give children money (an external reward) or a hug (an internal reward) based on whether or not they have finished cleaning their room (a condition). On the other hand, unconditional rewards are given in response to a child's effort and cooperation rather than focusing on an end result. The parent who gives a child praise or money for each A on her report card is using a conditional form of reward. Parents who show their approval of their child's effort and hard work, regardless of the letter grade, are displaying an unconditional reward. This doesn't mean that children are allowed to perform a task in a sloppy manner or leave a task half-done. It does mean that parents praise their children for their effort and then instruct them on how to finish the task correctly or assist them in completing the task. An unconditionally rewarding parent might state their appreciation for their child's hard work during the course of the school year and then talk about some ways to help him achieve higher grades, such as hiring a tutor or spending more time with him on his homework.

Rewards help children become more responsible. This in turn leads to greater self-esteem. But if children only receive conditional rewards, then they will soon learn that it is better not to try than try and fail. They will avoid taking risks because that could mean feeling insignificant or not worthwhile. Unconditionally rewarded children have a more consistent and stable sense of self and are generally more willing to try new tasks. This is because they have learned that it is the effort and not just the end result that is important. The bottom line on rewards is that they change behavior. However, they do not discriminate between good and bad behavior. That is the job of the parent. In fact, it is possible to reward good behavior in the wrong way. This is done by overdoing external, conditional rewards. External, conditional rewards are a good place to start, especially with a child who is difficult to handle. Parents need to remember that external or conditional rewards are just a starting point and that internal, unconditional rewards are the destination. If you work towards this end, fading out external, conditional rewards over time, you will achieve more lasting and positive changes.

Ages: All; High Love, High Limits.

Rituals: Allow nontraditional and traditional families to form collective identities, facilitate healing, celebrate life changes, and pass on expressions of beliefs. Rituals include daily activities, even if they are taken for granted, such as getting ready for bed, eating at the table, and watching a television program. They can also be much more elaborate, although not necessarily more symbolic, such as weddings, funerals, bar mitzvahs, graduations, and religious ceremonies. Regardless of their format, rituals are an important aspect of our social lives, and parents can utilize this hidden resource in developing more intimate families. Family therapists have used the concept of rituals to help families that have been hurt by past actions toward one another or by an unexpected traumatic situation. Wedding vows have been restated by stepfamilies and have included all family members, including the children. Letters of anger and sadness have been written to unknown mothers and fathers and then ceremonially burned or destroyed as an act of saying goodbye. Marriage bands have been melted down or thrown into the middle of lakes to break emotional ties and symbolize the need for an emotional divorce, even after families have already been legally divorced. Again, how one performs these valuable tools is not as important as finding a way to signify a gain, loss, or both in the lives of families. See also **bedtime** and **mealtime** ritual parenting tools.
  Ages: All; High Love, High Limits.

Rubber and Glue: Inspired by the children's rhyme: "I am rubber and you are glue. What you say bounces off me and sticks to you." We are not recommending that you chant this rhyme to your children, but you can use its inherent wisdom to deflect children's argumentative behavior. When children complain or argue, parents can be "rubber" and respond "nevertheless" or "regardless" and reiterate their original directive. You don't need to get mad or argue with your child. This reduces you to the level of the child and rarely solves a conflict. Parents can use this tool to stay firm and consistent in their directives to children and not back down. This teaches children that parents mean what they say and will, over time, increase cooperation from them since arguing gets them nowhere. This tool can be merged with other communication parenting tools, such as **reflective listening,** to increase its sophistication and effectiveness.
  Ages: All; High Limits.

Saying "No": Reduces confusing or mixed messages, if used properly. When parents say "no," they usually mean "maybe." Some children will interpret "no" to mean "ask me later" or "go ask the other parent." To get respect, a parent's "no" must mean "no!"

So how do parents say "no" to their child? Use a firm tone of voice that is slightly above your normal speaking voice but not at the level of screaming. Parenting partners who agree will be more effective when saying "no." If possible, parents should put their heads together to decide on various issues, such as eating all dinner before getting dessert or staying up late on a school night. Children will be less likely to manipulate parents when they know they are in agreement.

Some children will react to a parent saying "no" by throwing tantrums and verbally abusing the parent. This is most likely in the case where parents have not been consistent in making "no" mean "no" and the child is not used to being frustrated. When this happens, it is important that parents do two things: Stay calm and stay firm. Keeping calm will eliminate any negative emotion the child might be seeking and staying firm will communicate to the child that the parent is serious. Let frustrated children vent. If they become abusive, physically or verbally, tell them to take a **time-out** to cool down. Use the **time-in** parenting tool to discuss with them why they took a time-out and discuss their feelings of frustration (see the **reflection** parenting tool).

A sensible approach is to give your child a short, clear reason for your negative response. Once you have done so, there is no need to continue discussing the decision. Use the **broken record** parenting tool here.

Ages: 2–5, 6–12, teenagers; High Limits.

School Daze: Use with your children to make sure they have a positive school experience. Some children find school an exhilarating challenge, while others are overwhelmed. Parents of young children can help them by being more involved in school. If you have the time or a flexible work schedule, you can participate in the classroom one day a week. This affords you the opportunity to observe your child and to help the teacher, who probably has his or her hands full. You can see what problems your child has adjusting to the school routine and find ways, by modeling the teacher, to help your child. Your presence also gives the younger child a feeling of security to know mom or dad is close by. Unfortunately some parents do not have this flexibility to take off a day and participate in their child's classroom. You can still stay involved by attending parent/teacher conferences, calling the teacher periodically to see how your child is doing, and keeping informed about overall school events as well as your child's individual performance.

Parents can also reduce their child's school daze by helping them learn good study skills and overcome homework malaise. Self-discipline can be a difficult trait to build, but it is crucial to academic success. While IQ is important, a child's feeling of confidence in herself and her ability to master a subject is also critically important. Make sure your child knows how to study and finds it a positive, rewarding experience. You can do this by using the **homework helper** parenting tool. In addition, you should encourage children's natural curiosity to learn. Provide opportunities to discover new things. Get excited about your child's projects, both at home and at school. Post school work on the refrigerator door as if they are pieces of famous art work. And talk regularly with your child about his feelings about school. Is he afraid of another student? Does he think the teacher is nice or mean? What is it like riding the bus, or eating school cafeteria food, or playing at recess? Who are his friends and why does he like them? Even busy parents can find time for these discussions. Use the communication parenting tools listed here to validate a child's feelings about school without getting caught up in them at the same time. Remember that empathizing with a child (hearing about feelings and acknowledging their validity) is different from sympathizing with a child (feeling what they feel, be it mad, overwhelmed, or dazed). The former allows the parent to help solve problems while the latter gets parents caught up emotionally in the problem.

Ages: 6–12, teenagers; High Love, High Limits.

Selfishness: For those who are permissive in their parenting styles. Permissive parents are high on love (relationship discipline) and low on limits (action discipline). They frequently feel as if they are a slave and martyr to other family members, particularity their children. They have fallen for the mistaken belief that if they love their child, they must constantly give to their child, even when they have nothing more to give. Some limits on this type of love are necessary. Selfishness is one way to set these limits on "overloving."

By nature of their parenting style, permissive parents will cringe at the term *selfishness.* To them it implies they love themselves over their children or, on an even deeper level, they would be a bad parent. On the contrary, selfishness implies that in order to give to children, parents must first give to themselves. Another way of saying this is that parents can't give what they don't have; to give to others, they must give to themselves. This creates a greater balance of wants and needs between parent and child.

Selfishness can be used in many different ways. On one extreme, parents can give themselves a time-out when things are getting hot and heavy between them and the child. Parents can tell their children that mommy or daddy is angry and needs to take a time-out and cool down just like they have to when they are feeling or acting that way. Put on the egg timer for 15 minutes or so, just as when a child is in time-out, and go take a bath or lay down and breathe deeply. At the other extreme, parents can make plans to leave the children with a baby-sitter (or wait until they are at a friend's house or at school), be determined (because parents will think of many reasons why they shouldn't) and go do something selfish, such as seeing a movie, visiting a friend, or working out at the gym. How parents use this tool is less important than simply doing it. And doing it means more than one time per month or year. Be selfish at least once a day for a few minutes each day. If this is too much for permissive parents, then work up to it gradually, by starting off with one time per week and then moving to 2 days, and so on.

Ages: All; High Love, High Limits.

Selective Ignoring: Pretending that your child's inappropriate, attention-getting behavior doesn't exist. Much of children's misbehavior is due to their need for attention—positive or negative. By ignoring inappropriate behavior and simultaneously paying attention to appropriate behaviors, a parent can teach children right from wrong. Parental attention is a powerful internal reward, but all too often parents respond to their children's pleas for attention and ignore their more appropriate behaviors. This is because appropriate behavior is often quiet, respectful, and nonviolent. In a parent's hectic life, inappropriate behavior can end up demanding attention more readily. Recognize your child's attention-getting behaviors by observing the *intent* of that behavior and the *feelings it stirs up within you.* Children whose actions appear to be pleading, "look at me," are most likely displaying attention-getting behaviors, especially if those behaviors provoke in you irritation or annoyance.

Is it wrong for a child to want a parents' attention? Of course not, unless they are striving to get it in an inappropriate manner. Selectively ignore the inappropriate behavior and pay attention to the appropriate behavior. Some behaviors cannot be ignored. For instance, children who are hitting one another or destroying property cannot be ignored. But parents can prevent negative attention from undermining their efforts to correct their children. Deal with the aggressive or destructive situation with as much businesslike demeanor as possible. Keep your voice firm but neutral. Don't grab or yell at the child. If you must put a hand on the child, do it in a controlled manner. Otherwise, what might have started out as mischievousness can end up as attention-getting if parents supply negative attention to the behavior. Use the **redirection** or **positive expectation** tools listed here to teach more appropriate ways to get a parent's attention. Also, see the **negative reinforcement** and **triggers** parenting tools for more information on what might be reinforcing children's inappropriate behaviors.

Ages: All; High Love.

Separation Serenity: How to cope with children's separation anxiety. It helps to ease the distress of saying good-bye to children when going off to work or going out for an evening alone. As society changes and more mothers enter the workforce (through choice and out of necessity), separation anxiety is becoming a major concern for both parents and professionals. Longer durations of separation are occurring for children at earlier ages. Separation anxiety is universal to infants of all cultures and speaks to a fundamental, biological mechanism in children. It proves that children form strong, healthy attachments to their caregivers and indicates a type of survival instinct in children. In addition, researchers have discovered that reuniting is as an important skill for parents as managing the good-byes of separation. How parents and children interact when they come back together indicates the strength or weakness of the children's attachment to their parents. Children who are comforted when mom or dad returns are said to be more securely attached than children who react coolly toward mom or dad or are ambivalent—demand to be picked up and then fight to be put down.

The most effective way to create separation serenity instead of separation anxiety is to leave the child in a familiar place, such as home. If it is not possible to do this—if parents must leave the child in a day-care provider's home, for example—then it is important that the parent spend some time with the child in the new environment to let the child build some familiarity and comfort in that place.

Another way to create separation serenity is by controlling how parents share their feelings about the separation. Because of their strong attachment, emotions between parents and children are contagious. Parents who feel wretched for leaving their children with a baby-sitter for an evening at the movies create more distress in children, who have their emotional antennas out and are picking up guilty feelings from their parents. Cheerful, positive parents create children with less fears and more security than ambivalent or distressed parents. Perhaps children look to their parents for indications of whether or not they should be afraid and trust the baby-sitter.

In addition, most baby-sitters and day-care providers report that children's tears turn off soon after parents leave and that staying too long to comfort the child actually makes the situation worse. Because children have short attention spans, they quickly adapt to the situation by focusing on a toy or other children. A helpful day-care provider can support separation serenity by distracting and engaging the child in an alternative activity. Some parents worry that their child's separation anxiety is abnormal. Children experience this anxiety mostly through age 4. By age 4 months, as the child learns to distinguish between the human world and the nonhuman world, the separation anxiety process already has started. By 8 to 10 months, the child recognizes a difference between herself and her parents. She also distinguishes between people she likes and those she does not. Consequently, some people frighten the child and others will not create any distress. By 18 to 20 months, the child's sense of herself has become even more distinct. Children who are sitting across the room from a parent will be comforted by a parent's smile as much as if they were sitting in their lap. By age 2 1/2, children can feel comfort out of their parents' sight. They can take mental pictures and emotional feelings of security with them and not need as much visual or physical contact to feel secure. By age 3 1/2 to 4, children have learned to use these mental pictures and emotional feelings to form chains of reasoning about themselves and the world. They can state: "Mommy or daddy will be back later to pick me up. I can wait for them." or "I don't want to wait. I'm mad at them for leaving." These feelings may come out symbolically through play as one toy animal eats the other or leaves the animal alone on a chair across the room. What is significant about this stage is that the child can separate thoughts and feelings as different from one another and has a more solid sense of security. This sense will enable him to form positive relationships with his peers.

If children do not feel secure at this age or display hostile or out-of-control hysterics when parents leave, it may be necessary to contact a professional to help the child and the parent create more secure feelings.

Ages: Under 2, 2–6; High Love, High Limits.

Sexual Education: Teaches children about the changes they are experiencing in their own bodies and about appropriate sexual behavior. The first task is explaining about the physiological changes adolescents go through, while the second is about a family's values. The bottom line is that parents make the effort and take the time to talk to their children instead of letting them learn false information elsewhere. This can be difficult for parents who did not have this talk with their own parents or, if they did, found it too embarrassing and awkward. Obtaining printed or video materials designed to help parents educate their children will make this task somewhat easier. But parents will still need to initiate and perform the task. Children become naturally curious about reproduction and sexual behavior as early as 4 years of age. Parents who are prepared to answer children's questions by becoming informed themselves will handle this situation more confidently.

Some guidelines for talking about sex with children include:

1. Be prepared by researching good material on sex education for children.
2. Be honest, simple, and direct when talking about sex.
3. Accept that having one "big talk" may not be enough and that several "little talks" may be necessary.
4. Use children's natural curiosity to initiate the communication.
5. Be sensitive to the child's comfort level as well as your own.
6. Don't push children to talk, watch, or listen to sex education material if they are not ready for it.

Ages: 6–12, teenagers; High Love, High Limits.

Signs in the Window: A nonverbal, communication parenting tool. This tool uses written media to communicate rules, boundaries, or information to children in a humorous and/or less threatening manner. Signs are used all the time in the business world. They simplify communication by not having to repeat a message over and over again to different people. For example, a sign in the window might state: "Open for business" or "Out to lunch" or "Help wanted." Parents can use this form of communication with their children. Put a handwritten sign on the refrigerator door that states: "Gone fishing (for supplies)." Or put one on the bedroom door that says: "Do not disturb" when you need some peace and quiet. For younger children, use drawings of a child playing with a ball with a large X through it on the front door to indicate no playing with the ball in the house. If the child is still confused (maybe you're not that great of an artist), use the opportunity to communicate verbally the rule about not playing ball in the house. This tool is limited only by a parent's creativity or artistic ability. But since it is designed to be humorous (see the **humor** parenting tool), stick figures are encouraged.

All; High Love, High Limits.

Squatter's Rights: For parents who disagree on how to discipline their children. At best, this is a way of compromising parents' diverse methods to balance love and limits and to prevent confusion on the part of the child until a better agreement can be found. Essentially, this tool states that whichever parent is currently disciplining the child has the right-of-way. The other parent, new to the situation, is not allowed to interfere unless what the other parent is doing is illegal or immoral. Other than those two exceptions, the other parent must not interfere so as to prevent confusion and conflict from affecting the family. This tool may be difficult for parents to employ. It will be especially difficult to use if parents are separated or divorced and are angry at one another. If that is the case, they must remember to keep the best interests of the child in focus and not allow their emotions or past hurts to take over the situation.

After the parent with squatter's rights is finished disciplining the child, the other parent can request a conference with the parent to discuss other ways to discipline. This prevents the child from "dividing and conquering" during the situation and puts up a reassuring front for the child. The reality is that the disciplining parent is probably doing just fine, even if he or she is approach-

ing it differently then you would. But if your partner asks for help, then you can intervene. See the **tag team** parenting tool for what to do next.
Ages: All; High Love, High Limits.

Storytelling: An excellent way to teach positive behavior to young and older children alike. Parents can use their imaginations or find a book that deals with a problem they are having with their children. Many bookstores and libraries carry specialty books for children on various issues and lifestyles. If you choose to use your own imagination, here is a simple suggestion for doing so: Ask the child to make up a story. Suggest a couple of fictional characters and a general theme, such as a family of bunnies on a picnic. After the child has told her story, retell the story again to the child but modify it to incorporate some recent problem situations at home. For example, you might retell a child's bunny story by talking about how the bunny children disobeyed their mommy and daddy bunny and got lost in the woods and became very frightened and couldn't find their mommy and daddy bunny. Then they remembered that the mommy and daddy bunny told them that if they every got lost, they should stay in one place. So they sat down and sang some bunny songs to comfort themselves. Soon their parents found them and they were so happy, the little bunnies never disobeyed their mommy and daddy bunnies again.

Parents can use this tool in two ways: to deal with a current problem they are having with their child, and as a prevention tool. Parents who face an existing problem can try to educate their child about why they are telling him to do or not to do something important. In some ways, this is a younger version of the **reasoning** parenting tool. Be careful to not scare the child or make your story morbid. Create a happy ending that includes a moral lesson, such as, "...and so the bunny children always told their mommy or their daddy bunny where they were going before they ran off to play." Add puppets and dolls to illustrate the story for more color. Young children are very comfortable with fantasy (until about 6 years of age), and stories are an excellent way to enter their world and balance love and limits.
Ages: Under 2, 2–5; High Love.

Structured Activities: Provide bored and restless children with constructive, appropriate releases for pent-up energy. Parents can research their local library or ask an early childhood professional, such as a preschool or elementary school teacher, about some age-appropriate activities they can incorporate at home. Too many parents use television and computer games as babysitters for their children. While these things may not be bad in and of themselves, they must be balanced with age-appropriate physical activities. Sit down at the end of the day with your children and plan a list of activities for the next day or upcoming weekend. Planning activities is an excellent tool for strengthening the parent/child bond. If necessary, use the **problem solving** parenting tool to come up with a list of activities. Also see the **family meeting** section for a broader use of this parenting tool.

Ages: 2–5, 6–12; High Limits.

Supply and Demand: Uses the principle of loss and gain in motivating children. It has been said that people are motivated by two things: the opportunity to gain and the fear of loss. Similarly, the term *supply and demand* is used in the marketplace to describe what motivates value of a product or service. The higher the supply, the less the demand, and the lower the supply, the higher the demand (and price).

Parents can use these principles of motivation by giving children opportunities to gain money, time, or other privileges for appropriate behavior. If children clean their room, they get so much allowance, extra time playing, or a smiley face sticker on their behavior charts. For more information, see the **rewards, behavior chart,** and **privileges** parenting tools.

But for some children, the opportunity to gain is not sufficient motivation to clean their room or behave appropriately. What these children may require is the feeling of loss or the lowering of supply to increase demand. For example, children can be given a certain amount of poker chips or money (in coins) in the morning and have them taken away through the day for not following through with cleaning their room completely or acting inappropriately. Another example is using this tool on a family vacation by giving children a certain amount of money in coins before you leave; tell them that this money is all they will get for buying souvenirs they want or paying for activities they may wish to engage in. If children misbehave on the vacation, a coin is taken away, and they have less money to spend. For some children, the fear of taking things away that they already have is more motivating than the idea of performing a task in order to gain a reward. This may be due to their personality or temperament. Either way, it may prove more effective than handling rewards when children do not respond with much demand when given the opportunity to gain.

This tool can be combined with the **privileges** parenting tool, so that a child can earn rewards and lose rewards for appropriate or inappropriate behavior. This tool is also effective with groups of children; the parent gives all the children points, poker chips, or money ahead of time and takes away a counter for each misbehavior. In this situation it may be useful to have a **family meeting** to discuss what will result in removal of a reward and how many rewards will be taken away for certain behaviors.

Ages: 2–5, 6–12, teenagers; High Limits.

Swinging to the Mood Music: For parents of older children who are experiencing mood swings. Mood swings are the ups and downs preteens and teens go through on a daily basis. As their bodies and minds transform from childhood to adulthood, they shift from irritability to joyfulness to depression, all within a few moments. Many parents are left scratching their heads wondering what will happen next, perplexed by the strange dance of adolescence, and helpless over how to cope with it. You can swing gracefully through the "mood music" played by your child by keeping in mind the developmental forces at work in the child and not blaming him for rapid shifts in mood. It's OK to allow him to have a "bad day" from time to time.

Preteens and teenagers don't usually know why they feel the way they do. That is because the hormonal changes that are occurring in their bodies can make them more irritable or yes, even lazy. Parents who keep in mind that developmental forces are at work can better "swing with the mood music."

Therefore, it is important not to blame adolescents for their mood swings. That isn't an excuse, though. They can still take responsibility for how they express their mood, even if you are not blaming them. For more information, see the tool on separating the **deed from the doer.**

Everyone has a bad day. You can reframe your child's mood music as their response to a bad day. Or a bad moment (even if it is multiple moments through the day). The optimistic parent will acknowledge that the likelihood of many moods through the day or week—some of them positive and some of them negative. Accept their negative moods and wait for the positive ones to come. And they will come!

If they don't come and the child continues to display a negative mood for a long period of time, consider consulting a professional to see if something else is the problem. Depression is not uncommon during adolescence, but it can be treated successfully.

Ages: teenagers; High Love, High Limits.

Tag Team: Enhances parents' cooperation in balancing love and limits together. Parents often have different styles of disciplining their children, each with its own strengths and weaknesses. These strengths can be complementary if parents are aware of them and use them wisely rather than reacting to one another and label each other's strengths as "abusive" or "worthless." This tool uses an old wrestling term that refers to how one teammate signals another teammate that he or she needs assistance. The teammate signals the other by reaching out and tagging the other's hand. This allows the other teammate to enter the ring and contest the opponent. If no signal has occurred, then the other teammate is not allowed to enter the ring. Parents, must not interfere with their partners who are currently engaged in disciplining the child—however different that style might be—unless they signal for help.

Two points are crucial for this tool to work. The first is that the parent "in the ring" must be willing to ask for help, and the second is that their partner must not "enter the ring" unless signaled to do so. The best signal is to verbally state one's need for help, not in an angry, whiny, or sarcastic manner, but as a simple "Would you please come and help me with this situation?" Parents can also work out a nonverbal signal, such as hand waving or nod of the head. Verbal signals will be much clearer and less confusing than nonverbal signals. See the **Squatter's Rights** parenting tool for more information on compromising parenting styles in the heat of the discipline "match."

Ages: All; High Love, High Limits.

Thinking Out Loud: Models to children how to solve problems. Parents might think out loud about how to fix a flat tire, how to rearrange the living room, or what to fix for dinner. Children who are nearby will often add their own suggestions. Acknowledge these suggestions without judgment. Continue thinking out loud, using their suggestions and weighing the pros and cons. Hint at more practical solutions to stimulate their problem-solving skills. Act excited about the suggestions that children offer. Use the **humor** parenting tool to play the role of the "lame" parent. This encourages children to rush to the parent's rescue and participate in the problem-solving process. Soon they will be using the process on their own.

Ages: 2–5, 6–12, teenagers; High Love.

Time Cushions: Time management tool that parents can use when attempting to juggle too many responsibilities. A time cushion allows for more time than might actually be needed to accomplish an activity. Parents can allow a liberal amount of time both before and after picking up the kids from day care. This will allow them to greet their children in a less stressful mood and deal with any last-minute crisis at work or on the road to the day care. Children pick up on their parents' frenzied feelings and often respond in kind. Parents and children may complain, whine, or argue with one another, with both sides totally oblivious to why they are acting that way.

Ages: All; High Limits.

Time-In: Use immediately after a **time-out.** This tool provides the educational component to what is basically a punishment-only method. Time-in instructs the child as to what behavior the parent expects from the child. During a time-in, the parent sits down face to face with the child and *restates* the reason she was sent to time-out. Asking a child to tell you why she was sent to time-out is a frustrating situation, at best. Most children develop spontaneous amnesia. Small children with very short attention spans may actually have forgotten why they were in time-out. Older children will selectively forget or, due to the stress of the moment, be unable to access the information. Instead, simply restate the reason for the time-out and then *state the appropriate, expected behavior.* For example, if a child is sent to her room for writing on the wall, then you could remind her that paper is used for writing on, not the wall. See the **redirection** and **positive expectations** parenting tool for more information on negotiating this step. Complete the time-in tool by giving the child a hug or soft pat on the back. Because of the isolation or punishment nature of time-out, children often need to be reassured that they are still loved and accepted.

Ages: 2–5, 6–12; High Limits.

Time-Out: Allows children a cooling off period during which the child is separated from other people and things. The children are given a chance to calm down and think about their out-of-control actions. Of course, this assumes children are old enough or do not have a disability that prevents them from conceptualizing the appropriateness of their actions.

Unfortunately, time-out has been billed as the magical wand of behavioral change techniques. Professionals are too quick to suggest that a parent use time-out without first explaining how and when it should be used. Consequently, many parents use this tool inappropriately or with a child who does not respond to this form of discipline. Thus, parents end up even more frustrated, using a tool that doesn't work.

But time-out does work in some situations and with some children. The two most frequently asked questions by parents regarding time-out are: "Where should I send them?" and "How long?" The best place to send a child is to a chair or separate room away from other people and things. Some parents send their children to bed, which has been known to create bedtime fears and sleeping problems. In addition, most children's rooms are mini-electronic storehouses. The idea behind time-out is to isolate your child, not provide her with entertainment. The rule of thumb for the length of a time-out is one minute for every year of life. For example, if your 5-year-old is throwing a tantrum, you would place him in time-out for approximately 5 minutes. Putting children in time-out for too long or using it too much will render it ineffective. It might also feel more like punishment than discipline. Time-out is best used as a teaching tool, not a prison sentence. Too many parents use time-out more for themselves than for their children. Because they are so frustrated, parents will place children in their rooms for an hour or more. If parents need a break, they should use the **removing yourself from the situation** parenting tool.

If your child has a difficult time staying in one place for even a short time, try a **rapid time-out.** Place the child in a chair for a few seconds and state "You are in time-out because of _____", and then hug him and let him go. This version of the time-out parenting tool is useful for hyperactive children, who cannot sit still under the best of conditions and often throw tantrums, run away, or tear their rooms apart in frustration when under "house arrest." Follow either format with a **time-in.** (See **freeze play** for another form of time-out.)

Ages: 2–5, 6–12; High Limits.

Touching: Use to calm a needy child, reinforce a fearful child, or offer an unconditional reward for a child's effort. Touching is an important part of the parent/child relationship and is vital to a child's emotional well-being. Touch communicates many things to a child, the most important one being "I love you!"

Children have different levels of tolerance for touching, though. Some need lots of touching, while others want very little. This may be due to many different reasons including age (younger children are more apt to want to be touched than older children), temperament (some children are extremely sensitive to touch), and the situation (older children may be embarrassed by a show of affection in front of their friends).

You can give your child a hug, pat him on the back, or put an arm around his shoulders. This tool does not give parents permission to inappropriately touch a child or touch a child without permission. Children's bodies are their property and should be respected. Communicating this to children will empower them to resist others who might wish to touch them inappropriately. While most children welcome a hug or pat on the shoulder, some, especially older children, may want to give their permission to be touched anyway.

Ages: All; High Love.

Triggers: Make use of *behavioral stimulus controls*. This is the technical jargon for people or things in a child's environment that cause the child to act in a prelearned manner. The trigger is usually reinforcing to children's behavior in and of itself. When children are exposed to these triggers, they respond in an automatic manner. The responses are learned behaviors to positive or negative experiences they have had in life (see **rewards** and **negative reinforcement**). A child who has been spanked may flinch when the parent raises a hand, even to wave "hi" to the child. Children who have been sent to their beds for time-out may develop sleeping problems due to the negative association between the bed and punishment.

Even more frustrating is when parents themselves are the trigger. A father may complain that the child behaves worse with him than with her mother or that the child behaves worse at home than at school or the doctor's office. This may be due to the fact that the child has *learned* to behave in a certain manner with one parent or in a particular environment and another way with the other parent or environment. They may accept limits with one person or place but act out of control somewhere else with someone else.

Understanding the concept of triggers makes the child's behavior less confusing. Children learn what is expected of them and what one parent will tolerate and another will not. Parents can control this stimulus response in their children by controlling how they are positively or negatively reinforcing their children's behavior. Parents can observe what goes on with their partner or other environment where the child behaves appropriately and attempt to recreate those triggers in their interaction with their child to create a more positive balance of love and limits. They can also experiment with themselves (i.e., what they do and say that may be negatively affecting their interaction with their children) until they find the negative trigger and can change it to something more positive.

Ages: All; High Love, High Limits.

Verbal Warnings: Brief statements to let your children know they are on "thin ice." A verbal warning might include **describing** a problem situation, stating a **positive expectation,** and/or counting aloud to 3. When using the last method, be careful to not let the child manipulate the situation by waiting until you get to 2 before he or she complies. Schools use this tool with great success. Some of the formats used successfully by schools include the check mark, color zones, and number cards methods.

The check mark method uses checks marks after a child's name to warn them they are getting close to serious discipline. Teachers place these check marks in a public place to incorporate peer pressure. The method begins with writing the child's name on the blackboard (or a refrigerator notepad at home) for the child's first mistake. This is followed by check marks next to the child's name with consequences listed for each one. The more check marks, the more severe the consequence. Parents can use colors just as easily. For young children, parents can use the colors of a street light to indicate how close to a consequence they are. A green card is a first, cautionary warning of undesirable behavior, followed by yellow and red cards to indicate more seriously undesirable behavior. In the color zones method, parents tell their children, "You are now walking in the red zone!" to warn them that their behavior needs to stop. Finally, the number cards method uses plain 3 × 5 cards with large numbers written on the front and a consequence on the back. Some parents use a variety of number 1, 2, and 3 cards with various consequences written on the back and allow children to choose their own consequence. After a child has gotten a number 1 card for the day, he will pick a number 2 card for the next undesirable behavior during that same day and so forth. Each card has a consequence that must be completed. Perhaps it is a 10-minute time-out or missing out on a privilege. A new day means a clean slate and starting at number 1 again. Extra incentives can be given to the child for not pulling a number 3 card or getting in the red zone for a prescribed period of time.

The overall benefit of verbal warnings is that they allow children to monitor their own behaviors. The permissive parent has a concrete tool to use to overcome inconsistency, and the authoritarian parent can delegate the responsibility of desirable behavior to children, even letting them choose their own consequences.

Ages: 6–12; High Limits.

Wants List: Helps keep a lid on children's endless list of wants. A child's desire for a new bike, toy, or pair of jeans, in itself, is not wrong. We all have a list of things we would like to own. But when these wants get out of control, parents need to limit their children's excessive cravings. The demand for things often increases between the ages of 7 and 10. This is due developmentally to cognitive changes that make children more aware of other circumstances that are different from their own. The result is often a lot of comparisons between what one does and does not have compared to other children.

One way of dealing with these demands is to ignore them. Viewing a child's wants as a cognitive exercise of comparisons and not feeling the need to respond to these cravings is one way that parents can cope with a child's wants. For more insight into this method see the parenting tools on **reflective listening, selective ignoring,** and **wishes.** Another way of dealing with a child's wants is to make a family "want list." This tool allows wants to be expressed openly without any feeling by the parent to fulfill them all. Whenever children say they simply must have the hot, new computer game or the colorful, new doll, suggest that they write their wish on the want list and place it where everyone can see it, perhaps on the refrigerator. Instead of reacting to a child's demands, the parent can redirect the child to "go, write it down on the want list." Parents can put things down on the want list, too. This demonstrates that parents often make do without things they want as well. Use the want list as next year's birthday or Christmas list, but don't be surprised if the child no longer wants those items anymore.

Also, use the list as an educational tool. Use the **Description** parenting tool to notice how wants come and go, how some can be acquired with effort and savings and others cannot, how circumstances differ from family to family, and how important things, like love and relationship, are free and last a long time.

Ages: 6–10, teenagers; High Love, High Limits.

Wishes: A talk tool that acknowledges children's wants without giving into their demands. Everyone has needs, wants, and desires. For example, hunger is a need, a turkey sandwich is a want, and a full turkey dinner with all the trimmings is a desire. Let's face it, most parents cannot give their children all of their wants all of the time. Even if they could, it would probably be a bad idea. Unfortunately, children may have to settle for getting a need filled instead of a want or a desire. Using the food example, children may have to settle for the turkey sandwich or whatever leftovers are in the refrigerator instead of the full turkey dinner.

Wishes are unique in that they acknowledge children's desires as healthy and valid even when they cannot have them. For example, a child who wants a pair of $200 tennis shoes may have to settle for a less expensive pair. When children realize they cannot have the expensive shoes they may sulk, throw a tantrum, or become verbally abusive to parents who "never does anything nice for me." To avoid this power struggle, try a response like this: "Wow! Those are great looking shoes. And wouldn't it really impress your friends when you show up at school with those shoes? I bet you could jump at least 8 feet straight up in the air with those shoes. But unfortunately I only can afford those shoes over there. Which one of those shoes would you like?" Such a response uses several other parenting tools, such as **redirection, reflective listening** and **choices.**

Another example would be in the situation where a parent and child are on a trip, and the child begins whining for something to drink even though nothing is available for miles. You might use this tool to fantasize what it would be like to drink a tall, cold, thirst-quenching, sparkling glass of soda. Use the **humor** parenting tool here. The actual desire can be met now in fantasy and later when you get to a store.

If a child is persistent and will not let go of a wish, use the **broken record, problem solving,** or another parenting tool that deals with power-struggling children.

Ages: 6–12, teenagers; High Love.

References

Bandura, A. (1977). *Social learning theory.* Englewood Cliffs, NJ: Prentice Hall.

Baumrind, D. (1971). Current patterns of parental authority. *Developmental Psychology Monograph,* 4 (4, Pt. 2).

Bowen, M. (1994). *Family therapy in clinical practice* (pp. 198–205). Northvale, NJ: Jason Aronson.

Bradshaw, J. (1995). *Family secrets: What you don't know can hurt you* (cassette recording). New York: Bantam Audio Publishing.

Carter, B., & McGoldrick, M. (1989). *The changing family life cycle: A framework for family therapy (2nd ed.)* Boston: Allyn & Bacon.

Coontz, S. (1992). *The way we never were: American families and the nostalgia trap* (pp. 23–41). New York, Basic Books.

Cosby, B. (1986). *Fatherhood* (pp. 57–59). New York: Dolphin.

Covey, S. R. (1989). *The 7 habits of highly effective people* (pp. 156–158). New York: Simon & Schuster.

Darling, N., & Stienberg, L. (1993). Parenting style as context: An integrative model. *Psychological Bulletin, 113* (3), 487–496.

Dickinson, E. (1900). *The complete poems of Emily Dickinson* (p. 686). Edited by Thomas H. Johnson. New York: Little Brown and Company.

Driekurs, R. (1964). *Children: The challenge.* New York: E. P. Dutton.

Ellis, A. (1975). *A new guide to rational living.* North Hollywood, CA: Wilshire Book Co.

Faber, A., & Mazlish, E. (1980). *How to talk to kids so kids will listen and listen so kids will talk* (pp. 1–46). New York: Avon.

Faber, A., & Mazlish, E. (1987). *Siblings without rivalry: How to help children live together so you can live too* (pp. 85–106). New York: Avon.

Fine, M., & Henry S. (1989). Professional issues in parent education. In: *Second handbook of parent education.* Academic Press.

Freud, S. (1905). Three essays on the theory of sexuality. In *The Standard Edition of the Complete Psychological Works of Sigmund Freud* (Vol. 7, pp. 125–245). London: Hogarth.

Garrity, C. B., & Baris, M. A. (1994). *Caught in the middle: Protecting the children of high-conflict divorce* (pp. 19–20). New York: Lexington.

Ginott, H. (1969). *Between parent and child.* New York: Avon Books.

Glick, P. C. (1991, October). *Address to the annual conference.* Stepfamily Association of America, Lincoln, NE, quoted in Harway, M. (1996). *Treating the Changing Family.* John Wiley & Sons, Inc., New York, p. 52.

Glick, P. C., & Lin, S. (1986). *"Recent change in divorce and remarriage." Journal of Marriage and Family, 48,* 737–747, quoted in Harway, M. (1996). *Treating the Changing Family.* John Wiley & Sons, Inc., New York, p. 52.

Goldenberg & Goldenberg. (1991). *Family therapy: An overview* (3rd ed., pp. 38–44). Pacific Grove, CA: Brooks/Cole Publishing Co.

Gottman, J., & DeClaire, J. (1997). *The heart of parenting: raising an emotionally intelligent child.* New York: Simon & Schuster.

Hall, E., Perlmutter, M., & Lamb, M. (1982). *Child psychology today* (pp. 370–373). New York: Random House.

Harway, M., & Wexler, K. (1996). "Setting the stage for understanding the changing family," quoted in Harway, M. (1996). *Treating the Changing Family.* John Wiley & Sons, Inc., New York, pp. 3–16.

Hendrix, H. (1988). *Getting the love you want: A guide for couples* (pp. 208–209). New York: Henry Holt.

Imber-Black, E. (1989, July/August). The power of ritual—lasting rites. *The Family Therapy Networker,* 39–46.

Imber-Black, Eran, & Roberts, Janine (1987). *Rituals for our times: Celebrating, healing, and changing our lives and our relationships.* (pp. 3–23). Harper Collins Publishers, New York, N.Y.

Jacobs, J., & Wolin, S. (1989, July/August). The power of ritual—lasting rites. *The Family Therapy Networker,* 41.

Kantor, D. (1975). *"Inside the family"* (pp. 10–22). San Francisco: Jossey–Bass Publishers.

Kübler–Ross, E. (1969). *"On death and dying"* (pp. 38–42, 50, 85–88). New York: Macmillan Publishing Co., Inc.

Lamb, M. E., & Baumrind, D. (1978). Socialization and personality development in the preschool years. In M. E. Lamb (Ed.), *Social and personality development.* New York: Holt, Rinehart & Winston.

Leman, K. (1985). *The birth order book.* New York: Dell Publishing.

Lombardi, L. (1995). How Parents Discipline Their Kids. *Child,* March, 16–19.

McKay, M., Rogers, P., & McKay, J. (1989). *When anger hurts: Quieting the storm within.* Oakland, CA: New Harbinger Publications.

Minuchen, S., & Fishman, H. C. (1981). *Family therapy techniques* (pp. 16–20, 146–160). Cambridge, MA: Harvard University Press.

Moses, K. (1989). *Shattered dreams and growth: A workshop on helping and being helped* (cassette recording). Resource Networks, Inc., Illinois.

Newman, M. (1994). *Stepfamily realities: How to overcome difficulties and have a happy family* (pp. 49–63). Oakland, CA: New Harbinger Publications.

Nye, F. I., & Berardo, F. M. (1973). *The family: Its structure and interaction.* (pp. 12, 247, 373–404). New York: Macmillan Publishing Co., Inc.

Olson, D. H., & Defrain, J. (1994). *Marriage and the family: Diversity and strengths* (p. 9). Mountain View, CA: Mayfield.

Parish, T., & McCluskey, J. (1994). The relationship between parenting styles and young adults' self-concepts and evaluations of parents. *Family Therapy, 21* (3), 223–226.

Peck, M. S. (1978). *The road less traveled: A new psychology of love, traditional values and spiritual growth* (pp. 15, 16). New York: Simon & Schuster.

Satir, V. (1972). *Peoplemaking.* Science and Behavior Books.

Sears, R. R., Maccoby, & E., Levin, H. (1976). *Patterns of child rearing.* Stanford, CA: Stanford University Press.

Shapiro, J. L. (1993). *The measure of a man: Becoming the father you wish your father had been* (pp. 55, 56). New York: Berkely Publishing.

Spock, B., & Rothenberg, M. B. (1992). *Dr. Spock's baby and child care* (6th ed., pp. 24–27). New York: Pocket Books.

Thomas, A., Chess, S., & Birch, H. (1968). *Temperament and Behavior Disorders in Children.* New York University Press, New York, pp. 180, 181.

Toman, W. (1969). *Family Constellation* (pp. 24–125). Springer Publishing Company, Inc., New York.

Uriquiza, A., & McNeil, C. (1996). Parent-child interaction therapy: An intensive dyadic intervention for physically abusive families. *Child Maltreatment, 1* (1, May), 132–141.

Watkins, H., & Bradford, M. (1982). Child maltreatment: An overview with suggestions for interventions and research. *Family Relations, 31* (3), 323–333.

Watlawick, P., Weakland, J., & Fisch, R. (1974). *Change: Principles of problem formation and problem resolution.* New York: W. W. Norton.

Weiner-Davis, M. (1995). *Change your life and everyone in it* (pp. 132–157). New York: Simon & Schuster.

INDEX

Behavior penalties parenting tool, 158–59, 164
Behavioral terms for goals, 16–17
Beliefs. *See* Values
Biological versus nonbiological children, 23–24, 63, 64
Birth order, 29–34
Blame, 44, 89, 104, 106, 130, 133
Blended families, 33–34, 62–63
    See also Nontraditional families
Blending, 41
Body language, 125
Boundaries in family systems, 35–36, 38, 83, 129
Bowen, Murray, 4, 25, 48, 50
Brazelton, Dr. T. Berry, 13
Broken record parenting tool, 37, 54, 159, 160, 161, 180, 208, 212, 228
Buddha, 18

C

Call the police parenting tool, 160
Capitalism, 110
Caring cyle of communication, 126–28
Change, 153
    long-term, 105
    in parenting styles, 5, 100, 142–44
    in values, 5, 11, 81
Cheerleading parenting tool, 160
Child abuse, 85–94, 110–11
    causes of, 87–89
    cycle of, 89–90
    prevention of, 90–94
Child labor laws, 110
Child (magazine), 2
Child support, 63
Child-centered parenting style, 97
Childhood, concept of, 109–10
Childhood rituals, 72
Children
    biological versus nonbiological, 23–24
    depression in, 65
    manipulation by, 37, 45, 143
    motives of, 122–24
    philosophy of, 109–10
    reaction to saying "no", 37
    revengeful, 98
    safety of, 25
    submissive, 97–98, 142

temperaments of, 121
    See also Siblings
Choices parenting tool, 53–54, 159, 160–61, 170, 180, 228
Choosing your battles parenting tool, 55, 161–62
Chores parenting tool, 161–62
Circles. *See* Family meetings parenting tool
Circular approach, 23
Closed systems, 35–36
Coercive or vicious cycles of interaction, 86–87
Cognitive approaches, 4
Cognitive therapy, 73–74
Cohesiveness as a family funtion, 60
Communication, 132, 141
    in authoritative parenting, 104
    aversive or positive, 125
    caring cyle of, 126–28
    complementary, 49, 52
    democratic process of, 105
    in family systems, 22–23
    mixed or double messages, 36
    open, 11, 94
    in permissive parenting, 122
    in relationship discipline, 8
    verbal or nonverbal, 125
    vicious cyles of, 124–26
Community events, 132
Competition, 44, 52
Complementary communication, 49, 52
Compromise, 119
Conflict resolution, 50
Conflicts, 134–35
Consensus, 48
Consequences, 130
Consistency, 37, 54
    in authoritarian parenting, 100, 102
    of permissive parenting, 109
    and security, 103
Consistency parenting tool, 162
Control versus flexibility, 102–4
Conversation extenders parenting tool, 162–63, 171, 194
Cooperation, 2, 105, 126, 152
Coping strategies for parents, 92–92
Corporal punishment. *See* Physical punishment
Cosby, Bill, *Fatherhood*, 113

Courage to be imperfect, 76–77
Courage to change what can be changed, 151–52
Courtship, 80
Covey, Stephen, 37
Crisis-oriented approach to child abuse, 90
Cultures, 12, 79, 139
    See also Society
Cursing. *See* Dirty words parenting tool
Cycle of child abuse, 87–89

D

Daily living tasks as a family funtion, 60
Daily routines, 103
"Damnations", 74
Decision making, 129, 132
Deed from the doer parenting tool, 128, 163, 172, 192, 197, 221
"Defective" label of parents, 88–89, 90–91
Defensiveness, 105
Delay of gratification, 135
Delinquent behavior in children, 89
Demands versus expectations, 104
Democratic process of communication, 105, 120
Democratic style of parenting, 79–83, 129–53
    accepting different styles, 138–42
    beliefs causing family imbalance, 135–38
    changing parenting beliefs, 133–35
    changing parenting roles, 142–44
    doing it your way, 148–50
    effects on children, 130
    and the nontraditional family, 144–46
    seeking solutions, 146–48
    and the *Serenity Prayer*, 150–53
    value teaching, 130–33
Denial as stage of grief, 61, 66
Dependency, 129
Depression
    in adults, 65, 112
    in children, 65
    in grief, 68, 69, 70
Describing parenting tool, 159, 163–64, 188, 201, 226, 228
Detriangulation, 50–51
Developmental stages, 53
    and authoritarian parenting, 102–3
    of childhood, 109–10, 152

and fair versus equal, 120, 121
and goals, 17
identity formation, 10, 39, 151
Developmental transitions in family life cycle, 38–42
Diagnostic questions parenting tool, 121–24, 126, 164–66, 191
Dickenson, Emily, 99
Diet, 85
Differential reinforcement parenting tool, 155, 159, 166–68, 181
Differentiation process, 40
Dirty words parenting tool, 168, 189
Discipline
    action, 8–9, 83
    aggressive, 86–87
    debate about, 1
    definition of, 7–12
    and fathers, 113–14
    in the past, 95–96, 110
    relationship, 8, 83
    versus punishment, 100–102, 130
    See also Physical punishment; Punishment; Spanking
Discussion parenting tool, 169
Distraction parenting tool, 169–70
Divorce, 80–81
Divorce rate, 2, 45, 57, 112
Divorced families, 33–34, 62
    See also Nontraditional familes
"Doing a 180", 144, 153
Doing the unexpected parenting tool, 170–71
Downward influence of parental subsystem, 28–29
Dramatic play parenting tool, 171, 172
Driekurs, Rudolph, 76, 121–22
DRs. *See* Differential reinforcement parenting tool
Drugs and alcohol, 37, 38, 58
Dual-career families, 57

E

Ecological model of child abuse/neglect, 87–88
Edison, Thomas, 77
Education of children, 110
Elder care, 40
Ellis, Albert, 73, 74